ISBN 978-1-58023-417-7

Put your heart's desires into words — no one else can truly pray for you.

Have you lost faith in prayer? Do you wonder just who you are praying to and if it is worth the effort? Does your search for religious meaning take you anywhere but to synagogue and the traditional Jewish prayer book? If so, you're not alone.

This is a no-holds-barred look at why so many of us find synagogue services and prayer at best difficult, and at worst, meaningless and boring—and how to make it more satisfying. Rabbi Mike Comins draws from over fifty interviews with Jewish spiritual leaders from all denominations, as well as from their "best prayer practices." He offers a new and different response to the challenges of prayer to entice and inspire you to become a "prayer person," a person who engages in prayer to play the heart strings of the soul.

He then guides you in overcoming the obstacles to achieving a satisfying prayer life through twenty-four innovative and traditional practices, relating prayer to the needs of conscious living:

- Nurturing joy
- Increasing mindfulness
- Facilitating self-change
- Dealing with tragedy
- Responding to loss

Also Available

Award Winner

My People's Prayer Book
Traditional Prayers, Modern Commentaries
Edited by Rabbi Lawrence A. Hoffman, PhD

Winner, National Jewish Book Award
Each volume in this momentous, critically acclaimed ten-volume series provides the traditional Hebrew text, a modern translation, and commentary from all perspectives of the Jewish world that covers the prayer book's connections to the Bible, history, traditional law, kabbalistic wisdom, feminism, modern developments and much more. Volumes are:

Vol.1—The Sh'ma and Its Blessings 7 x 10, 168 pp, Hardcover, 978-1-879045-79-8
Vol.2—The Amidah 7 x 10, 240 pp, Hardcover, 978-1-879045-80-4
Vol.3—P'sukei D'zimrah (Morning Psalms) 7 x 10, 240 pp, Hardcover, 978-1-879045-81-1
Vol.4—Seder K'riat Hatorah (The Torah Service) 7 x 10, 264 pp, Hardcover, 978-1-879045-82-8
Vol.5—Birkhot Hashachar (Morning Blessings) 7 x 10, 240 pp, Hardcover, 978-1-879045-83-5
Vol.6—Tachanun and Concluding Prayers 7 x 10, 240 pp, Hardcover, 978-1-879045-84-2
Vol.7—Shabbat at Home 7 x 10, 240 pp, Hardcover, 978-1-879045-85-9
Vol.8—Kabbalat Shabbat (Welcoming Shabbat in the Synagogue)
    7 x 10, 240 pp, Hardcover, 978-1-58023-121-3
Vol.9—Welcoming the Night: Minchah and Ma'ariv (Afternoon and Evening Prayer)
    7 x 10, 272 pp, Hardcover, 978-1-58023-262-3 $
Vol.10—Shabbat Morning: Shacharit and Musaf (Morning and Additional Services)
    7 x 10, 240 pp, Hardcover, 978-1-58023-240-1

Making Prayer Real

Leading Jewish
Spiritual Voices on
Why Prayer Is Difficult
and
What to Do about It

Rabbi Mike Comins

For People of All Faiths, All Backgrounds
JEWISH LIGHTS Publishing

Making Prayer Real:
Leading Jewish Spiritual Voices on Why Prayer Is Difficult and What to Do about It

Library of Congress Cataloging-in-Publication Data
Comins, Mike.
Making prayer real : leading Jewish spiritual voices on the difficulty of prayer and what to do about it / Mike Comins.

p. cm.
Includes bibliographical references and index.
ISBN 978-1-58023-417-7 (pbk.) 1. Prayer—Judaism. I. Title. BM669.C66 2010
296.4'5—dc22

2009050594

ISBN 978-1-68336-187-9 (hc)

Manufactured in the United States of America

Cover Design: Tim Holtz

For People of All Faiths, All Backgrounds
Published by Jewish Lights Publishing
www.jewishlights.com

For Jody

Contents

v

Acknowledgments

A s I thanked nearly everyone I ever met in my first book, I will be brief this time around.

Have you noticed that when people get on the air, they thank the radio talk-show host for taking their call? My heartfelt thanks to Emily Wichland and the Jewish Lights staff for their encouragement and guidance in producing this book, and to Stuart M. Matlins, publisher of Jewish Lights, for taking my call.

Over and over in these interviews, I heard the wisdom of two great teachers distilled through the devotion and insight of their students. This book is a testament to their living legacy. On behalf of the many teachers quoted in this book, may I gratefully acknowledge the gifts of Abraham Joshua Heschel, of blessed memory, and Zalman M. Schachter-Shalomi.

Everyone I know who sincerely prays has some words of wisdom on the subject. How could it be otherwise? For every person I interviewed, there were another five I know who should have been interviewed, and another five hundred whom I don't know. Had I lived somewhere else, or been exposed to different people in life, other names would appear in the contributor list. To all those who are thinking, "Why didn't he talk to me?" I offer my apologies. Your wisdom is missed.

This book was written in a remarkably short period of time as I dropped everything and devoted myself to the project. I have been blessed with the support of an amazing woman, my beloved Jody. *Making Prayer Real* is her gift to the Jewish People. If you like the book and run into her at the farmer's market, please give her your thanks.

Preface

If you had asked me, when I was a teenager, why I didn't regularly attend synagogue services, the answer would have been quick and decisive: it's BORRRing!

And I actually enjoyed services more than most. I liked Hebrew and singing; they sparked memories of the fun I had at Jewish summer camp. For ethnic reasons, I was really into being Jewish, and Jews gathered at synagogues.

But my list of complaints was far more compelling. I could mouth the Hebrew, but for the most part, I could not understand it. I didn't know what I prayed when I prayed it, only afterwards when I read the translation. And after reading the translation, I often felt that it would have been better if I had never looked. Why do people think that praising God is such a great thing to do, as if God, being God, needs us to suck up and "worship" Him? Wasn't *worship* the term for a pagan's relation to an idol or an immature person's relation to a rock star? And why "Him" instead of "Her"?

And who was this God, who did miracles that I knew were impossible, like splitting the Red Sea? Why would the prayer book try to impress me by making such a big deal out of something so unbelievable, and then brag about saving us by recounting the drowning of an army's worth of Egyptians? The prayers were written a long time ago for a very different audience.

All the personal petitions are phrased in "we" language rather than "I" language, as if they, too, knew better than to ask for personal attention. "Want to cure disease?" we thought in the late sixties and early seventies. "Then put your faith in university research hospitals." So soon after the Holocaust, the idea of a God who looks out for righteous individuals, indeed any individuals, was clearly folly.

The creative English readings were often interesting. At least, the first one was. By the third creative reading, my mind was elsewhere. And if I had read it a few times before at previous services, my attention was gone from the start. I was taught to be independent, to value individuality, to be authentic; that is, to do things because I knew that they were right and true. And here I was, reading prayers—the thoughts of someone else—in unison with a hundred other people.

No one talked about God. Not even the rabbi pretended that we were there to pray to this God that few believed in. Like most of us, I was there not because of the prayers but despite them. There was a perverse logic at play. If I do something so clearly unenjoyable as plodding through the service, I'm really demonstrating my loyalty to the Jewish community. Why else suffer through this?

The best part of the service was the sermon, because our rabbis knew better than to talk about anything spiritual. Instead, they spoke about politics, Israel, saving Soviet Jewry, Vietnam. The times were hot, and so were we. And then there was the *oneg* after services. Lots of brownies, plenty of friends, and, most fun of all, Israeli dancing. There were rewards for our suffering. But not enough to draw me to services when I didn't have to go.

Thirty-Five Years Later

Today, when I'm not spending Shabbat in nature, I attend a traditional egalitarian service with a full Torah reading. It takes more than three hours, but I do not wear a watch and it never ends too late for me.

If I'm really good, I rise early enough to meditate before leaving for services. On the drive over, I sing Jewish chants with my wife, Jody.

I enter the "sanctuary." It has no stained glass windows, no elaborate ark, no fancy pews; it is just a meeting room at a community center, some folding chairs around a few tables on a simple tile floor. I am happy to see my friends, the people who will be there for me in hard times, as I will be for them; the people whose singing and dancing transformed my recent wedding.[1]

Even though I am a bit late, I go back to the first prayers in the prayer book, the Siddur, because they are my favorites. I bless the *tallit,* feel it drop over my shoulders, and pray the morning blessings. Then I join in the singing during the first part of the service, largely psalms. In between songs, when others are praying the words of the psalms, I close my eyes and sink into a basic meditation. I put all of my attention on my body.

As I sit quietly or sing songs from the psalms that I know by heart, my mind empties and my body relaxes more and more. I do not talk to others. I focus on listening—to the singing and to my heart. Body awareness is critical. Where the body goes, the mind mirrors and the heart flows. It is not mysterious or difficult or in any way esoteric. It's just another way of being in the world. My body feels a certain way when happy, a different way when angry or stressed. This is how my body feels when I'm open and present, ready to feel God's presence. In the words of Jewish mystics, I am the empty vessel that God's spirit might fill. More important, I am familiar enough with this state that I can get there anytime I make the effort.

With the *Barchu* prayer I bring my focus back to the prayers. I read them in a state of relaxed concentration, allowing the prayers in this section to do their job: to center me, to remind me of my place in the world in relation to God, nature, humanity, and the Jewish People. If a particular verse strikes me, I stop and dwell on it for a bit.

As the *Shema* prayer enjoins me, I continue to listen for what God may be sending my way this morning. Awareness still on my body, I feel the spirit of my fellow davenners, my fellow pray-ers. I soak up their energy, which energizes me. As I sink deeper into this unstressed, peaceful state of being, my better emotions naturally emerge. I remember why I married my wife. I feel love for her and for my friends, and for the people in this room whom I don't know at all. I even remember how important it is to show a little love for myself.

As we approach the *Mi Chamocha* prayer, I take a moment to think back over the week that has passed since last Shabbat. I do a quick internal check-in. Am I taking care of myself, getting what I need, treating others well, living a life of service?

The prayers themselves at this point, about God splitting the Red Sea, I find problematic. So I forget the particulars and go for the general. This prayer is about redemption. As we sing it, I lose myself in the music and ask: What would redemption look like in my life in the next week? How would I change the way I go about things? I try to think small. Could I greet a barista with a smile instead of my usual morning scowl? Could I pay just a little more attention to someone in my life?

Everything comes into focus as I take three steps back, then three forward, and begin the *Amidah* prayer by saying, *"Adonai sefatai tiftach"* (O God, open my lips). During the week, I would pray my requests amid the traditional prayers. It is not difficult. After a half hour or so of listening, I usually know what I need, and when you know what you need, you know what to ask for—what to put out in the world that you hope will be fulfilled. But it is Shabbat, and according to the tradition, even God, as it were, has the day off. So I refocus on my body and just experience the grand emotions that are now filling my soul. I pray the words of "just being," the biblical quotes that proclaim the holiness of the Sabbath.

In this alert but somewhat trance-like state, I am in touch with the big picture of what it means to live a human life: the grandeur, the tragedy, the dreams, the pain, the mystery.... Like clockwork, gratitude wells up, and the tradition knows, for it places my favorite gratitude prayer, *modim anachnu lach* (we thank you), right at this juncture. I thank God not for achievements or any of the larger things I am grateful for, but for the gift that comes in the simplest form, my breath.

The *Amidah* ends, the Torah service begins, and my mind kicks in again for the intellectual endeavor of reading Torah, but in this contemplative state, I soak it in before I start analyzing things. I work less at "understanding" and first try to "hear," to really listen to the words as if for the first time. As a person who naturally loves learning and philosophizing, this part of the service comes easiest to me. I eagerly await the insights of my fellow members of the minyan, one of whom will give a *d'var Torah,* a sermon, on the weekly Torah portion.

Being a Reform rabbi, I have many reasons for dropping *Musaf,* the repetition of the *Amidah* after the Torah reading. But my soul wants to continue in "prayer consciousness," to tap into and to extend the invigorating energy that is enlivening my body and relaxing my mind. A good prayer session builds, and now that I have spent two hours locating the best of myself—intellect, body, and heart—I am ready for my best praying.

I don't relate much to the words, the details of the sacrifice offered on Shabbat more than two thousand years ago in the Temple. But the theme is compelling, the climax of the whole morning. What am I willing to sacrifice for God? What am I willing to give to make the world a better place? Again, I think about what I can really do. What bad habit can I try to let go this week? What can I give to my loved ones? How can I respond better to an imperfect world? Calm and alert, but emotionally raw and defenseless, I offer my heartfelt prayer to make this life a good one.

The service thematically concludes with the *Aleynu,* the prayer for harmony and peace in the world. Filled with sadness and joy, I pray. If only it could really be!

Services aren't as lovely as I have described here every time, but neither is this an occasional happening that I attribute to the alignment of the stars, the luck of the draw or to a martyr-like perseverance (pray enough and occasionally something special will transpire). This is what happens most of the time. It does not depend on anything or anyone else but me. Usually I feel like God is really there; sometimes not. But when I make myself truly ready to receive God, it is always worth the effort. Getting in touch with my noblest emotions, and reaching toward the best aspirations of a human life, is its own reward.

Becoming a Prayer-Person

What a difference a few years makes! (Okay, a few decades, but who's counting.) What changed for me?

For years I attended services, when I attended services, because I liked the music, identified with the community, enjoyed seeing friends, and relished a good sermon and Torah discussion. Good reasons, indeed, but today all that is secondary for me. Now my central goal is to slow down, make some space for God, listen, and respond. My purpose is to interact with the Holy One.

Pursuing a direct relationship with God, something to which few liberal Jews of my generation aspired, brought me to the critical insight that changed my relation to prayer.

No one else can truly pray for me.

My prayer life changed when I took ownership of it and no longer left my heart's expression in the hands of rabbis, cantors, the Siddur, the building architect, the community, or whether a baby happens to be crying in the sanctuary today.

The Hebrew words *ani tefillah* appear in Psalms 109:4. Literally, they read, "I prayer," or in proper English, "I am prayer." Clearly this is an expression, and the phrase is translated "I am all prayer,"[2] or "I have nothing but prayer."[3] But I like to take the translation literally in order to make a Midrash, a poetic interpretation. To say "I prayer" is to say "I am a prayer-person."

Exactly what constitutes a prayer-person is a broad question; it is the subject matter of this book. But for now, let me propose a working definition. A prayer-person is one whose very life is a prayer, a form of heightened awareness for whom the skills of prayer are a means to a life of virtue, joy, and service.

Personal Ownership

Over a seven-year period, I led High Holiday services for the Jewish Community of Jackson Hole in Wyoming. Overall, it was a wonderful experience that I treasure and look back on with joy.

But like most human endeavors, it was not all fun. Every summer, when it came time to gear up for Rosh HaShanah, I suffered an initial wave of depression. Partly it was the terror of writing two major sermons. But mostly it was the thought of leading services.

During the year, I loved the services that I was privileged to lead. Over the months, the regulars studied Hebrew, learned the prayers, mastered the melodies, and further developed the wonderful sense of community that only grows in a place with so few Jews. At some point in every service, I would close my eyes, stop singing, and just listen. Whereas only a few people sang when I first arrived, now I bathed in a full congregational chorus. Amid my friends, I could relax. As the prayer leader, managing a public ceremony for tens of people, it is often impossible to let go and pray. But instead of the congregation getting in the way, I was lifted by their participation and singing. I was one fortunate rabbi.

Then came the High Holidays. The regulars were outnumbered by "once-a-year" Jews who didn't know the music, didn't know the liturgy, and didn't care much for prayer. The focus would not be on the prayers; it would be on the clergy.

While we all like a talented prayer leader, clergy-centered services are problematic. If I go to services expecting the rabbi to impress me with her words and the cantor to move me with his musicianship, I am like a critic at a movie. When a good film touches me, I am spiritually enriched. If not, not. It mostly depends on the film. But if I pray like a painter about to draw on her canvas, I am responsible for finding my inspiration and engaging the practice. My prayer may not always turn out great, but even "failure" moves me forward in the artistic quest. The critical point: it depends mostly on me—my longing, my desire, my creativity, my talent, my sincerity, my devotion to the art. We have a choice: to consume art or to become an artist; to consume the synagogue product or to become a prayer-person, an artist of the soul whose sincere prayer serves the community as much as the community supports our prayer.

"Once-a-year" Jews are more like moviegoers, waiting to be moved and entertained by a liturgical performance that was never designed to entertain anyone. Partly by adopting the theater-style seating of the general culture, often because we do not know what to do if left to our own devices, most liberal North American Jews depend on the rabbi and the cantor to give them a good and satisfying experience. If attendance figures are an indication, it does not happen very often.

So there I was leading High Holiday services, struggling with what so many rabbis experience today. Most congregants are comfortable with neither the traditional prayers nor prayer in general. But I am bound to this liturgy and we are here to pray. Give me a few months of class time and I know that I can help the people sitting in the pews before me. But they are not interested enough in prayer to attend a class. (Considering their experience so far, who can blame them?) So I lead prayers that I know most find boring, and there is little I can do to soften the blow.

I know that responsive reading in English is a spiritual dead end for most, but this is the only tool I have to engage most of my congregants during the service. I read to them, and they read to me in robust, earnest voices. They think I like this and apparently want to appear as if they enjoy it, too. In reality, of course, I know that we are all suffering and far from God, but I don't know what else to do. At least some of them might find a moment of inspiration that would not be available if we droned on in Hebrew the whole time.

The most these congregants can do is listen to the music (thank God for our wonderful lay cantor) and wait to see if they like the sermon. Depressing for them, depressing for me.

Toward a New Paradigm

Better music, better sermons, and better prayer books can only go so far. Many innovations have been tried around the world, and no doubt synagogue leadership will continue to think creatively about improving services. But deep and lasting change will only come when each of us takes ownership and responsibility for what only we can really guide: our inner lives.

Throughout this book, I discuss the specific problems that, in my view, need attention in order to improve the current situation. But the first thing that must change if we are to transform our personal prayer lives and synagogue services is our general attitude toward prayer and our expectations of clergy.

Becoming a prayer-person requires an appreciation of what prayer has to offer, sincere effort, and, for most of us, a willingness to try something new. But the first step is to accept responsibility for our own inner lives. Specifically, with regard to synagogue services, this means accepting a basic premise: *clergy are not responsible for what happens in my heart.*

For more than a decade as an Israeli yeshiva and rabbinical student, I met North American rabbinical students from across the theological spectrum as they studied in Jerusalem. Today I am an itinerant rabbi who teaches at numerous synagogues and participates in many a rabbinical conference and seminar. Even for a rabbi, I know a whole lot of rabbis.

The rabbis of my youth rarely talked about God or prayer; I can testify that the times have changed. Partly because of the introduction of women to the rabbinate, partly because spirituality has become acceptable in the general Western culture of the first world, rabbis are embracing their role as spiritual leaders. They believe in God, they grapple with spiritual issues in their personal and professional lives, and they are dedicated to a very difficult but holy job. More than a hundred rabbis (and another hundred cantors and Jewish educators) have participated in the two-year training program in complimentary but nontraditional paths to God, such as meditation, yoga, Jewish chant, contemplative prayer, and more offered by the Institute for Jewish Spirituality.

I am privy to endless conversations about synagogue services. Rabbis are obsessed with the subject, because they are frustrated as heck. Here is my conclusion. In the past, spiritually minded laypeople often felt held back by their seemingly nonspiritual rabbis. Many left Judaism for Eastern paths. Today, for the most part, it is congregants who hold rabbis back. Not every rabbi, of course, is a spiritual seeker, but compared to yesteryear, a surprisingly high number of them genuinely seek the Holy One.

At least, I think that this comparison is valid. I have often criticized the rabbis of my youth for their seeming lack of spirituality. But now I'm not so sure. In the God-is-dead sixties, if there was something laypeople had no patience for, it was God-talk. Rabbis, those who want to keep their jobs anyway, can only go so far beyond their congregants. In the late sixties and early seventies, rabbis who talked spirituality were isolated. American Jews weren't having it.

Thankfully, those days are over. Today, laypeople, cantors, Jewish educators, and rabbis are all exploring their relationship with God. While each rabbi and cantor is different and I cannot speak for them all, my belief is that in many congregations, nothing would make the clergy happier than members pushing for a deeper spiritual experience at services. Nothing would please rabbis more than to teach their congregants prayer in a classroom and then pray together as partners at services rather than entertain them from the pulpit. Nothing would make clergy happier than to embrace their congregants as allies in the spiritual quest, fellow travelers on the same soul-path, rather than once-a-year consumers of High Holiday services.

As I travel the country, I already see significant movement in this direction. It is my prayer that *Making Prayer Real* will aid in this sacred endeavor. Please, God, may clergy and laypeople, together, become the prayer-people that we might be, and may the synagogue be our spiritual laboratory and home.

INTRODUCTION
The Problem with Jewish Prayer

I learned about prayer in a sweatlodge, before I identified very Jewishly. It was with a group of people who met once a month in a forest in New York, and there was one sweat that was scary hotter than ever before or since. It brought up this primal fear. Suddenly, someone in the sweat lodge cried out the *Shema*. Before that moment, I didn't realize that everyone there was Jewish. It was a *Shema* that was so powerful that it shifted us into this sacred space where none of us were afraid anymore. It was a very powerful experience of prayer. And it's with me anytime I say the *Shema*. It came from the place, we're going to die, and then it shifted us to that place of unity with God. There I was with a minyan of Jews. What I learned in the sweat-lodge is how real prayer could be and however real it is, that's how powerful it is. As a rabbi, that became my value: I wanted to make it real. It didn't matter if it was fancy or articulate, it had to be real.

RABBI SHEFA GOLD

Few would argue with the claim that the Jewish People suffers from an ongoing crisis of prayer. Traditional Jewish prayer works best for traditionalists—that is, ultra-Orthodox Jews. In the Modern Orthodox world, and in ultra-Orthodox communities as

1

well, the men pray three times a day and the synagogues are full on Shabbat, but many observers attribute this more to sociology than theology. Many traditional Jews pray to fulfill the commandment. They attend synagogue out of fidelity to God, love for the community, and commitment to the observant life (and maybe to hear a good sermon). Connecting with God is another matter. Many rush through the prayers, succumbing to the time constraints imposed by the sheer mass of liturgy on the one hand and duties to family and work on the other. A certain kind of popular theology is offered to justify the situation. Prayer is viewed as a demonstration of fidelity to God and the tradition, with little expectation of feeling God's presence. Rather, we listen for God, and God speaks to us, through Torah study and fulfilling other commandments.

In the liberal Jewish world—here I refer to Reform, Conservative, Reconstructionist, Liberal, and Renewal synagogues and prayer groups that serve more than two million non-Orthodox Jews—relatively few people attend services on a regular basis. To know this is true, you only need think of the logistical gymnastics it takes for synagogues to seat their members on Yom Kippur, the one day when everyone shows up. The entire membership structure and building requirements of liberal synagogues would have to be reconceived if eight of ten members actually attended Shabbat services, as they do in Orthodox synagogues and on Sunday at Christian megachurches. If a liberal synagogue draws 10, maybe 20 percent of its members with any kind of regularity, it is considered a success.

The main reasons for this dismal state of affairs are well known. The prayers are in Hebrew, a language in which liberal Jews lack fluency. More important, most liberal Jews do not believe in the all-powerful and the all-knowing, the rewarding and the punishing, the you-can-trust-in-Me God that the Siddur, the Jewish prayer book, has in mind. There is little belief in the efficacy of traditional Jewish prayer, especially in our post-Holocaust world.

These are indeed daunting problems, but I believe that there is much more to the story. The problem, as I see it, is that people do not really understand the problem. And without a proper diagnosis, there is little chance of finding effective medicine. Here is my litany of the maladies that afflict Jewish prayer services.

Too Many Words

When I participate in a typical traditional service most anywhere in the world, I have two problems:

1. The prayers are said too fast.
2. It takes too long.

I'm hoping you had a small laugh, and that you can see the problem. When I read through prayers at breakneck speed, there is little chance of feeling God's presence. And if that is the case, however long it takes is always too long.

Speed-davenning (praying) is a well-known phenomenon in the Jewish world. People race through the Siddur. Otherwise, praying three times a day would be an inordinate burden. In my experience, people have little expectation of meeting God during speed-davenning. Theirs is the spirituality of obligation.

But less traditional Jews do not fare much better when it comes to inviting God's response. It is nearly impossible to listen to another while talking. Yet liberals read or speak nonstop at their services, leaving no space for God. The notion of *listening* for God is seldom taken seriously.

What happens when we pray words from a prayer book? Here, the insights of neuroscience are instructive. On the left side of the brain, we process abstract thinking such as math, logic, and language. When we leave words behind and our intuition, creativity, and emotion find expression, the neurons are firing on the right side of the brain. You should not take the left/right division too strictly, nor think that the intuition/intellect divide is hard and fast. Philosophers and neuroscientists remind us that it is not. But for our purposes, this general description of brain function is valid.[1]

The question is this: when our prayers are truly heartfelt, which side of the brain should be working? In my teaching I have asked this question many times, and I always receive the same answer. Moving, meaningful prayer is emotional. Not over-the-top crying or laughing-out-loud emotional, but heartfelt. As opposed to the fruit of dispassionate, intellectual analysis, the feelings and insights of "God-moments" swell up in a process that is clearly intuitive. The right side of the brain is engaged.

But what is the first thing that we do in a synagogue service? We open a book and begin to read words. We immediately activate the rational, analytical left side of the brain, the home of language and reasoning.

This is why English readings, no matter how beautiful, get old fast. This is why speed-davenning the Hebrew is so unfulfilling.

There are methods for overcoming this problem. For those who know the prayers by heart, especially non-native Hebrew speakers, the liturgy can serve as a mantra meditation. But the more popular way to activate both sides of the brain while reciting a traditional or contemporary prayer, the tried and true method of bringing words into heart-space, is one you are likely thinking of already. That way is music.

It is no coincidence that the most successful liberal synagogues, such as Kol HaNeshamah in Jerusalem and Bnai Jeshurun in New York, and the Shlomo Carlebach–inspired and various soulful musical shuls (synagogues) and devotional prayer groups in the Orthodox world, make their services into one long song. Prayer bands are sweeping the Jewish world and almost every liberal synagogue in a big city has at least one service a month with live, contemporary music.

Why does music change the character of the prayer experience so thoroughly? This brings us to our next point.

Neglecting the Body

Emotions and feelings are intimately connected with the body. We know this in part from scientific studies. As an outdoor educator, I am most familiar with research on the effect of nature on brain function. When people hike in a place where their senses are fully engaged, as opposed to reading a book or watching television where vision is two-dimensional, their concentration and memory skills significantly improve. According to child advocacy expert Richard Louv in *Last Child in the Woods: Saving Our Children from Nature-Deficit Disorder,* nature calms autistic children. People score better on memory and understanding tests after taking a walk in nature. Through the placebo effect and many other studies, the medical community has learned that the mind-body connection is real, and should not be ignored in treatment.

We also know the mind/body, heart/body connection from our own experience. When we are angry, our muscles tighten. When we are grateful, our bodies relax. When we want to know if someone is lying, we listen to their words, but we pay attention to their facial expressions and body language. As my Buddhist meditation teachers are fond of saying, the mind has many ruses, but the body never lies.

Clearly, our emotions play out in our bodies. Nevertheless, we usually fail to take this into account, consciously anyway, when we plan synagogue services. As a result, we suffer in at least two ways. By constraining our bodies in the formal structure of theater-style seating, we prevent bodily movement and hence limit emotional expression. More important, we give up on one of the few strategies that can reliably prepare our hearts for the encounter with God. For just as the mind affects the body, so, too, the body affects the mind.

As any yoga or tai chi practitioner will tell you, consciously relaxing your body has the immediate effect of relaxing your mind and calming your emotions. Though physically tired, most people feel emotionally refreshed after exercise, as physical activity usually improves emotional sensitivities and well-being. Ever wonder why ultra-Orthodox Jews shuckle (sway) so fervently when praying? The wise use of our bodies during prayer can evoke the feelings and encourage the emotions that we seek. This is the secret of why music profoundly influences prayer. It engages much more than the sense of hearing. Music flows through the body and induces a change in a person's emotional state. Unsurprisingly, many prayer bands jack up the volume, just like at a club or concert, to ensure the effect.

I enjoy a good prayer band as much as anyone. I think it can genuinely help people to pray, especially when a person is beginning to get serious about prayer. But if we were able to create the same effect through our own song, we would not be dependent on loudspeakers or even choirs and cantors. And if we could relax and energize our bodies on our own, our prayer experience would not be thwarted by music we don't particularly like, or a lack of singing when the attendees are apathetic, or the negative effect of a dispassionate rabbi or an endless recitation of English readings.

Engaging the body is the most dependable way of moving us from the left to the right side of the brain.

Prayer Book Trumps Prayer

Nine times out of ten, would your wishes, feelings, and needs be best expressed by someone else's words or your own? I'm rather certain that you would choose the latter. If prayer is meant to be from the heart, then the difficult challenge is to put our deepest longings and wishes into words. Most of the time, our own words get closest to the mark (even though they, too, are often inadequate). The task of putting our higher desires into someone else's words is exponentially harder.

Yet, if your Jewish education was like mine, you were taught prayer book before you were taught prayer, if personal prayer was in the curriculum at all.

There is, of course, much to be gained from praying other people's words, particularly the prayers of the traditional liturgy. Prayer must be modeled for us if we are to discover our own possibilities. As one woman put it to me, "You don't start out as a great chef. You learn how to cook by following recipes." And sometimes we really do find that a great poet can express the longings of our hearts better than we can. As this book will demonstrate, I do not believe in throwing out the traditional prayers or making whole-sale changes to traditional Jewish liturgy.

But we shoot ourselves in the educational foot when we forget this simple truth. Prayer is a difficult enough subject to teach as it is. Why focus on the harder task of teaching the prayer book to the exclusion of the easier one—that is, spontaneous, personal prayer?

At my religious school, the answer was obvious. The teachers were like the people they served. They did not go to services themselves, and they did not pray privately (unless they were keeping it a secret). Like most in the community, they didn't think that prayer does much. For them, teaching the prayer book was a way of avoiding the issues that personal prayer would inevitably bring up: to whom am I praying and what good is prayer?

Herein lies the core of the problem. For many observant Jews, prayers are said without any expectation of a discernable response. Most liberal Jews are uncomfortable with the very idea of prayer. They are not sure what it really does, and whether it is worth the effort.

Through the late Middle Ages, most people believed that God exists and listens to prayer. Putting individual belief into communal context was not much of an issue. Today, however, when most Jews do not have such beliefs, to act as if we assume they do shows a preference for avoiding the key issues of prayer rather than confronting them.

A personal relation to transcendence is at the heart of what makes prayer worthwhile.

And in placing prayer book before prayer, we ignore the fact that a person who values prayer in general acquires just the kind of knowledge and experience that enables the appreciation of traditional Jewish liturgy. Developing your own prayer voice and personal, outside-the-synagogue prayer skills not only enriches your life but also shines a light on the poetry, insight, and beauty of the Siddur.

To become prayer-people, we must cultivate the art of putting our heart's desires into words—our own prayers as well as the prayers of our people.

People Don't Think Prayer Is Answered

The greatest stumbling block is the difficulty people have with the most basic question. What use is prayer? Indirect answers (to fulfill my obligation, to identify with the community, to sing, to say *Kaddish* for a loved one, to see my friends, to hear the rabbi's sermon, to enjoy the cantor's artistry) are good and true, but not enough for most to become regulars at synagogue services. We want to know. Does God answer prayer? How can you tell the difference between God's communication and your own imagination?

All kinds of strategies are employed to avoid giving a straight answer. My favorite: It's a mystery. We can't know the physics of prayer; to describe it actually cheapens the whole thing. Talk about what the prayers mean, but stay away from the how and the why.

This argument makes sense to a lot of people. But frankly, it has never worked for me, and from what I can tell, it does not work for most Jews. For me, faith requires some real-world plausibility, if not outright evidence. I do not need the kind of proof that a physicist would verify, but I have to have some idea of why this activity is worthwhile and some criterion to judge if it is working. Otherwise, I have other things to do with my time.

The most convincing and oft-repeated justification for attending services that I heard in my youth was some version of this: the act of prayer itself is the answer to our prayers.

Today I have real respect for this statement, now that I think God is real and the act of praying itself actually changes the world. (More on that later.) But this is not how it was explained to me growing up, where explicit talk of God was studiously avoided. The statement was purely psychological, as prayer does not affect anything outside of us. (It was a popular approach because it did not depend on a God whom most believed did not exist.) So when I prayed for the health of a sick friend, for instance, the purpose of the prayer was to make me aware that I should pay a visit to that friend.

While the psychological effect of prayer is certainly valuable and true, it was not enough to motivate me to pray regularly. Did I really need a prayer to know that I should visit a sick friend?

Prayer is intended to be a conversation with God. If we take this proposition seriously, then theology, in the form of down-to-earth, straight talk about how God acts in the world, needs to be on the agenda.

Services Are an End unto Themselves

In today's consumer environment, liberal synagogue services are often compared with other leisure-time activities (to which they typically lose out). And so rabbis are forced to judge their services' success by whether they have provided an enjoyable experience. The discussion turns to the quality of the music, the sermon, the architecture, the social scene. The ultimate criterion: the number of people who attend. Partly because it is difficult to judge, mostly because we are not used to thinking spiritually, we rarely ask, "Has this service helped people connect to God?"

Of course, rabbis, cantors, and synagogue leaders naturally concern themselves with sermons, music, architecture, and the logistics of synagogue services. This is what they are responsible for; here they have some degree of control. But when the goal is to interact with God, the ultimate criterion for success is what happens *outside* of the synagogue. Am I kinder and more aware? Am I living a life of service? Are my relationships improving? Am I coping better with the stresses of life? Am I identifying my true goals and achieving them? Does prayer help me to mourn and grieve my losses in a healthy way?

The result of this basic disconnect is that Jewish prayer is unwittingly taken out of its proper context. At its core, *prayer is a means to an end, and not an end in itself.* In contemporary lingo, it is a means of spiritual growth to transform ourselves and to change the world. In the language of Jewish tradition, prayer is a means to personal and communal redemption.

Instead, most Jews attend synagogue for social reasons, or to receive some kind of positive intellectual and/or aesthetic experience. This is well and good as far as it goes, but when we approach services as if we were attending a concert where we get to sing along, we limit the power of the experience. And when our primary concern is to teach and learn, to gather as a community, or otherwise to tend to the needs of cultivating Jewish identity and community (again, laudable goals in themselves), we judge success by the wrong criteria (the numbers attending an enjoyable Shabbat service). We take prayer out of its proper context and make services an end unto themselves. With attendance in mind, we turn to all kinds of entertaining strategies to lure various demographics into the synagogue, from tot Shabbats to famous speakers, which ironically might make it harder for people who are sincerely trying to pray.

One key to revitalizing Jewish prayer and prayer services is to restore their context as the means to interact with God and cultivate the virtues of a passionate Jewish soul. While the methods may be modern, the goal is ancient: to enable the personal encounter with the Holy One that can transform a life and better the world.

Entering the Debate: On the Difficulty of Jewish Prayer

Please allow me a disclaimer. I have no problem with those who attend synagogue services to fulfill their obligation, to identify with the community, to sing, to say *Kaddish* for a loved one, to see their friends, to hear the rabbi's sermon, to enjoy the cantor's artistry. I also have no problem with those who have no need of God to motivate their prayer practice. On the contrary, I do not know where we would be if people did not attend synagogue services for those reasons, as I did for many years. Nor do I mean to imply that everyone's spiritual experience is identical, or that one person's way to God is more valuable than someone else's. There are people who indeed connect to God through a liturgy of creative responsive readings or through the unadorned traditional service, not to mention through intellectual stimulation from the rabbi or the aesthetic enjoyment of great architecture and the cantor's voice. For what I'm claiming here to be right, it is not necessary to say that what works for others, especially for those who love and enjoy their synagogue services just the way they are, is wrong.

Indeed, I interviewed fifty spiritual practitioners and teachers in preparation for this book. As one might expect, some took exception to my point of view.

While Cantor Ellen Dreskin agrees that a person should take responsibility for his or her prayer life, she reminds us that this is not so easy for one unfamiliar with synagogue services.

> I'm not clergy-centered, because I am familiar with the prayers. I have worked hard on it. But for new people the clergy are crucial. Our whole purpose as prayer leaders is to help people connect to the words. In your Introduction, you say the setting doesn't matter, but if I'm new to the activity of communal worship, I need all the help I can get. It is like an apprenticeship. In a place where real serious davenning is happening, it rubs off. [For more on this theme, see Rabbi Lawrence A. Hoffman's comments on pp. 191–192.]
> CANTOR ELLEN DRESKIN

Plenty of devoted pray-ers, such as Rabbi Laura Geller, are moved by creative English readings.

> For me, a lot depends on the prayer book. When I'm sitting in the congregation I'm often off with the poetry and reflections and meditations.
> RABBI LAURA GELLER

For Rabbi Elyse Frishman, editor of the North American Reform Movement's new prayer book, *Mishkan T'filah,* asking people to develop their personal prayer voice outside of the synagogue is not the first place we should look for a solution, because it may not work.

> Judaism emphasizes communal worship. This allows us to finesse our difficulties with God and with our own lives.

Rather than focus on the challenge of the moment, communal prayer helps us to listen to others, for example, with the *Mi Sheberach* for healing. This is the essence of spirituality, which I understand to mean the deepening of healthy relationships. These relationships begin with one another; from this can grow our relationship with God. Additionally, when we realize through our prayers that we are part of something greater than ourselves—whether a community and/or God—the impact of our personal suffering is softened. Thus, one result of effective communal prayer will be to reinforce our sense of purpose and our connections with one another and God. When a prayer book offers language to achieve this, it is a meaningful contribution to the Jewish People.

RABBI ELYSE FRISHMAN

I see the value in their points of view, and I think that they respect my opinion as well. For the main rule about a spiritual practice is, does it work? And what works for me may not work for you. In fact, different things work for the same person on different days, even in different parts of the same service. So while some of our respondents were quite committed to one particular method or approach to prayer, most adopt multiple modalities for themselves, and most are happy, not sad, when people find a way to pray for themselves that is different than their own.

Having said that, the debates represented in this book are real. I stand by the above diagnosis, and I believe I speak for the majority of Jews who do not find Jewish prayer life compelling.

Here are additional reasons, provided by our community of teachers, on why so many Jews struggle to pray.

Stranger at Home

People hate being ignorant. If you don't know Hebrew, even if you go to a Reform service, it's an immediate feeling of, "I'm a PhD in neuroscience but I can't figure out what page we're on." Especially men. It's very hard for adult Jews who are literate in everything else to become illiterate publically. And it's misguided expectations as well. Congregants walk in and they expect the spiritual high they get when they go to Yosemite or the Rocky Mountains, inside an urban synagogue!

RABBI ELYSE GOLDSTEIN

Part of the disappointment for Jews coming to synagogue is that they're supposed to feel at home but they don't. They feel like strangers. They don't understand what's going on, and yet this is supposed to be their spiritual home.

RABBI NAOMI LEVY

Prayer Book Blocks Prayer

The prayer book is the major impediment to prayer. There are many images of God in Jewish tradition. The ones that got fixed in the prayer book are images of God as a "power over" as opposed to "empowering." While I think that subsequent generations of prayer books are trying hard to overcome it, the fact is, when people confront prayer, particularly on the High Holidays, they see God's kingship in such an overwhelming way that it interferes with their ability to connect to God, or to validate experiences that actually are connections to God but don't fit that model.

RABBI LAURA GELLER

Dumbing It Down

The problem with Reform liturgy is that we assume that we should always give people an exciting new experience. There were ten Friday night services in *Gates of Prayer* [the Reform prayer book], which had the unfortunate side effect of preventing anyone from memorizing the liturgy. And it sort of turned everyone into dummies who had to be told when to stand up and when to sit down. I'm always struck when the leader of the service says, "We now rise for the *Shema*." Why are you telling me that? I've been coming here for thirty years.

I know we stand up for the *Shema*. Only Jews tell one another when to stand. People in every other religion assume you know what to do, and if you don't, you're smart enough to watch and see what everyone else is doing.

RABBI LAWRENCE KUSHNER

Where Is God?

My students write papers on their moments of closeness to God, very rich papers. Rarely do those moments take place in synagogues. I don't have a sense that God is very much present in the synagogues I go to, and I travel around the country to a lot of them, Reform and Conservative, and I go to Orthodox synagogues. Now this may be my skewed experience, but I don't think that whatever it is that Jews associate with spirituality is to be found in the synagogue.

RABBI NEIL GILLMAN, PHD

Power and Vulnerability

I don't think people in the liberal world know how powerful a prayer experience can really be because they don't trust that people really *want* to pray. It's assumed if you don't believe in a petitionary God, you don't need to be vulnerable. Rabbis themselves are afraid to be vulnerable. They are afraid to make davenning into a deep, transformative experience. So they make it into entertainment.

RABBI DAVID INGBER

The Clash of Values

If you're working your whole life so that you can be an executive at GM, and become a member of the Brentwood Country Club and send your kids to Princeton … I think that American Jews have bought into secularism and academia and titles and the outer symbols of a particular kind of success, of which prayer is a challenge and a repudiation. Assimilation has good and bad [aspects]. I think our whole-

sale embrace of Western materialism and degrees as a means
of worthiness has been a bad thing.

RABBI BRADLEY SHAVIT ARTSON

Avoiding the Issue

We fail to examine and work deeply with our own individual
experience of prayer. We are not taught how to do such
examination in our normative Jewish educational institutions.
We prayer educators don't know how to educate toward such
discovery and articulation. Teacher and student alike are
afraid of what they may find, or more likely may not find,
upon such examination. We are still traumatized by our sense
of God's betrayal during the Holocaust. Who dares to open
their heart in prayer?

RABBI NANCY FLAM

About the Book

I realized early on that this book would serve readers better if it
included more viewpoints on prayer than my own. Hence the
interviews and the special character of this book. It is neither a
straight one-author narrative nor a typical anthology. *Making
Prayer Real* is a hybrid. I am presenting a specific approach to the
problem of Jewish prayer, but it includes a range of opinions and
variations.

As a result, opposing methods are presented, sometimes side
by side. For instance, some of our teachers believe that learning
the cognitive meanings of Hebrew words is a waste of time. The
purpose of Hebrew prayer is to serve as a mantra. Others find the
meanings of the Hebrew words essential. Most of our teachers
actually use both approaches.

You will notice quite a difference in the tone of our teachers'
comments. Most were interviewed orally; some preferred to
respond to my questions in writing. Some switched mid-course. I
preferred to keep their language despite the stylistic inconsistency.

Another thing you should know is that these were not journalistic interviews. Sometimes different comments were merged together, as oral interviews can jump around to different topics frequently. The responses were sent back to our contributors for their final approval and, if desired, rewording. The goal is to provide the best information in readable form.

In addition to the interviews, I asked some of the teachers to share their insights in a more focused and deliberate way. Their reflections are found throughout the book, particularly in chapter 1, which is a collection of five short pieces on the efficacy of prayer by four contributors and myself.

A difficulty inherent in interviews, especially when a rabbi converses with another rabbi, is the use of jargon. Many Hebrew terms are thrown out as if everyone understands them. For the most part, I have translated the terms immediately, but this was not always possible without making the text difficult to read. Please make use of the extensive glossary. If you are not familiar with the major units of the Jewish prayer service (*Shema, Amidah, Kaddish*), it will be helpful to glance at chapter 16, where they are briefly explained, and to refer to the glossary. One more note: the word *daven,* Yiddush for praying the traditional Jewish prayers, has entered the American Jewish lexicon. You will see it conjugated as an English word, such as *davenning* or *davenned* (praying, prayed).

Another kind of jargon is the mentioning of well-known teachers and rabbis in Jewish history. Two names stand out: Abraham Joshua Heschel (1907–1972), in my opinion the greatest Jewish thinker to live on American soil, was one of the few to write about spirituality in the God-is-dead fifties and sixties. He influenced nearly every one of our teachers, and they refer to him often. When the name "Zalman" appears in a quote, the reference is to Rabbi Zalman M. Schachter-Shalomi, the father of the Jewish Renewal movement. At age eighty-six as of this writing, he is still sharp as a tack and graciously agreed to my interview request. Trained and ordained through the Chabad branch of the Hasidic

community, he left the ultra-Orthodox world to inspire a generation of Jewish spiritual seekers in the sixties and seventies, many
of whom had left Judaism for the spiritual paths of the East. With
his sharp intellect, passion for God, and unrelenting commitment
to the truth—whether the spiritual truths of the heart or the truths
of modern science and democratic values—he has helped to revive
Jewish mystical thought without returning to a worldview from the
Middle Ages. Many of our teachers studied at his feet. Other names
include the Baal Shem Tov (Master of the Good Name), Rabbi
Israel ben Eliezer (1698–1760), founder of Hasidism, the popular
movement that captivated the Jews of Europe by reframing Jewish
mysticism and revitalizing Jewish prayer; and Rabbi Nachman of
Breslov (1772–1810), a prominent Hasidic rabbi famous, among
many other things, for his practice of freely talking to God, called
hitbodedut (see practice 12).

Finally, let me direct your attention to the Practices section
and the extensive annotated list of Resources at the end of the
book. You might want to take a quick glance before proceeding.
They are grouped at the end for ease of use, but if you would like
to get started before reading this book from cover to cover, there
are suggestions for practice and resources (books, DVDs, and websites) relating to most every chapter.

Making Prayer Real

Taking on Jewish prayer as an adult may seem overwhelming at
times. The solutions offered here certainly require an investment
of thought and a modicum of effort. There is no switch to be
thrown, no wand to be waved. But becoming a prayer-person is
not a one-time decision or a one-time activity that must be completed in a certain time frame. There is room for flexibility. Every
step brings its own reward. Plus, there is no need to be overly
serious about it. Good prayer is sincere but playful, full of improv-
isation, and fun! Most important, the payoff can be enormous.
Prayer can change your life.

PART I

The Spiritual Dynamics of Prayer

The above diagnosis of the problem of Jewish prayer shapes the structure of this book. Instead of prayer book, we start with prayer; instead of Jewish liturgy, we start with prayer in general; and instead of communal worship, we begin with personal prayer. My hope is that the knowledge and perspective gained in parts 1–3 will help you relate to traditional Jewish prayer in part 4.

We start in chapter 1 with the most basic questions. Why pray? Does prayer work? Chapter 2, "What Is Prayer?," begins our exploration into the dynamics of prayer. The approach is functional and practical. What are the goals of prayer, what motivates prayer, and how does it work?

1

The Efficacy
of Prayer

Does Prayer Work?

Rabbi Aryeh Ben David

Does prayer work?
Is it efficacious?

Garrison Keillor, the American storyteller, writes of a mythic town called Lake Wobegon, where "all the children are above average." Perhaps it would be nice to live in such a place. Unfortunately, it is mythic. Still, we often yearn to live in such make-believe places and lead make-believe lives. I do.

People ask, "How is everything?" and I respond, "Great, fine, thank God." It is so easy to escape from our realities, to deny our realities, to become strangers to ourselves and to our souls. Is everything really "Great, fine"?

I am fifty-four years old, and for a fair portion of my life I have lived in Lake Wobegon. I pretended that everything was fine—work, family, health, livelihood. Why? What compelled me to live a fairy tale? Sometimes the fear of things not being perfect was too frightening for me. Often I was playing a role. People looked at me as "the teacher," "the rabbi." As a community role model and a representative of Torah I thought that I had to have answers and my life had to be exemplary.

Prayer brought me back to reality. Prayer brought me back to myself, to the inner chamber of my soul. Prayer introduced me to the life that I was actually leading, rather than the life I thought I was supposed to lead.

Noted Israeli rabbi Dr. Eliezer Berkovits writes that "it is the need alone that God desires.... Prayer is a cry. It is not a memo, a list of things I want, a liturgical recitation. It is a cry of my most needful needs."[1]

Why do I cry out? Will my heart-wrenching yearnings be fulfilled? Will I receive answers for my longings?

Maybe, maybe not.

But this is not really the goal. I call out because I need to call out. Because life, with all of its wonder and beauty, can also be devastating. Because there are failures and insecurities, doubts and disappointments. I need to encounter and express my vulnerabilities, my failures, my shortcomings, my worries. I do not want to lead a fake life. I want to live a life of personal integrity, wholly accessing all of my being.

With whom can I do this? With whom can I call out, without hesitation or concern of being judged or disregarded? With whom can I express the fragility of my life? With my friends? When they ask, "How are you doing?" can I reply, "I think I have failed one of my children, my body is showing worrisome signs, my wife and I seem to be missing each other, and I have an overall feeling of dread"? Will my friends ever ask me again?

With my wife? I have been married for almost thirty years. My wife is one of the world's great listeners, nonjudgmental and loving. Yet when and how can I bare my soul without qualification or second-thought? How often? Is she ready to hear me at precisely the moment I need to unburden myself?

I have a relationship with God, a personal relationship. God knows where I am.

In fifth-grade Sunday school they taught me that God was omniscient. That was a pretty big word for a ten-year-old. I had no idea what they meant. But now it comes back to me. God knows. God already knows. And precisely because God already knows, I can cry out.

There is no embarrassment—God already knows. There is no shame—God already knows.

I call out to escape being held prisoner in Lake Wobegon. To stop being a stranger to my own soul.

I call out to God from the deepest inner chamber of my being, expressing my greatest fears, disappointments, failures, worries, anxieties—not in order to have my problems solved, not in order to receive something, but in order to fully encounter myself. If I cannot admit this and articulate this, then I am held in the perpetual captivity of denial.

Rabbi Berkovits writes that we need to "tumble into the presence of God."[2] Not enter or stand in the presence. Not even be in the presence. We need to tumble. Imagine for a moment that it is a beautiful day and you are standing on the top of a grassy hill. You throw up your hands and tumble down. How did it feel?

Free. Scary. Out-of-control. Exhilarating. Joyful. Bouncy and dirty. Losing breath and laughing.

In the synagogue during prayer, at certain points I will simply put the prayer book down, take a deep breath, and tumble. I will ask, "Okay, Aryeh, where are you really? There are so many gifts, so many things to be thankful for, life itself. And there are also demons and fears. And struggles—that I have faced and I have lost. Where are you?" And I tumble. It is not scripted. I never know where I am going and if it will hurt. It is free and scary and exhilarating. And sometimes I feel like I have grass stains on my soul. But precisely because I lose control and do not try to censor my words, it is authentic.

And like a child running to a parent, a lover in the arms of a beloved confidante, suddenly the fears and struggles do not seem as daunting.

A while ago my wife and I decided to have a special night and go out to a romantic restaurant. We made all of the arrangements, went out, and—it was closed. All dressed up and with nowhere to go, we ended up getting a piece of pizza and sitting on a park bench. And—it was fine. Because with my wife, with the depth, honesty, and love of this relationship, it is really just about being together, candlelight or pizza.

So it is for me with prayer. I have a relationship with God. It is an intimate relationship. I know there are many people for whom the songs and the dancing enhance the quality of prayer. I am not one of them. In any synagogue, at any time, I can find the moment to put down the prayer book and open the inner chamber of my being. I can tumble into the presence of God.

I imagine that it would have been nice to have lived in Lake Wobegon. I still like to think that my children are above average.

But living my own authentic, struggling life is a very powerful place to be. Prayer has offered me a unique opportunity to witness my own struggles, to encounter my own soul, and to live with God as my confidante.

For me, it works.

Choosing Life: Prayer and Healing

Rabbi Anne Brener, LCSW

One day recently, I struggled with painful aftereffects of chemotherapy. My most life-sustaining efforts, walking and writing, felt challenged.

That morning I hobbled downstairs, holding tight to the banister. I sat on the couch and read a book of blessings made for me at a rabbinical conference when my cancer was first diagnosed. My friend Riqi decorated a scrapbook and left it for attendees to inscribe with prayers and wishes on my behalf. I read their words, as well as the prayers and blessings of others, written on ribbons and cards, which decorate my home. I pictured the friends, acquaintances, and strangers who have sent me these loving acknowledgments. Then I read the latest edition of *The Outstretched Arm,* a publication of the National Jewish Healing Center, which explored the theme of Shabbat and healing. The words soothed me. When I came to the end of the publication, I realized that, for the entire time I had been reading, I had not been aware of my pain.

Recently a study was released asserting that prayer does not work. Skeptics were emboldened. "You see," they said smugly. But those of us who have basked in the glow of prayers, rested on their wings, been buoyed by the love they convey are not deterred. We know that while prayer may not effect a permanent cure, it can certainly bring healing. That healing may only last a second or be more enduring. But it is healing just the same. Prayer often enables us to change tracks when we feel pain. Our focus diverted, perhaps only briefly, we align with relief. This brings us closer to a *refuah shleimah,* a complete healing. This morning's reading, which transported me into a zone of healing, was a lot like praying. To paraphrase Rabbi Zalman M. Schachter-Shalomi, it was less of a vending machine experience (you put in your prayer and get what you prayed for) and more of a flight path experience (you are transported into another place).

Prayer may or may not involve God. I pray when I glance at the *Mi Sheberach* list on my computer desktop and feel connected to those for whom I wish healing. I am soothed by the knowledge that there are people praying for me. I breathe more deeply, and on that breath, there is relief. When my kitty purrs, our connection feels like prayer. Each gaze at my daughter is a prayer.

Liturgical prayer can be an affirmation of faith such as the statement of the weekday *Amidah,* which requests of God, "Heal us and we will be healed," or the *Mi Sheberach* [prayer for healing], where God is named as the one who heals both body [*refuat ha-guf*] and soul [*refuat ha-nefesh*]. Prayer can also be a response to the liturgy—not just a positive one. Recently, during the morning service, I had difficulty rising on my toes as we said *"Kadosh, kadosh, kadosh* [Holy, holy, holy]*"* during the *Kedushah* prayer. I cried out in my heart, "Is this what You want? That I'm not even capable of properly praising your name?"

My expression of desperation and anger as a form of prayer is consistent with ancient Jewish understanding. There is a midrash in which Rabbi Johannan used ten words to describe prayer, many of them taken from the biblical description of the emotional state of the Hebrews trapped in the depths of slavery.[3] Those words are *cry, lament, groan, sing, encounter, trouble, call, fall, pray,* and *supplicate.* Almost all of those were present in the question rising from my pain.

As I came upstairs to write, my feet hurt less. Expressing how I felt, I prayed with my fingers and, as I typed, my fingers felt less pain. Sometimes prayer tricks me. After complaining about my situation, the pain seemed miraculously ameliorated. I was embarrassed, thinking that in my crying out I had been overdramatic. I feared burdening those who care for me. Forgive me, if your prayers work. And thank you to all of you who have sent blessings or prayers on behalf of myself. They sustain me.

Why Pray?

RABBI RAMI SHAPIRO

I'm new to prayer. True, I was raised on Davvenen and *tefillin,* and I have spent a lifetime reading aloud to God from a Siddur, but prayer—actually talking to God—was reserved for emotional foxholes and college finals.

For me, God is Reality, everything that was, is, and will be. God is not a being but Being itself. God is *Ehiyeh asher Ehiyeh* (Exodus 3:14): not the fixed and static "I Am That I Am," but the fluid, creative, unbounded "I Will Be What I Will Be" that burns through theological speculation and leaves the seeker in a joyous freefall of not-knowing.

I had no need to pray to God, for there was no Other "out there" to whom to pray. Meditation made more sense, and I took that up with a vengeance. Yet after decades of sitting on cushions and, as I got older, chairs, I felt called to pray. Something was missing in the silence of meditation. While formal prayer was for me a musical score without rests, and hence merely noise, meditation had become a score without notes, and hence merely quiet. I valued the silence, but I wanted the sound. I wanted to talk to God, yet having for so long focused on the nondual No-thing, I just couldn't talk to the supremely dualistic Something.

All that changed in the late 1990s when God began talking to me. "If I am truly nondual as you claim, then I am Other as well as Self, the Many as well as the One, the Wave as well as the Ocean. Do not proclaim My creativity and then imprison Me in your lack of it."

I actually heard this. I was experimenting with Reb Nachman of Breslov's *hitbodedut* practice, isolating myself with God for an hour or more each day, and pouring my heart out about every aspect of my life. I did this for weeks before I heard what the ancient rabbis called *Bat Kol,* the Daughter's Voice, an auditory meeting with God. For me, the Voice was clearly female, and it heralded an encounter with *Shechinah,* the feminine Presence of God, that led me to the Divine Feminine, God as Mother.

"You see, Sweetheart, if I am all things, I am self and other, and that which transcends them both. Don't see me in the tree—see me as the tree. Don't see me in yourself—see me as your self. I am both formless nonduality and the splendor and gore of infinite variety. When you sit in silence and your story fades, you and I fade as well, leaving only formless bliss. But when you pray, chant, and talk to Me, you and I arise together to chat. The silence is true, and so is the talk. Just don't be attached to either."

So began my daily conversations with God, the Divine Mother, an all-embracing presence whose unconditional love burns away the self-serving dramas of my life and leaves me without defenses or hideouts. Her answer to my prayers is always the same: "Sweetheart, drop the drama and look at the truth, then you will know what to do, even if you choose not to do it. Here, let me help you."

God's help is rarely pleasant. Having my story wrenched from my grasp, being stripped naked emotionally and intellectually and forced to see what *is* rather than what I so desperately want there to be, is humbling and often terrifying, and always profoundly liberating. And it is done with such love and compassion that in the end I fall into Her arms in selfless surrender.

"I won't clean up the messes you make," She tells me, Her voice always soft, compelling, and (sometimes frighteningly) inescapable. "And I will be with you while you make them and with you while you unmake them. I will never condemn you, but I will laugh at you. Learn to laugh with me and you won't make so many messes in the first place."

I think the Mother and laughter go together. Sarah laughed and denied it (Genesis 18:12). She named her son Laughter (Isaac) but feared when he played with Man-of-God (Ishmael; Genesis 21:9). In this she brought much suffering to the world, a suffering that lingers even now. In her shame and fear she taught us how to fall from grace, and hence how to return to it as well. Recovering laughter and learning to play is key to spiritual maturation. But today's religion and formal prayer leave little room for play.

At its best religion is myth, jazz, poetry, and play. We make it up, and it makes us up, and in this sacred invention is the possibility of discovering that God is all. But when we take it too seriously we rob ourselves of joy, lose all hope of discovery, and suck the very life out of faith. It is like graduating from stickball to the major leagues; the game is no longer played but managed. We boo and cheer but we no longer laugh.

It is the same in the prayer services I experience in synagogues around the country. Everything is so serious, scripted, and safe. There are no surprises. We know exactly what is coming and what to do when it comes. We call out that God is one (*Adonai echad*) and rarely notice that God is the very one sitting next to us and in front of us and behind us. We say that God's love is unending (*ahavah rabbah*) yet never let it sear away the narcissism and self-pity that fuels the false self we insist upon calling "me."

I value synagogue and liturgy for the community they offer, but when it is God I seek, my shul is the forest, my liturgy the chanting of Her Names, and my prayer the unscripted dialogue of Psalms 42:7: deep calling to deep.

Praying with the Divine Flow
RABBI MIKE COMINS

G rowing up, my Jewish experience was very positive, but it was ethnic, not religious. I liked Hebrew; as a high school student I worked hard to free Soviet Jews; I fell in love with Israel and moved there at age twenty-six. I stayed for fifteen years.

Prayer was always part of my Jewish life. I was a Reform Movement youth-program junkie, and that's what we Reform Jews did. I loved the singing services at summer camp. I had powerful moments of prayer with groups in Sinai, at the Western Wall. And I remember wonderful davenning with my housemates at the Jewish co-op at UCLA. Praying alone in the Sierra, with a minyan of mountains and stars, I was moved to tears.

And yet I had no *personal* connection with God through prayer. So much so that when I interviewed for rabbinical school, I declared that I would never be a pulpit rabbi, as that would be hypocritical. I wanted a rabbinic education to become a better Jewish educator.

I must have had a connection with something, however, because in Israel I davenned regularly, sometimes three times a day when I was at the Pardes Institute of Jewish Studies. My home in Israel was Congregation Kol HaNeshama, a Reform synagogue in Jerusalem, where services were always spirited and moving. I loved how it felt. Praying was definitely an entryway into holiness. Transcendence was happening.

But a dialogue with God? *Nada.* The personal God my friends believed in, Orthodox and Reform alike, was not a possibility. For me, the Siddur was like a passport or an entry ticket, not much more. I didn't believe the theology. I liked the meanings of some of the prayers and hated others, but it didn't seem to matter much. I was connecting with my ancestors and with my people, and I loved Torah study. That's what made it meaningful. I was still a spiritual seeker, as always. I looked for God in the Talmud at Pardes; I tried Western philosophy and theology at the university. But I was a wannabe when it came to God, wondering if the divine lightbulb would ever light up.

Eventually I grew tired of davenning. I was conflicted on my ordination day. I wouldn't exactly call it a crisis of faith, since I never really had any, but the title rabbi presented me in public as something that I definitely was not.

Fortunately, life changed shortly thereafter when I discovered the Judean Desert. Back in my first spiritual home, the wilderness, I read nonacademic books on Jewish mysticism (thank you, Lawrence Kushner), and suddenly, as I like to put it, God kicked in. I hated the academic study of Kabbalah at Hebrew University with a passion. But the understanding of God as an impersonal vitality or force, whom I could nevertheless relate to personally, made enough sense in my head that I now had permission to seek God by way of my body, which brought in my heart. What a difference! I had been in touch with God all along, but misguided expectations, Western religious bias (nature equals paganism), and a lack of teachers who could translate the traditional prayers into a theology and language I could accept left me gasping. Now, the Siddur took on new life.

I left Israel in search of teachers, Jewish and non-Jewish, who could articulate what I was feeling. My first stop was the Rockies, where I heard about a vision quest guide named John Milton. He prepared us for four days of fasting and meditation in nature to connect with "Source" by teaching us qigong, a Daoist body meditation. We were supposed to exchange *chi* (energy) with trees. I thought about leaving after the first day. It may sound strange for a person who now relates to God as a force, but *energy* was one of those New Age buzz words that made the hair bristle on the back of my neck. Maybe I was overly defensive because I knew how far I had already strayed from classical theology.

In any event, I had come too far to turn back. Somehow, I suspended disbelief. Maybe because it wasn't so far from what I read in the works of Kabbalistic and Hasidic rabbis that I had just begun to appreciate. Maybe because it was based on the same theories of Chinese medicine behind acupuncture, which cured friends with difficult illnesses after Western medicine had failed. Maybe because I had practiced tai chi for close to a decade in Jerusalem. Introduced to it by friends, I found tai chi a relaxing body practice to balance my endless hours of study as a rabbinical student. (Floor hockey was my other passion.) Whatever the reason, I took to qigong like a fish to water. Immediately, I could feel *chi*.

I'll never forget the first time I proceeded as instructed and reached my heart and hands toward a towering, centuries-old pine tree. The floodgates opened. I couldn't believe it. For four days, I did it over and over and over, with trees, with rocks, with the moon and the stars, because everything I thought about how the world works was crumbling. All the theology I had studied, even Martin Buber, rested on the Cartesian distinction between spirit and matter. God is extra-dimensional, outside time and space, a being unlike anything we normally perceive.

But energy was everywhere. I could receive it, bathe in it, direct it. Suddenly, Jewish mysticism really made *sense*. *Chi* is so much like what the Kabbalists call the *shefa*, the river of divine light that permeates the universe. Rabbi Nachman called it *chiut*. *Chi, chiut; chiut, chi*. Looking back, I now knew that from my childhood trips in the Sierra Nevada mountains onward, I had regularly experienced transcendence. Now I knew how. Through my senses!

I soon encountered Sylvia Boorstein and her teachings of Buddhist mindfulness in Jewish circles. For the first time, I sat in silence with other rabbis, listening for God. I prayed the Siddur, one word at a time, for an hour every morning. A few months later I began a six-week silent meditation retreat under her tutelage at a

Buddhist retreat center. It was there that I embraced personal prayer for the first time. (Oh, God, six weeks! What was I thinking? Help!) But more important was the meditation, observing the interaction between my mind, my body, and the world. I saw that emotions always play out in the body. I experienced the feel of fear and love, sometimes as sensations in specific parts of the body (mainly the chest), and sometimes in general "body-moods." I saw that when I did something to purposely change my emotional state, my body changed, too. I learned to gauge my emotions though body awareness and saw that different emotional states viscerally affected how I perceived the world around me.

I discovered that anger and fear cause the body to contract. The outside world is pushed away when I take a defensive posture. And when I move into mindfulness, waiting until my body relaxes and paying attention to how my heart feels, peace and love arise on their own. Open to the world, I feel the *chiut* streaming around me and into me. For me, compassion and grace feel a certain way on my skin.

What I now knew, in my body as opposed to in my intellect, was the veracity of certain teachings from Hasidic rabbis and Martin Buber, both interpretations of Jewish mysticism. Various Hasidic rabbis spoke about *devekut* (cleaving to God), about a mental state in which we are constantly aware of the Divine, whether praying in a synagogue or doing the dishes at home. They taught various meditative practices, such as singing a *niggun* (a simple, wordless melody) over and over again, to focus our awareness on the potential holiness all around us. Another name they used was *mochin d'gadlut* (literally, "big brain"), meaning "expanded consciousness." They contrasted our normally self-absorbed, defensive, contracted selves with the open-hearted, egoless, spacious, and loving mode of being that enables a person to be in God's presence.

Buber called this I-Thou relation. When you perceive the world through deep, nonjudgmental, sympathetic listening, authentic relation arises. A new mode of being emerges from a newly opened window—Buber called it the Between—where the subject/object distinction disappears and the reality of time and space fades, as we find ourselves in a moment of eternity with a thou. In every moment of genuine relation, wrote Buber, God is here. To enter I-Thou, teaches Buber commentator and Harvard professor of education Nel Noddings, we must enter "receptive mode," where we ethically validate and listen deeply to the world around us.[4] Receptive mode, it seems to me, is the secular version of *mochin d'gadlut.*

Like Buber, and unlike the Hasidim, I experienced I-Thou as a deepening of experience in this world, particularly in nature, rather than the mystical union with God that comes from overcoming materiality. But unlike Buber, and like a number of Hasidic rabbis, for me I-Thou was accompanied by an increased charge of *chiut*, of divine energy flowing in my body and in the world around me. *Mochin d'gadlut* and "receptive mode" are terms that I will return to in this book, as for me, attaining this state is the purpose of many spiritual practices, including prayer. Especially prayer.

I knew from meditation that I could use my body to observe and affect my emotions. Since I learned what peace feels like, I could see if a prayer for peace might actually bring peace to me. And I could use prayer, particularly in the form of meditation and chant, to bring myself to a peaceful state. In receptive mode, I could pray for peace from a peaceful heart. I could send *chiut*, the divine energy in my heart, to others.

Does prayer work? Without a doubt. It changes me, tangibly. Because I know how to carefully observe my physical and emotional self, I can watch its effect over and over and over again. I can relax into a meditative state by praying the prayers or chanting a chant until I feel the flow of *chiut* increasing as I draw it to me. It only happens when my body is relaxed and my heart is open. Being in *mochin d'gadlut* is its own reward.

Do my prayers change anything in the world around me? I can only assume so. For everything we do sends energy of some kind into the world. The more good energy I send, the more there will be. Since mind and body are not separate, there is a cause and effect relationship between thought and the material world. But this can't be measured, at least not today. So when I pray for a friend to overcome illness, I don't believe that I am influencing the decision of a divine mind that this one shall live and this one shall die. But I am sure that the divine energy is always there, and we can tap into it. When we do, we immediately feel a difference. And just as I can draw it in, I can send it out to affect the world, through prayer.

Surrendering to the Preposterousness of Prayer
JAY MICHAELSON

For many Jews, traditional prayer is a relic of an older form of religion, with a place of prominence in Jewish life but rife with outmoded ideas, language, and forms. Secular Jews, of course, object to the notion of "God," the deity to which Jews are supposedly praying. Progressive religious Jews object to the theology of a God who selectively listens to prayer—particularly after that God chose not to answer the prayers of the innocent victims of genocide. Other progressives take issue with the gendered language of prayer, with the ethnocentric orientation of traditional Jewish liturgy, or with many of the petitions of the Siddur, such as those asking God to smash our enemies. And rationalists and agnostics of all stripes often find it hard to square the notion of a God who hears and answers prayer with anything remotely resembling a philosophically reflective Jewish theology.

Surprisingly, traditional texts tend to agree. While popular discourse is full of exclamations that prayer changes the mind of God, elite literature tends to focus on how it changes the person doing the praying. Even those texts which do suggest that prayer changes reality do so by means of theological-mystical doctrines such as the Kabbalistic understanding of theurgy. Some Kabbalists believe that prayer is effective because of the combination of letters, for example, while others hold that it works because of the symbolic correspondences of words. But almost none say that God hears prayer in the ordinary senses of those words; it fits neither theology (mystical or philosophical) nor the experience of a people persecuted for many centuries.

But the mind—theology, explanations, rationalizations—is not why we pray in the first place; the heart is. It takes only a moment's review of the Psalms, still the urtext of Jewish prayer, to see that Jewish prayer is, at its core, devotionalistic in nature. Even Maimonides, the great rationalist, understood prayer as a time for the heart to open. And while the mind may know rational skepticism, nondual panentheism, and other -isms and -ists, the heart knows that it yearns, a desire that includes a yearning to have a yearned-for. Yes, devotion implies a devoted-to. It implies duality and a primitive, problematic notion of God. But who except diehard atheists can really say that, when the chips are down, they don't turn to a primitive theological idea of God? In the hospital, in the trenches—at such times theology goes out the window, and the heart cries in a language the mind can neither approve nor understand. And similar, though gentler, yearnings are with us all the time: to articulate our hopes, to feel that we are loved, to express gratitude. None of this depends on theology.

Devotion can be embarrassing for thoughtful people. We are trained, those of us who read literary magazines and have a stake in culture and art, to develop our minds, and we are rewarded, with money and degrees and plenty of approbation, for displaying the mental dexterities that show us to be successful and advanced human beings. Sure, there is talk these days of emotional intelligence, and elite culture is itself a concept increasingly under attack. But there persists not only the concept but also rewards for certain kinds of rational behavior in businesses, universities, professions, politics.

So who wants to admit that we remain, on a primal level, in some need of primitive notions of prayer and supplication? All the more so because those who *do* admit such a need often seem weak-minded or brutish or both: fundamentalists, New Agers, the various dope fiends of religion and spirituality—these are the people who *need* to cry out to God. The only question for the thinking class is which is worse: the nasty dogmatism of the Evangelist or the fuzzy banality of the California-spiritual.

But let's admit our basic human needs—albeit with a healthy dose of ambivalence, humility, and even insecurity. Let's concede that traditional prayer is intellectually incoherent. More than that— I'll concede that, at times, it is spiritually counterproductive. If everything happens as it must, rather than how we'd like it to, then what is the point of wishing really hard for it to be otherwise? Indeed, to do so increases delusion, craving, and the denial of What Is—perhaps our best translation for the Ineffable Name, YHVH. Let's not deny that there's something a bit vulgar about a prayer for a person's own well-being, especially when it's simply for a fatter paycheck or thinner romantic partner. In fact, let's give up on prayer as making any sense at all.

But let's not stop praying. Ironically, the very act of admission— of surrendering the pretension of sense-making and admitting that yes, dammit, I want to pray; I want to yearn; I want to ask that all-powerful Mother or Father figure for what I need most—this very act is the gateway to authentic prayer itself. Giving up the attempt to square the circle, to make all the parts fit, is a great release of inhibition and the pretensions of knowledge. A great "I don't know" replaces the arrogant (and ridiculous, if we consider the limits of human knowledge relative to the size of the universe) claims to metaphysical certainty. This "I don't know" is not defeatism; it is the negative theology of the Cloud of Unknowing, the limits of reason according to Kant, the limits of language according to Wittgenstein, the mystery of Being according to Hegel and Heidegger. This "I don't know" is the absurdity of Zen, the transrational of Ken Wilber, the transcendent *keter* of Kabbalah, the impossible unity of emptiness and form. It is that toward which art gestures, the mystery that is rendered banal by explaining, the poetry lost in translation.

From this unknowing springs a kind of permission given by the mind to the heart. Of course, prayer is absurd. Its language is primitive, outmoded, and ridiculous—nearly as ridiculous as love itself. Nor is it strictly necessary. But to those of us who seek to be connoisseurs of the self, to know the intimations and stirrings of our souls, to go without the self-abnegation of prayer is like forgoing music or wine. Yes, life goes on. But without the heart being allowed to cry in the modality of prayer, some of its flavors are drained out, like the industrial foods that pass for produce today.

And so prayer flows from surrender—at first, the mundane surrender of the pretension that I am too sophisticated for prayer, or too intelligent; then, the surrender of the attempt to make it all work out theologically; and finally, the surrender of the "I" itself. In the progressive Jewish world today, you often hear a language of wrestling: with problematic texts, with ideas, with that in which we don't believe but with which we struggle. But if everything is God, the wrestling of Jacob with the angel is the wrestling of the One with the One. It is not a contest; it is an embrace, an act of love in which God is the only lover. It is a divine role play, one moment taking on the submissive role, allowing, begging, being pressed to the ground, and the next assuming the active role, insisting, demanding, expressing the will. It is none other than the drama of prayer itself, once the demands of the intellect bend to the dance of the imagination.

This is prayer set loose from the repressive shames of the self and the preposterous fantasies of theology. It is the heart dancing, imagining, and of course, projecting. Unlike naive prayer, it does not assume the existence of a separate deity who will answer the petitions of the sufficiently pious. Unlike rationalized prayer, it does not masquerade as meditation or magic. And unlike the avoidance or hesitation of the overly uptight or sophisticated—the religious equivalent of hipsters too cool to dance to simple music—it does not submit the needs of the heart to the cynical auditing of the intellect.

To be sure, the edifying notes of chorus-sung hymns can elevate the refined soul to heights of aesthetic pleasure. So, too, can the dull responsive readings of American Judaism inculcate, in some, the ponderous ethical values of tradition. But give me the guts and tears and life-blood of a prayer unashamed of its nakedness, pleading and demanding, shuckling and clapping, or at times at which the soul is in constriction, just going through the motions in the hope that something, somewhere, will loosen.

Is prayer preposterous? Is it susceptible to dangerous fanaticism and pathetic delusion? Is it, like other erotic acts, unsuitable for polite conversation? Of course. But I, too, am often preposterous, susceptible to danger and error, and impolite. I am also, often, trapped, running to and fro in the service of pointless demands that need to be forcibly interrupted. When enlightened consciousness arises, then, yes, there really is no need for prayer. But the rest of the time, I need to do work to see the obvious—and the type of work varies with the type of lack I experience. Sometimes, the mindful space of meditation quiets the nonsense that masquerades as sense, so that the sense that looks like nonsense can remind me of its truth. Sometimes, the body is the key. And sometimes, what's needed is the courage to give the heart its due. Sometimes I need to pray even for that.

2

What Is Prayer?

It's very surprising for people to learn that very few rabbis, Jewish philosophers, or theologians really have a conventional view of prayer, namely, that we ask for something and God gives it to us, or doesn't. It's really striking. The Kabbalists have all kinds of ways in which prayer can have an effect, but not the standard "you speak and God listens" model. Likewise in the philosophical tradition, and even in the rabbinic tradition. In the last two thousand years, reflective Jewish religious thought actually does not give a lot of space to what 99 percent of us would immediately assume is the point of prayer.

JAY MICHAELSON

As we read in the previous chapter, the question of whether or not prayer works depends on what a person believes about God and God's relation to the universe. While this is not a book about theology, we cannot discuss prayer without acknowledging that it means different things to different people.

"Conventional" prayer, to adopt Jay Michaelson's term, is the presumed traditional take on the world. We pray to change God's mind, for God has the power and desire to intervene in the world. This view is represented in *Making Prayer Real,* and not only by Orthodox Jews. At the opposite end of the spectrum, usually mystics and contemplatives (including the rationalist, philosophic variety), God does not possess at least one of the "all" attributes that make the suffering of the innocent so problematic: all-knowing, all-powerful, all-present (past, present, and future), and all-good. God lacks either the decision-making kind of mind we humans possess, or the desire to intervene in the course of the world, or the ability to do so. For them, prayer is directed at the human heart, the only place it can affect. Others take a middle position of one sort or another, believing that prayer indeed aims to change humans, but this has a cosmic effect on the world and on God, who does have the power to intervene in worldly affairs. This is the neo-Hasidic, mystical position that I accept. We shape the flow of divine energy in the world through the internal struggles of our hearts. Most of the teachers interviewed for this book accept some version of the latter two positions.

The purpose of this grossly oversimplified typology is to recognize that prayer takes different forms in Jewish tradition, drawing on different experiences and subsequent explanations of how God works in the world. But the differences should not be overemphasized. When we turn to the main questions of this book—how prayer functions and what it tries to accomplish—there is a surprising amount of agreement. Even the mystics, who see no separation between themselves and God, find it useful to employ the second person "You" language of address that assumes a dualistic understanding of God as other. And of course, those who believe in the "conventional" take on prayer have no reason, or desire, to deny the effects of prayer on the human heart.

One way to get to the bottom of what prayer is, is to ask, what does prayer do?

All prayer—when we pay attention, whether personal or liturgical—is ultimately a form of speaking the truth. It makes us aware of what is going on in our lives in this moment—so that we can see clearly and respond appropriately.

RABBI JONATHAN P. SLATER

Prayer changes and affects the person who prays because prayer opens the heart. Prayer lets down the barriers between our intimate longings, our private pain, our anxious clutching fears, and everything else. The very interiority of a prayer experience (even a prayer as brief as "Wow") opens and exposes our tender hearts.

RABBI SHERYL LEWART

Underneath its stated intentions of praising, thanking, or beseeching God, underneath its functional goals of fulfilling our religious obligations, spurring us to action, bringing us comfort in times of stress, improving our character traits, or bonding with the historical and the present Jewish community, prayer is first and foremost a spiritual practice that lays the foundation for attaining any of the above. In its essence, prayer is the practice of becoming more aware and more compassionate. It is a way of speaking truth and opening the heart.

How does prayer accomplish this task? Particularly for those who do not hold a traditional theology, we must ask, how does prayer actually work?

Aligning with God

I like the Leona Medina image. If you saw somebody pulling a boat to the shore and were mistaken about mechanics and motion, you might think that he was pulling the shore to the boat. And that's what prayer is like. You think that you're pulling God to you, but in fact, if you pray well, you pull yourself to God.

RABBI DAVID J. WOLPE

For most, particularly the mystics, prayer is understood as a method to attune or align ourselves with God.

Prayer can be taking that contemplative moment before a meal or a boardroom meeting. We can say to ourselves, "I'm going to take a moment and center myself—what am I about to do and why?" In this moment we are locating a self often buried under the mundane. Prayer gets us in touch with that deeper self.

RABBI SHAWN ZEVIT

The one who prays is like the shofar. The shofar itself has no independent significance or power. It is only meaningful when someone blows into it. The sound that emerges is recognized and has a meaning. We are the shofar—and it is God who moves through us, "blows" on us to generate the prayer that emerges. Thus, prayer is the closing of a circle, the making of a connection between self and Self, creating a united whole.

RABBI JONATHAN P. SLATER

One method of aligning with God is to change our usual perspective and bring attention to matters of the holy.

What prayer means to me is turning myself so that I'm no longer the center of the story. I'm reminded of that kid's book *Zoom,* where you start out looking at a farmhouse, and then you go back and see that it's really a picture on a wall in a room, and then you go back further and see the room is in a house, and further and further until eventually, you're seeing this from "God's perspective." And suddenly, the universe is completely different and the place of that farmhouse is a completely different story. At my best, prayer is about getting out of my own way and, as much as possible, trying to see the world for a moment through the metaphoric eyes of God.

RABBI LAURA GELLER

Practically speaking, the most important way to examine a religious question is, "How does this actually work?" Prayer is a spiritual technology. It changes the heart. Before prayer, we might be thinking about business relationships or the mortgage or whatever else, and then during prayer, our mind is turned, either by a formal liturgy or our own intentions, to other subjects more essential, more real. The mind has been cleansed in a way. I like to joke that prayer is the original mental floss.

JAY MICHAELSON

You Cannot *Think* God

None of the teachers interviewed see prayer as an intellectual experience.

If you ask most people, it's the sound of the prayers and the music of them and not the cognitive content, and frankly, although we comment on them all the time, the cognitive content of many prayers is not so impressive. Other parts of the tradition are much more impressive. It affirms certain beliefs, but it's not supposed to be intellectually tantalizing. That's not the purpose of it. In fact, if it were, it would sort of defeat the purpose of it.

RABBI DAVID J. WOLPE

Indeed, the liturgist uses words and concepts, as does the poet, not to convey information but to evoke emotion, to both embody and celebrate the Divine-human relationship.

I'm not trying to understand the words. I'm trying to be the words.

RABBI SHEFA GOLD

I don't pray to God with my prayers. I experience God through my prayers, with my community. When my voice is joining with twenty other people's voices, chanting the *Amidah*, I experience God through that moment. I'm not praying to God for something to happen.

RABBI JAMIE KORNGOLD

The *Is* and *Ought* of Prayer

So little of Jewish prayer is actually asking for things, especially on Shabbat, when most attend synagogue services. What do we want when we pray?

> I'm davenning to not want anything. Not davenning to want what I don't have, but to want what I already have. And so prayer becomes an hour of gratitude practice and a sense of being able to be with the real and come out of my antagonistic posturing to what has been given. A softening to what is, so that I can be with what is.
>
> RABBI DAVID INGBER

In this sense, prayer is a true source of peace. It helps us to accept what we might prefer to deny. But at other times, the same honesty and acceptance that lead to equanimity goad us to rebel against the way things are.

> Prayer isn't only comforting, it's also disturbing. It can stir up parts of you that are more comfortable left dormant. That's not always easy. I think that one of the reasons to shy away from prayer is that you don't want to hear that part of yourself and prayer brings it out.
>
> RABBI DAVID J. WOLPE

This, too, is prayer, a point usually missed, and certainly not advertised in the synagogue bulletin. Real spiritual practice is often painful, particularly at the beginning, when we have the courage and honesty to see ourselves in our folly as if for the first time. An open heart is not only more receiving of love; it is more sensitive to pain, especially our own.

Dr. Heschel writes that embarrassment and shame are what hold us back from praying our deepest prayers. For me, the point of spiritual practice is to keep dancing on our own edge. As we practice, we can look for where we've fallen into a place of comfortability. What might we still be afraid of expressing or ashamed of showing?

RABBI DIANE ELLIOT

Authentic Prayer Is Dangerous

When prayer works, we see the world and ourselves with increased clarity. One way to remain in denial about our deficiencies is to rationalize our current state as the way things should be. Paradoxically, sometimes to accept what is, is to accept that we need to change. Real prayer is not complacent.

I'm unimpressed by the idea that prayer is just to make you feel good or feel better. Prayer is also supposed to challenge you. I appreciate the quote, "Prayer comforts the afflicted and afflicts the comfortable." I like that a lot. There's often too much emphasis on feeling good. It's all about changing yourself in order to change the world. When you walk out a better person, prayer works.

CANTOR ELLEN DRESKIN

Rabbi Ethan Franzel brings a mystic's perspective to prayer.

The Baal Shem Tov talks about the body and prayer. Just as in the act of lovemaking there needs to be a friction, there needs to be movement to generate the heat and the passion, so the body needs to be involved in prayer as well. Lovemaking is really an act of intimacy, of knowing another, of merging as close as you can, literally, physically. Spiritually speaking, the act of giving yourself up, of subsuming your identity, of throwing your lot in with who you truly are, which is God, is the most intimate act that you can do, which is why it's so scary.

RABBI ETHAN FRANZEL

Genuine prayer is honest, and when we're honest, we do not know what we will uncover. We do not know which emotions will be triggered, or what insight may come. But in community, human or divine, we need not feel alone to face the music.

Often prayer is simply a sigh of release, an acknowledgment that we are not always in charge of our lives. A feeling of accompaniment rather than abandonment invites us to share intimacies and probe the dark places. As we sense the presence of a loving, nonjudging, patient soulmate, we grow in optimism and confidence. No matter how difficult the situation, we recognize the psalmist's words as our own. "Even though I walk through a valley of deepest darkness, You are with me" [Psalms 23:4].

RABBI SHERYL LEWART

Prayer as Spiritual Practice

We end this chapter by restating the premise of this book. Prayer comes alive when we take responsibility for our own inner lives.

I would suggest that we need to reconceive prayer as not about addressing the Divine Being with praise and requests. Rather, we should see prayer and the time set aside for prayer as time devoted to our spiritual work. It is time for reflection, a precious gift to ourselves amidst our busy lives. The liturgy should remind us:

1. There is something larger than ourselves in the universe—what many of us call God. It is an important perspective that also reminds us that we are not alone.

2. It should be a time to reflect on the spiritual issues in our lives. To think about how to improve my ethical qualities to be more like the person I deeply desire to be.
3. It is an opportunity to express gratitude for the blessings in our lives—most of all the blessing of life itself.

This is in fact a reconstruction of the traditional forms of rabbinic prayer: *shevah* (praise), *bakasha* (request), *hoda'ah* (thanks). Reframing *bakasha* as focusing on spiritual growth rather than asking God for things is a critical redefining of prayer.[1]

RABBI MICHAEL STRASSFELD

One reason prayer is difficult is because we don't know what we're doing. I'm not talking about Siddur literacy or synagogue skills. Most of us are unfamiliar with our own internal dynamics as pray-ers. One way to understand prayer is that it is a transformation of consciousness. So we need to ask ourselves, "Where are we starting from? Where are we trying to go? What are the prayer strategies or practices that we know from experience are likely to take us there?"

Prayer needs to be understood as a spiritual *practice* just as we might understand the practice of meditation or yoga. But in order to do this, we need to know what we're practicing *toward,* what we're practicing *for.* We need skilled guides and teachers to help us. We need patience, determination, and faith in the practice. And we need to know if, over time, we're making any progress.

RABBI NANCY FLAM

The rest of *Making Prayer Real* is devoted to meeting the challenge that Rabbi Flam has set before us. With our community of teachers, we turn now to the spiritual dynamics of the practice of prayer.

3

Yearning

When I'm on top of the world, it's easy to forget gratitude and humility. So the greatest gift of longing is just to tap into your inadequacy or the world's inadequacy, the home-sickness your heart has. That opens the doors of the heart; that's where prayer life begins.

RABBI TIRZAH FIRESTONE

Prayer expresses desire. Holy desire: for an end to an illness or for a peaceful world, to live in joy and to behave well, or to find connection with God. We start by asking, where does holy desire come from? Why do we yearn? For what do we long?

Longing and Belonging

Longing is the impulse that started the process of creation. Not God's will, but God's desire. So I understand longing as a language that is hard-wired within us, who were made in the image of God. Longing is how we communicate with Source, the way we bring the energy of creation into the world. So when my prayers really come from that longing place, they have the greatest power.

RABBI NADYA GROSS

In the heart of our souls, there is an existential longing that most of us sublimate, a place we often only face with mortality, for as much as we're surrounded by friends and family, dying is the one place that is truly ours to navigate. You can find your dream job or live in your dream place, you can marry your dream partner, and you think the longing would be gone. But it's not.

RABBI SHAWN ZEVIT

Our tradition tells us that the soul has its own yearning, its own longing for union with the Divine. Longing to connect with another and longing to connect with the Eternal, with God. If we ignore that yearning, we can have everything and still feel empty. That's why as a society we can have so much and still feel like there's a hole, an emptiness that can't be filled. *Tzama lecha nafshi* [Psalms 63:1, My soul thirsts for You] is describing that hunger.

RABBI NAOMI LEVY

Prayer is about longing and belonging. To "belong" is to "be-in-longing." Praying is being able to say, *"Ribbono shel Olam,* Master of the World, I belong to you, and I am in-longing for you. I believe that You long for me, and are in-longing for me." When we can identify where we belong, to whom we belong, to whom we are in-longing, then our lives have been transformed.

REB MIMI FEIGELSON

Prayer and Love

We cannot speak much about desire without turning to the strongest of the noble emotions, to love.

For me, prayer is all about yearning. In a way, when we really pray, we expose ourselves to the humility of that deep longing.

What do we long for? Love. Not much more than that. We long to know that we are loved in such a way that we matter. That Someone cares when we're in distress. It takes courage to humble ourselves so much, in pining for love. It takes courage to pray.

RABBI ZOË KLEIN

I use a myriad of images to think of Divinity at different times in my life, but mostly, I speak to God as one lover to the other. I find that for myself, this has the most comfort and the most power. I recognize, theologically, the problematic with it, but as Reb Zalman [Schachter-Shalomi] once said, I don't let my theology get in the way of my spiritual life.

RABBI LAVEY YITZCHAK DERBY

The Seed and the Fruit

Part of what davenning does is reorient us toward our deepest yearnings, our real wants. Yearning is both a seed and fruit. Yearning is true when it's something that fills you with wholeness, and yearning itself fills you with wholeness much like what you imagine and yearn for. It's a funny thing. When you yearn for wholeness, the yearning itself brings you wholeness.

RABBI DAVID INGBER

This is an important, if paradoxical, truth about the efficacy of prayer, one that I resisted for much of my life. It seems too easy, and too self-serving. But that was before I prayed with sincerity. Just as recognizing the source of a problem can solve the problem, recognizing the depth of our desire for peace or love can actually evoke peace or love.

The experience of longing I can only describe as an exquisite pain that brings intense joy. Finding the longing is already finding the connection. Prayer is one of the ways I get there.

RABBI NADYA GROSS

Stay in Touch with Your Longing

Yearning can reveal the gap between where we are and where we ought to be. Sometimes longing is painful, but as Rabbi Nadya Gross reports, we might experience our pain with compassion. We can feel the pain of where we are, but we can also experience the joy of getting honest and knowing where we want to go. We can hold on to longing and let it be our teacher.

> I can't always tell you what's missing, but it's staying with "missing," with "longing," that gets me in touch. And if we don't try to solve the question right away, if we don't look at prayer as being the answer, but at prayer as being a conversation, we can enter a dialogue.
>
> I liken this process of being with missing or longing or disconnection with the universe's black holes. At first when we looked at black holes, we only saw the absence of light. Until we pointed the Hubble telescope at them. Then, voilà! Thousands of galaxies. There were fireworks going on in there. All these worlds of light. All these worlds of possibility that we could not see—not because they weren't there, but our capacity and vision were not strong enough to penetrate the veil. That's what prayer can reveal, if we get in touch with our longing and peer into what may at first seem like nothingness.
>
> RABBI SHAWN ZEVIT

Yearning seems to be one of those things we are either born with or not. Many people feel quite at home in the world and don't live with a sense of something missing. Those raised in a happy and healthy home may well wonder what all the commotion is about. As long as they are living in honesty rather than denial, they certainly shouldn't feel bad about it.

For others, yearning is always present. Here the question is whether longing is healthy and holy or self-centered and destructive. Do we long for virtue or vice, for peace or for power, for joy or for pleasure, for the good of others or only ourselves? The choice is ours.

Many consider music to be the most powerful language of longing. Rabbi Shefa Gold, a pioneer in the ecstatic practice of Jewish chant, focuses on holy desire in her teaching. Her latest book, *In the Fever of Love: An Illumination of the Song of Songs* (Ben Yehuda Press), is a commentary on the biblical book of longing and desire.

Longing: Fuel for Spiritual Practice
RABBI SHEFA GOLD

When I sit down to meditate or pray, I address myself to God, saying, "I just want to BE with You." In that moment of focused intention, I turn away from the surface of things and I turn toward that which is essential. I open up the treasures of my depths; I unlock the power of longing.

That power sustains me in my practice, fuels the passion of my prayer life and sends me to a state of attentive, vital, open, loving expectancy. That power is critical to my spiritual practice.

Years ago, when I was first stepping into the blessing of being a teacher, Reb Zalman Schachter-Shalomi gave me this one assignment: "Go to your people and awaken the power of yearning."

The Song of Songs, the sacred text of yearning and consummation, says, "I was asleep, but my heart stayed awake. There it is ... the sound of my Lover knocking" [Song of Songs 5:2].

All of us are asleep to some extent, lulled by the constant din of media and commerce. We are constricted by past disappointments, habituated to a narrow version of reality, blind to the unexpected.

And yet each of our hearts is imprinted with a memory of Home, a knowledge of the Infinite, and a Great Love. Inside each of our hearts is a spark of holy desire, waiting to be ignited into flame.

I take two approaches to this work of awakening the force of longing. I believe that both are necessary.

One approach is in really knowing, experiencing, and expressing the pain of separation from God, from the Oneness. The pain of separation becomes the motivating force that finally turns us toward our Source and sends us on the journey to freedom. When the Israelites went down into Egypt, it took them four hundred years to realize that they were enslaved and to cry out to God. It was that powerful cry that set in motion the process of liberation. And when Moses began to act, life only got harder and more oppressive.

So too, when we awaken to the pain of separation, all of our well-built defenses begin to crumble; places in our hearts that had been shut down by disappointment or despair are suddenly feeling again. Our former numbness is replaced with the excruciating anguish of isolation and alienation. The pain shows us just how far we have strayed from our own truth. We were unconscious and hurt those that we love the most. We became strangers in the land of our own lives. These realizations have the power to strip away our excuses and defenses, to turn us toward God, to send us on a new path. In our brokenness, we find the force of longing that can move us to wholeness.

Every tragedy that I suffer in life opens the possibility of soul growth as I choose the option that affirms life and deepens compassion, rather than the one that leads me to bitterness.

This approach to the cultivation of longing would not be very popular or sustainable if there wasn't also another approach to this most essential spiritual work. The other way, equally rigorous but sometimes more attractive, is ecstatic practice.

Through prayer, chant, Shabbat observance, dance, drumming, breath, visualization, or focused intention, it is possible to receive a glimpse of the Promised Land. That glimpse is the momentary identification with a state of consciousness that is abundantly flowing with milk and honey, with the realization that God is right here, embracing us. In that glimpse we see and know our Oneness with creation and with the Source of all. We are nurtured by milk that flows directly from the breast of God, and we taste the honeyed sweetness of existence itself.

It may just be a moment. And that moment may be terrifying, as the boundaries of ego dissolve to reveal the wide expanse. However terrifying or delicious that glimpse may be, we can take the memory of that state back into the wilderness of our lives. That memory can be used to awaken the power of longing, the force that will sustain us on this journey. The memory of expansiveness sets up a painful dissonance with the narrow constructs we have built. As old and limiting beliefs shatter, we are propelled onto our path—sent by the impossibility of going back into slavery, drawn by the beauty of our vision of the Promised Land, and inspired by the taste of freedom. That memory becomes the compass that can guide us, as we learn to love and be loved, as we choose life again and again.

4

Gratitude

The Sufi poet Rumi said your depression is related to your refusal to praise. Heschel reminds us that all of Jewish prayer is praise. Praise is an antidote to depression. When I pray the words of praise, the clots of dissatisfaction soften. The flow of energy pulses with vitality. I am re-energized.

RABBI MARCIA PRAGER

It's easy to pray with a kvetch. Demanding. Victimy. Praying from that place engenders separation, not connection. There is a real wisdom in the Torah of gratitude, that the first thing you do when you get up in the morning is say *modeh ani,* I'm grateful.

RABBI TIRZAH FIRESTONE

G ratitude is the everyday heart opener of spiritual practice. While the heart responds in more dramatic fashion to major life events, good and bad, there is nothing like saying thanks to ground the more routine, and thus the more difficult—and the more important—rhythms of a regular spiritual practice.

It is not coincidental that Jewish services begin with prayers of gratitude, for expressing thanks immediately changes our mood.

As far as I can tell, it is impossible to experience gratitude and anger at the same time.

> We tend to notice only when something is broken. When I'm sick, I feel, "Oh, if I was only healthy." When I have bronchitis, "Oh, how wonderful breathing is." I had asthma as a teenager; boy, did I learn about the gift of breathing. I promised to myself, "As long as I live, I will never forget what a gift it is to breathe!" But I don't have asthma anymore. How easy it is to forget. Every day my mom calls me and cries about the macular degeneration that is gradually robbing her of eyesight. It reminds me that I am so grateful to see! When I sing prayers of gratitude for the gift of standing, the gift of walking, the gift of clothing, the gift of food, the gift of my eyesight and my easy natural breathing—for that measure of well-being that enables me to say, "Thank you, God! Enough still works that I'm still here," my heart soars and all grumpiness departs.
>
> RABBI MARCIA PRAGER

Prayers of gratitude keep us from taking things for granted.

> "Barchu et Adonai ha-mevorach," the call to prayer says, "Let us bless Adonai, who is blessed." This sounds initially like a tautology (which is why, perhaps, so many translations "fudge" the Hebrew). But we don't regard it as tautological or redundant to curse what is cursed. We can vent and complain and pass judgment all day long! The Barchu reminds us that it is vital to bless what is blessed. We do it to acknowledge the good, to recalibrate our standards, to inculcate and express gratitude, to experience—and not overlook—our blessings.
>
> RABBI DEBRA ORENSTEIN

Anytime I am truly mindful—when I leave behind thoughts of past or future, move beyond my own story and receive the world around me—something wonderful happens. My heart fills with gratitude. (Especially if I am with my beloved Jody or out in nature.)

That's how it feels, but in reality, I think the metaphor of "filling" is mistaken. The natural attitude of the heart is already gracious. But it is usually hidden by fear, tension, and the busyness of our lives. A better metaphor might be that prayer "uncovers" what is already there.

> Gratitude or praise practice uncovers the everyday gifts of life. As Reb Zalman [Schachter-Shalomi] would say, gratitude is like wifi. You can use it to log on anywhere, anytime. I employ the practice of blessing during the day to keep me aware of the gifts.
>
> RABBI DAVID INGBER

Humility

Gratitude is also important because it requires humility. A prayer from humility's opposite, arrogance, would be an oxymoron.

> Prayer teaches us the art of humility and surrender. The Talmud teaches us to stand in the presence of God with our heart looking up toward the heavens and our eyes looking down. It teaches us to embrace the unknown and to muster up our faith in moments of doubt, pain, and anxiety. It reminds us that we are part of a greater existence.
>
> REB MIMI FEIGELSON

> Has prayer changed me? It requires humility, gratitude, modesty. It requires a sort of smallness rather than bigness. It's not about making big theological statements; it's about how can my very next move, very next thought, very next smile, very next encounter, be more compassionate, more gracious, more skillful, more helpful, more understanding, more heartfelt.
>
> RABBI NEHEMIA POLEN, PhD

Gratitude soothes tension, creates a feeling of spaciousness, and directs us toward *mochin d'gadlut,* toward expanded consciousness.

> The major focus of prayer is learning to express gratitude, to feel the goodness of our lives, to pause to count our blessings, to feel grateful. And when we feel filled with gratitude, there's a natural next step. How might we share the goodness we've received with others?
>
> RABBI ELIE KAPLAN SPITZ

When we are in touch with our sense of yearning and gratitude, we establish the conditions from which prayer might flow. Tapping into our natural generosity, quite literally, opens the heart to our loved ones, to people everywhere, to God.

Yearning and gratitude comprise the emotional foundation of a prayer practice. Now we move to three foundational skills that propel prayer forward: cultivating *kavvanah,* engaging our bodies, and learning to listen deeply.

5

Kavvanah

I relate to prayer as an action that we initiate from our humanness. It is an offering, a practice. A gathering of intention or *kavvanah*. The Hebrew word for sacrifice, *korban*, coming as it does from the same root as the word for "coming close," seems apt.

RABBI MYRIAM KLOTZ

In Jewish spiritual practice, *kavvanah* is a central term. It has such a long history and so many meanings that it defies easy translation into English. It might be rendered "intention," "focus," "concentration," "purpose," or "sincerity." It is a goal and a method, a value and a virtue, an attitude and an attribute.

And then there is the original meaning. *Kavvanah* is an archery term, "aiming" an arrow toward the target or, more generally, pointing something in a particular direction. In modern Hebrew, the term is used for tuning an instrument. It is related to *chet* (sin), which in its original archery context means "to miss the mark." Over time *kavvanah* assumed the wider meaning of mental aiming, of intention. Skillful mental aiming, of course, has many facets, and so one Hebrew term came to include numerous attributes of spiritual practice.

59

Intention

Intention is the first step in performing any spiritual practice with awareness. Much of Jewish prayer and ritual explicitly seeks to establish proper intention. We say a blessing to express our intention in ritually drinking wine or eating *challah* bread. We study Talmud and pray for wisdom with the intention of acting with integrity in our daily lives.

> What I teach people is that you need to bookend all of your spiritual actions with intention, *kavvanah,* actually saying what you intend, which will change your state of being, and end with *hoda'ah,* with gratitude. So whether praying or meditating or chanting, or even teaching and learning, I begin with intention and end with thanks.
>
> RABBI ETHAN FRANZEL

Intention harnesses our yearning, our holy desire, and gives it structure. This aspect of *kavvanah* shapes a spiritual practice by delineating the target and declaring our desire to hit it. It might also articulate the steps we need to reach the goal.

Intention, then, creates the path. Focus and concentration keep us on track.

Focus

> The biggest insight I ever had about prayer is that it's a form of meditation, meaning that it involves a *continuous* focus. Once you understand that prayer is a meditation, almost everything else follows. If you pray *continuously without interruption*—without engaging in conversation or looking around aimlessly—but think about God and godly things for twenty minutes or a half hour or for a two-hour service, something happens. You elevate.
>
> MAGGID YITZHAK BUXBAUM

Formal meditation has helped me to develop *kavvanah*. Not only has it improved my concentration skills, but it has also taught me how to be kind to myself.

> One of the things you learn in meditation is how to set an intention and keep coming back to it, recognizing when your mind is wandering and bringing it back to the intention. This is something that is not always recognized in prayer. Like meditation, prayer is a concentration practice, coming back again and again and again, without judgment, without brutalizing yourself. That opens the heart.
>
> RABBI SHEILA PELTZ WEINBERG

Once you know that even the most experienced davenner will find him- or herself lost in thoughts about work, a college football team, or last week's episode of a television show, you can forgive yourself for your wandering mind. In fact, as experienced meditators will tell you, the more self-judgment and self-criticism we direct at ourselves, the more angry and tense we become. Often, the harder we try to concentrate in response, the more the mind wanders. For most people, the mind cannot force focus on itself. Rather, concentration *arises* when we are relaxed and "drop in" to prayer. When you find yourself lost in outside thoughts while praying, the best advice is to refrain from self-bashing and gently, lightly, return to your davenning.

Sincerity

> You can't be mealy-mouthed and half-hearted saying the prayers. A little with *kavvanah* is better than a lot without. One minute where you really mean what you say is better than a million mumbled words!
>
> MAGGID YITZHAK BUXBAUM

For prayer to work, you have to mean it. As we will see later, many people refrain from any relation to the meaning of words, particularly Hebrew words, when they pray. The words serve as a mantra. But when we are speaking words in prayer with awareness of their cognitive meanings, we need to speak with sincerity.

The challenge is twofold. The first task is to figure out what we really believe. This is easier said than done. Often we are unaware of our own deepest truths, the real motivations behind our actions and the foundational emotions underneath the ones we feel on the surface. The gift of prayer is that, like meditation, psychotherapy, and other methods of introspection, it can help us to reveal ourselves to ourselves. The key is honesty.

> Sometimes I worry that people use the concept of *kavvanah* as a kind of mental trickery. In other words, they think, if I do this or repeat that, I will be ready for prayer. But intentionality is nothing if not honesty. You cannot fake the intentions of your heart. I find my *kavvanah*, therefore, through trying to be deeply honest with myself and with God. If I know I've done something wrong, I whisper to God and myself about that. If I desperately need help, while I might not admit it to any person, I will beg God to help me. I express all my vulnerability and fears and helplessness in prayer. How do I prepare for that? I just tell myself, "You are in a sacred space. Be honest." And I am.
>
> RABBI ZOË KLEIN

Putting the Heart into Words

I'm part of nature but a form that has thought, and can praise. For other species it's just being, but there is an excitement about our ability to reflect and to say whatever starts with "Wow!" and goes on. It can be awesome or horrific or terrific or wonderful, but something that evokes our ability as human beings to find words to express. That's something very special. That's why I find a lot of the sense of prayer in modern poetry.

MELILA HELLNER-ESHED, PhD

The second challenge in speaking with integrity is connecting our hearts to our mouths. How often have we sat in a synagogue service, or even in private worship, and gone through the motions with little effort, little affect, and hence, little effect? Our lives are filled with words said by habit with little thought, intention, or sincerity. This is often necessary and healthy in our daily lives. How difficult life would be if every word were said as if in a court deposition. But when it comes to prayer, if we can't put heart into words, we know we shouldn't have bothered.

What does it feel like?

I think most of us know when we are speaking sincerely. Once we take our own words in prayer seriously, we become aware of what it feels like for us. For me, there is an emotional charge in dramatic moments, a certain emotional tone for less dramatic moments. For many, body awareness is a fruitful tool for connecting the heart to words (see chapter 6 and practice 6). For others, sincerity is experienced as a lack of distractions, as pure, concentrated devotion. The Talmud states that once we have started to pray the *Amidah,* we may not stop "even if a snake has wrapped itself around one's heel" (Mishnah B'rachot 5:1).

Another passage has always been theologically troubling to me.

> They tell of Rabbi Hanina Ben Dosa that he used to pray over the sick and say, "This one will live," or "This one will die." They said to him, "How do you know?" He replied, "If my prayer is fluent in my mouth, I know that he is accepted; and if it is not I know that he is rejected." (Mishnah B'rachot 5:1)

It sounds as if Rabbi Hanina Ben Dosa has godlike abilities. But my experience of sincere prayer has changed that understanding.

When I enter the "zone" of prayer and the words flow effortlessly, it feels like I am tapping directly into divine energy, as though the walls have dropped and I am truly attuned to God. In such instances, the words seem to say themselves. My desire is God's desire. Yes, peace is possible, love is real, the mountains sing, and I can change. When discursive thought returns, I can only look back in delight. Rabbi Hanina Ben Dosa's prayer, it seems to me, was not a manipulation but a reflection of the divine will.

Attaining *Kavvanah*

Our teachers share their methods of cultivating *kavvanah*.

Train Your Soul to *Kavvanah*

Rabbi Ethan Franzel accesses the fruits of past practice to jumpstart his present praying.

> It's no small thing to change your state of mind or state of being. When you learn guitar, you develop muscle memory. You have to play the same chords over and over and over, but eventually your fingers just know it. It's the same with your mind and your soul and your heart. So when I begin a prayer service, I always close my eyes and breathe deeply because those very acts put me into my soul muscle memory. This is what creates *kavvanah*.
>
> RABBI ETHAN FRANZEL

The Power of Place

> I find myself in a state of prayer mostly when I'm in nature. What is a state of prayer? The ability to be connected to my heart, to the great expanse, which for me creates the religious setting or sentiment. The invitation to move into that state is stronger outdoors than when I'm in a building.
>
> MELILA HELLNER-ESHED, PHD

When I go into a place that I'm used to praying in, filled with vibes, for lack of a better word, of past prayer and the expectation of what will happen that day, then I do feel in a dialogue with God.

RABBI RICHARD N. LEVY, DD

Listen to the Words
It's kind of a back and forth. If I can focus in on the words, that helps me realize where I am, in whose presence I stand. Then, the sense of presence brings me back to the words.

DR. TAMAR FRANKIEL

In the course of this book, we will explore many other methods for attaining *kavvanah,* for *kavvanah* is the foundation for every kind of prayer. In the meantime, we conclude with Rabbi David Wolpe.

Just Pray
Prayer is surprising. Sometimes I don't feel like going to the minyan, but then I end up having a more powerful experience than on other days when I go willingly. So I don't think that the mind-set you enter with is necessarily determinative of the mind-set you end with and I'm not sure what mind-set you should enter with. Prayer is various enough that you can take it in various directions.

RABBI DAVID J. WOLPE

6

Engaging the Body

The body has become important for me in my understanding of prayer and ritual. We live in our bodies, and I think our bodies and souls are not naturally separate. Anything that makes prayer more vivid to our bodies, like music or drumming, is powerful. For me this goes back to the womb experience. Much of what comforts us comes from the womb, like rhythmic sounds of drumming or the sense of free motion or the idea that we're connected to something larger than ourselves.

RABBI JILL HAMMER, PHD

Judaism is a very intellectual religion. Purposely or inadvertently, this cultural trait often informs Jewish prayer as well. Yet primarily, most of our teachers think that prayer is not an expression of discursive thought. So if the thinking mind is not the preferred means to express the heart, what is the alternative?

There is in the body-doing great wisdom that can never be fully put into an ideology, a package, a speech. It has to be done. And Jewish praying is doing. I'm deeply aware that Jewish prayer is physical. There's a fascinating rule in Jewish prayer that you have to pray loud enough that you can hear your praying. You do not and should not pray loud enough so that your neighbor hears what you're praying, but you should hear your own praying. It has to be aspirated. It has to be verbalized. Your mouth needs to be moving, air needs to be flowing through you. It can't be just conceptual.

RABBI BRADLEY SHAVIT ARTSON

Obviously, silent prayer is not without merit. What changes when we pray out loud?

People have used my translations of Hebrew prayers and wrecked them, because they make them for the eyes, to look good on the page. I make them for the mouth. When you make it for the mouth, you move from the cerebral into the affective level. If the ear hears what the mouth is saying, then the mouth will be saying what the heart wants it to say.

RABBI ZALMAN M. SCHACHTER-SHALOMI

The merging of heart and body through voice explains why music is so central to prayer, but other forms of body expression can enliven prayer as well.

My congregants know I'll start dancing, and I've learned not to be embarrassed. I do it alone, too. It's another way of being taken in by prayer.

RABBI LAVEY YITZCHAK DERBY

The movement of the body can generate the flow of consciousness and direct you. In fact, the Baal Shem Tov says that if you are particularly stuck in your prayer, you can accomplish that just by looking around at different things. Taking your eyes off whatever you're looking at now and looking somewhere else creates a new awareness in yourself.

RABBI ETHAN FRANZEL

Sometimes we can learn about our hearts by observing our bodies.

> When I pray, my body takes on a life of its own. Sometimes I sway horizontally, other times vertically. At times my hands are to my sides, at times they are in a beseeching position. There are times when they reach up, as if aspiring to reach where my words cannot go. I observe my hands, seeking to understand what it is that they are trying to tell me.
>
> REB MIMI FEIGELSON

> I've noticed that my body movement is often a measure of the depth of my prayer, rather than what I do to enhance my prayer. If I notice that I'm bowing deeper than I usually bow, it's because I'm really in a place of gratitude or humility or surrender.
>
> DR. LINDA THAL

Cultivating Body Awareness

As you have heard me say repeatedly, body awareness makes all the difference in my prayer life. Not only do emotions play out physically, but the body is the doorway into mindful presence, the home of *mochin d'gadlut* (expanded consciousness). Our thinking minds are constantly recalling the past or imagining the future, which is fine in much of our lives, but is usually counter-productive when our goal is to make ourselves available for an experience of God.

Unfortunately, getting out of our thinking minds is extremely difficult. We can't just say to ourselves, "I'll stop thinking and worrying now," and watch it happen. If only the mind worked that way! The usual strategy for escaping our minds is to engage in conversation or to spectate, becoming engrossed in a performance, a movie, or a good book.

But the more successful strategy is participating in sports or one of the creative arts. The more we concentrate on an activity through our senses, and the less we think about it, the easier it is to enter the "zone." You can spend quite a lot of time analyzing your golf swing, but if you think about it while you're hitting the ball, the results are rarely good. Instead, we rely on what our bodies have learned through repetition and practice to see us through. That's a large part of why we love team sports, dance, and music. We are thinking instinctually; we are in receptive mode.

The same strategy works with regard to prayer. By employing a method to focus on our bodies as they interact with the world in one way or another, we can leave thoughts of past and future behind, stay in the present, and become an I that might encounter the holy Thou. We examine three such methods.

Nature

No prayer should be in brick boxes. Nature is the true house of prayer. Failing access to nature, we should turn our shuls into planetariums. I'm serious!

RABBI RAMI SHAPIRO

First and foremost, nature is an optimal environment to learn prayer because there, unlike in a classroom, the question of God is not contrived. Most people respond spiritually to the beauty and power of the natural world.

Time and time again, people say to me on a hike or a ski trip, I've never experienced prayer like that. I think that's because the spirituality is already there. You already feel the awe.

RABBI JAMIE KORNGOLD

In *God in Search of Man,* Abraham Joshua Heschel illuminates why awe leads to God.

The meaning of awe is to realize that life takes place under wide horizons, horizons that range beyond the span of an individual life or even the life of a nation, a generation, or an era. Awe enables us to perceive in the world intimations of the Divine, to sense in small things the beginning of infinite significance, to sense the ultimate in the common and the simple; to feel in the rush of the passing the stillness of the eternal.[1]

Nature is the gateway to everyday awe. Our teachers provide other insights into the connection between prayer and the natural world.

> I think that you have to get away from brick and mortar at times, hopefully often. You are more able to witness the Tree of Life's roots not in bedrock but in soil. So much of prayer is breath, and all of breath is air, and air, the best air, is not in here. It's out there.
>
> RABBI ZOË KLEIN

> Prayer is about being part of the larger web of life. For me, prayer in nature and prayer about nature is where that consciousness lives. When I pray near a tree, I know that I'm not different from the tree in that we're part of the same ecosystem, both physically and spiritually.
>
> RABBI JILL HAMMER, PHD

> Anything I'm praying about, if I just go out into nature and sit down and watch, my prayer will be answered. It might be how the ants are moving, or how the tree is dying but there's another one growing nearby, or there's a plant growing directly out of a stone, or how the water is softening the rocks. Whatever I go out with, right around me, a lesson is given.
>
> RABBI TIRZAH FIRESTONE

One of the great gifts of nature is that it requires mindfulness. Far from hospitals, there are risks when we get lost in thought and fail to foresee weather patterns, remain alert for dangerous animals and plants, or stay on course. But even so, especially on clearly marked trails or when we hike socially with friends, mindfulness needs to be earned. Adventure Rabbi Jamie Korngold, my friend and colleague in outdoor Jewish spiritual education, explains how time in nature can be directed toward prayer.

> One of the difficulties of prayer is getting to a place where we are still enough and connected enough to pray. I think the liturgists understood that when they wrote the Siddur. There are all these beautiful psalms that are supposed to lead us up to a contemplative, quiet place. Except that for so many of us, they don't do that. They lie there dead on the page. So the outdoor experience enables us to get to that place of quietude the same way the psalms were intended. So I like to hike with a group for an hour before services, and then we start with the *Barchu*. We discuss this beforehand and set the intention for the hike. Otherwise the hike is just a hike, which is a different thing.
> RABBI JAMIE KORNGOLD

So many people spend time in nature and feel something spiritual but don't know what to do with it, or how to bring it home. That need not be the case.

> What we cultivate in wilderness is presence, and then from being present, we can create a connection—to ourselves on a deeper level, to the community, to God. Those are the two steps.
> RABBI JAMIE KORNGOLD

As my previous book is devoted to this topic, let me refer those interested in learning more about prayer and the natural world to *A Wild Faith: Jewish Ways into Wilderness, Wilderness Ways into Judaism* (Jewish Lights).

Music and Chant
The first time the Children of Israel engaged in communal prayer in their freedom was *Shirat Hayam* [the Song of the

Sea, Exodus 15]. Music touches us in a place that's beyond the rational mind, and it reaches into the heart. It is the language of the soul. We've all had the experience of knowing how a piece of music is a prayer in itself, without the words attached. We can pray through the music itself.

RABBI NAOMI LEVY

Music is perhaps the most pervasive form of embodied spiritual experience. It seems to move every single human being.

Music is intrinsic and essential, for me, to prayer life and the spiritual world. All people connect to melody. It opens us up, shifts us. Even people who have very little affect in their lives, who don't live with their hearts on their sleeves, will respond emotionally when they hear music they love. Teenagers, who don't want to show emotion because it's uncool, go to a concert and they'll be dancing, they'll be shouting, they'll be singing, they'll be showing *hitlahavut* [a Hasidic term for a fiery enthusiasm, ecstasy] that they'll show nowhere else. I always say that if you're thirsty, you can drink Coke, which will make you think you're quenching your thirst because it's liquid, but the direct line between point A and point B is water. For me, the direct path is music and the names of God.

RABBI ETHAN FRANZEL

For these reasons, music is an important element of synagogue worship. But music can impede prayer rather than further it. When music helps us to reach toward God, it is wonderful. When it functions to entertain us, we focus less on divinity and more on the musicians.

Because I'm a cantor, I'm not suspicious of a cantor's efforts. I don't assume the cantor is doing this to show off. I appreciate a skilled cantor or choir because they may be so much better than my limited means of expression and I'm open to that.

Listening with prayer sense, they take me places I couldn't go
by myself.
CANTOR ELLEN DRESKIN

A particularly effective way to harness the power of music for
prayer is to engage the practice of chant. As a student of the
woman who is leading the revival of Jewish chant in our day,
Rabbi Shefa Gold, I have learned a good deal about why and how
chant works.

Chant differs from song in that it purposely functions like a
mantra. A good chant melody is simple enough that when you
hear it for the first time, it is as if you already know it. A chant can
include an entire verse from Torah or the liturgy, but generally only
a few words are chosen. While musical and Hebrew abilities are
helpful, they are not necessary.

Why is chant effective? Not only is song a surefire method of
relaxing into *mochin d'gadlut,* singing allows us to playfully interact with words in the fullness of our mind/body/spirit. We take the
time to be with them, to discover what they might mean to us, and
to give them a chance to affect us.

When I look at a sacred phrase, I ask, what's the potential
here? What do these words do? Then I find out, by chanting
them, by dancing them, by taking them into my body and
seeing what is the effect of this. Do they have power? And
if so, what is that power? I like the language of medicine.
What happens when I apply this medicine? What changes
in me?
RABBI SHEFA GOLD

As Rabbi Gold likes to say, we do not think *about* the words or
their meanings when chanting. Rather, we embody them.

Chant is integrative. The music recalls body memories and
the sound itself is a very physical practice. My emotions are

totally engaged. The intellect is also engaged because of my curiosity into the words and these spiritual states, and it's also a practice. So all the different aspects of myself are activated, motivated, generated.

RABBI SHEFA GOLD

Chant is not only effective when chanting. When, in the course of synagogue service, we say words that we have previously chanted, they evoke memories and meanings of our past experience with them.

When I take the time to work with a word or a phrase—chanting it in my own time, rolling it around in my mouth, and letting it move through my whole body—then when I say the phrase quickly, all of that backstory is there for me. It can move me into a stream of consciousness.

RABBI DIANE ELLIOT

Yoga

Today, many spiritually seeking Jews engage in body practices from other traditions. Tai chi, aikido, qigong, yoga, the list is long. These practices can powerfully impact your prayer life. As yoga is the most popular of these body practices, I asked two rabbis who teach yoga, Myriam Klotz and Sheila Peltz Weinberg, to share their insights.

Yoga practice is a deep form of prayer for me, and I pray on my yoga mat almost every single day of my life. BKS Iyengar, a great yoga master in our time, says that we would be fooling ourselves if we said that we are only our bodies, yet that we'd be kidding ourselves if we believe that we can apprehend the soul apart from our bodies. Our physical experiences through our senses—what we see, taste, feel, hear, smell—have so much to do with the thoughts we think, the emotions we feel. How could we presume to fully come close to the

Energy that creates and sustains our every breath without bringing awareness of our bodies' truth in the moment, and without inviting our physical expressions as prayers to our Creator?

I think of yoga awareness as prayerful awareness. It is awareness of the Divine moving through me at every moment, not just when I am praying liturgical prayer in synagogue or on a mountaintop. So, for example, when I am in this moment, sitting at an Internet café typing these words, I connect to the posture of my body on this straight-backed wooden chair. I breathe into my belly and my heart and feel my shoulders relax.... I recall, I am made *b'tzelem Elohim*, in the image of God. I look up. I see my friend across the table. She, too, is made in God's image. I bow my chin slightly toward my chest, and in that subtle gesture, I offer a silent prayer for her well-being; I connect to the Divine inside my own skin, I offer up this moment as a prayer, bringing my deeper awareness present. This is but one example of how "informal" yoga and "personal" prayer intertwine off the mat, out of the synagogue.

There are times when I engage a physical posture and that very posture opens my heart to realms of feeling that I hadn't expected, and sometimes opens my mind to my soul in ways that are surprising and powerful. The act of full prostration—sometimes called child's pose in yoga—can catalyze a sense of drawing deeply inward. There have been several occasions when I have been in this posture and felt God's presence opening to me, or me into God's presence. It is a felt sense emerging from deep within me, and sometimes there are no words to accompany this feeling, but it is unmistakably a prayerful state.

Rabbi Myriam Klotz

Rabbi Klotz gives substance to the notion of a prayer-person. Any moment, any place, can be filled with prayer.

I have practiced and taught yoga for just over twenty years at the time of this writing, and I have been a rabbi for a decade. My prayer practice and my yoga practice deeply bow into each other, with great love, each giving the other permission to be fully what it is before God.

RABBI MYRIAM KLOTZ

Yoga has raised the bar. In the body, it's very hard to lie. I know what compassion feels like, and harshness, and I know how to balance between kindness and discipline and rigor. I know what it means to find the heart. It really works with Jewish ideas, and liturgy. Let's take *simcha,* joy, as an example. I bring *simcha* to my mind and body together through yoga. I try to make a strong container for joy. It's very powerful. It makes me feel much more alive, joyous, connected, free, all the things that I'm hoping for in prayer. In doing this, the quality of *simcha* breaks through the boundaries of ego. It's not about my projecting something, or needing something, or demanding or controlling; it's about entering the flow. It's completely intimate. My limited nature partakes of something tremendously expanded. It's divine.

RABBI SHEILA PELTZ WEINBERG

7

Listening for God: Silence and Meditation

Is God answering me? I would put it, God is always talking to me, but only occasionally do I listen.

RABBI ARYEH BEN DAVID

Another Zalman [Schachter-Shalomi] teaching is that when you are done praying, you need to sit down and be still, because that's as much a part of the prayer as when you are making noise. Zalman says that it may or may not be true that God answers prayers, but most of us hang up before we give God a chance to answer.

RABBI LAWRENCE KUSHNER

Prayer is usually conceived of as an act of speaking, even if speaking words silently in the heart. But as we saw in the last chapter, not all prayer fits this definition. While all agree that the judicious use of silence and meditation can prepare us for prayer, some people consider them forms of prayer in and of themselves. And if prayer is meant to be a dialogue with God, then should we not, as Rabbi Zalman Schachter-Shalomi suggests, stay on the line when we're done speaking?

Silence

Silence gives us a break from social life and the chattering of the world around us. So much of our lives is lived in a social context that many people are quite afraid to be alone. They cannot imagine themselves without something to do or someone to talk to. Even when we are alone, our thoughts are often dictated by what we will say to someone at the office or the gym. But those who use silence to look inward discover an amazing truth: I am more than my social life. Silence gifts us to ourselves.

Meditation is the activity most associated with silence, but simple quietude can help us to gather our *kavvanah*.

> If I rush in ten seconds beforehand, I'm so busy greeting people, the service starts and I'm supposed to snap to the world of prayer. For me, that doesn't work. Before the service begins, I need to get myself in the right frame of mind, to be open to whatever happens at that moment. I need to sit and concentrate. For me, everything that happens before *Barchu* is the most important part of the service.
> CANTOR ELLEN DRESKIN

> Every morning I turn my walk with the dog into a meditative walk, without any music, without any stuff in my ears. I don't take the Blackberry. It's silent. I listen to the breeze, the birds, see the new flowers. It's my time to notice the world. That place has infused my ability to come back to the prayer book.
> RABBI KAREN FOX, DD

For some, silence itself is a prayer, the prayer of just being in God's presence.

It works for me when I go from the place of yearning where I started, in small consciousness, to *mochin d'gadlut,* to expanded consciousness, where everything is possible and I become a channel for the *Shechinah's* desire. I'm not saying I get there all the time. Sometimes I'm just praying for my daughter to get a job or my friend to get well. But when it really works I just go into silence. There is an energetic shift, a real sense that a bigger mind has settled in and I'm serving needs bigger than my own.

RABBI TIRZAH FIRESTONE

Sometimes if I've come to *tefillah* [services] stressed, I'll just close my eyes and sit silently and listen to other people's prayer. The effect of closing my eyes is not so much the negative of closing anything out but the sense that in the dark, it's a bit like being in the presence of God before God started to create the world. So I find I close my eyes a lot.

RABBI RICHARD N. LEVY, DD

Meditation

Once silence banishes the external distractions by eliminating social life, a far more difficult threat to inner calm and presence arises. Our minds are full of internal distractions, the mental clutter and uninvited thoughts that just won't leave us alone. Meditation is the art and science of working with the mind. The goals and techniques vary, but the function is generally the same: to rest our frenetic minds and give our souls some peace and, in the case of the religious Jew, make some space for God.

For some, meditation is best understood as a partner and midwife for Jewish practice, particularly prayer.

It's good to see where you're standing before you start walking. Where am I right now? Is my mind calm enough and quiet enough to pray? There are times when I've gone to a Friday night service when I'm running late, and the service was over before I even realized that I hadn't arrived yet. So, certainly meditation helps get the most out of prayer by shaking off the travel dust and sitting still before you start the journey.

JAY MICHAELSON

I want to pray in a direction that leads to a direct experience of the Divine. The only place that can happen is in the present moment. Meditation techniques that bring your awareness to the present are a precursor to the possibility of having a direct experience of the Divine. It's not a sufficient condition; you could be aware of the present moment and hate it, but it's a precondition.

RABBI JEFF ROTH

Being able to sit quietly and really allow the mind to open, and connecting to the present moment experientially, cultivating an attitude that's not demanding in any way, not contracted, not pushing, puts me very close to the essence of liturgical prayer, which is opening to divine goodness. The words of the prayer book become filled with expansion and love.

RABBI SHEILA PELTZ WEINBERG

And as we saw above in our teachers' reflections on silence, for some the inner quiet and stillness characteristic of meditation is itself a prayer.

Sometimes meditation is the set-up. I notice what's bothering me and then, out of that, I can make my prayer. Sometimes meditation is just the quiet place, and that is a prayer.

RABBI KAREN FOX, DD

Thanks to the efforts of faithful Jew and master Buddhist meditation teacher Sylvia Boorstein, the dominant mode of meditation in the Jewish world today is vipassana, or insight meditation. Kabbalist and leading Jewish meditation teacher Rabbi David Cooper calls it the graduate school of meditative practices. Instead of focusing on an object or a mantra, you allow your attention to follow the most prominent sensation, which is often sensual but includes everything: emotions, feelings, mind states. It is a relentless pursuit of the truth of the moment, of understanding what is really happening by adopting the position of impartial observer.

> The most important thing is to acknowledge the truth of what is going on without judging it, in prayer or meditation. If I can do it, my experience is that that allows flow to happen, connection to happen, release to happen. If I get into a struggle and judge it or pretend it's not true, I contract. I can't open to the beloved Other.
> RABBI SHEILA PELTZ WEINBERG

Insight meditation is enormously valuable in many ways, but I find it particularly useful for doing *teshuvah*, the introspective work of repentance that is most prominent on Yom Kippur. We will explore more about *teshuvah* in chapter 13.

I think of a second form of meditation, where a person focuses exclusively on a mantra or an object, as programmatic. Here you can harvest the fruits of sustained concentration on a theme, a directed focusing of the mind for spiritual purposes. Much of Jewish meditation—repeating Hebrew phrases and words or closing your eyes and concentrating on Hebrew letters—falls into this category. See practice 4 for one such meditation practice. Since we dealt with some of the basic ideas in our discussion of chant and will do more with "mantra" prayer in later chapters, for now I refer you to the books on Jewish meditation in the Resources section if you would like to learn more about this practice.

For Rabbi Ethan Franzel, a programmatic form of meditation is the central piece of his spiritual practice.

I have a practice of meditation using the name of God, *Ehiyeh asher Ehiyeh* [I am that which I am (Exodus 3:14)]. It only shows up once in the Torah, at the Burning Bush. That name of God is always with me. I chant it, I use it for the focus of my meditation, and when I'm walking around, when I'm thinking, driving my car, I repeat it. It fuses itself into me. For me this is the greatest practice there is, because if God is one, then God's name is completely identical to God's essence. One is the other. Saying God's name is living within God's essence. It's powerful. Prayer is any moment that I redirect my mind toward its divinity.

RABBI ETHAN FRANZEL

One of our teachers actually reverses the usual sequence of meditation before prayer. Rabbi Linda Motzkin is a scribe. Several days a week she sits down with her calligrapher's quill and engages the sacred practice of writing a Torah scroll.

Others meditate to pray. I pray to meditate, to enter into this kind of writing meditation. I use the fixed, liturgical framework to slow down and gather my concentration so that by the time I'm through praying and ready to start my writing, I can be fully present. My consciousness for writing isn't where it should be if I haven't done my prayer preparation.

RABBI LINDA MOTZKIN

A third kind of meditative practice, well developed in Christianity, Sufism, and other spiritual traditions, is called contemplation. Like insight meditation, it is entirely open-ended, but it is not focused on ourselves. Rather, intention is focused on receiving something from outside of us. We wait for God.

There is a great teaching of the Maharal of Prague who says that we pray in order to empty ourselves of words, and the real prayer happens in the silence afterwards. Usually when

I'm feeling heartbroken, I will pour out my heart, in the words of the Siddur and in my own words, until I have no more words. Then I will just stand there, struck silent, and for me, that silence is as deep a prayer as any of the words I have said. And it's an opportunity to be there with the One and receive whatever there is to receive.

RABBI LAVEY YITZCHAK DERBY

This is the silence at the end of a chant, or at the end of a prayer, in which we simply wait in heightened sensual awareness (see practice 15). In some ways, this is the doctoral program of meditation. It requires great patience. And it's not always silent. Sometimes we repeat a word or two to stay focused. Rabbi Shefa Gold once taught her students to repeat the phrase, "Only You," in their minds during the silence after a group chant to invite God's presence. I use this phrase frequently. The exact words, of course, do not matter, so long as they help us to stay calm, alert and ready to observe whatever God may send our way.

The contemplative state is just an openness. A full being or full presence to the moment. It's beyond words. It's going through the words. Heschel talks about different levels of prayer. Song and tears and silence all have that quality of having gone through the words to another place that is more open, more receptive. The silence after a chant is a great example. I usually find that if we then chant again, I drop down further, and then really want another period of silence. Contemplation is that deep place of openness to what may come. But it doesn't have to be completely silent. Contemplation can happen through the Siddur, for example, when the words of prayer become mantra-like.

DR. LINDA THAL

8

Discerning Divinity

I've often heard the quote, in the name of different teachers, that when I pray I talk to God and when I study Torah, God speaks to me. I remember being puzzled when I first read Christian literature on discernment, contemplation, and listening for God. For a long time, I couldn't find something comparable in Jewish sources. I even had difficulty formulating the question. I asked my professors at the Jewish Theological Seminary, "Rabbi Nachman poured out his heart to God; did he ever stop and listen for a response?" They looked at me like they had no idea what I was talking about. "Where did that question come from?" one asked.

DR. LINDA THAL

The idea of listening for God in general, and contemplation in particular, brings us to a question I rarely hear discussed in Jewish circles. What might a response from God look like?

Our natural inclination is to suspect anyone who says, I prayed today and God told me to give you a call, or move to Honduras, or quit my job. If I were to say that I had an intuition that I should do any of those things, or that after months of thinking the answer suddenly popped up, or so many strange coincidences have happened that I think the universe is telling me something, people would understand. But saying God was involved brings up deep misgivings. Many of the people who openly claim to know God's will, it seems, do so for suspect reasons. It often means God is on our side; we can wage a war in the name of the holy; our values are above rational discussion; you're going to Hell, I'm not; or I'm on a mission.

But that is all the more reason to bring up the question. If there is a middle position between the fundamentalists, on the one hand, and the atheistic or agnostic position that God does not respond to prayer, on the other, we need to ask, how does God respond to prayer? What form does the answer take? How certain can I be that it is right? How can I tell the difference between God's communication and my own imagination? Perhaps we avoid these questions because they are so difficult to answer.

One position is not to worry too much about it.

I think that imagination is a very powerful instrument, a sacred faculty, so I don't mind if people accuse me of imagining God when I am davenning or doing spirit journey work. I would rather assume that God isn't talking to me directly, and rely on my imagination, than worry about whether God is talking to me. If God really wants to make God's self clear, then I'm sure God will do that.

RABBI JILL HAMMER, PhD

I don't know whether we can ever verify whether something is a product of our imagination or reality. God is invisible. It isn't a question that concerns me. If I feel a response from God, I see that as a response from God. Since my soul is intimately tied up with God, if I feel something in my soul, it is real.

RABBI RICHARD N. LEVY, DD

Point well taken. Still, discernment is a skill. Especially for those who struggle to feel what Rabbi Levy feels, or whose theology differs, we need to gain some insight into whether a particular thought or image or feeling that arises in our consciousness is the result of a connection with God, or the product of our fear and neuroses, or just another random thought. Here are some of the techniques of our teachers.

Observing What Arises

Prayer helps me to observe, sometimes, what's going on in my own head. Because it's memorized, I don't have to think about it. And that means that if I suddenly start thinking about my uncle, I think to myself, well, why am I thinking about my uncle now? Where'd that come from? So prayer becomes an opportunity for self-reflection, self-purification, self-understanding, and obviously the goal is to transcend self.

RABBI LAWRENCE KUSHNER

Serendipity

The one thing that really makes me sit up and take notice is serendipity. I'll be praying, and two minutes later the person I was thinking about walks in or something happens that is a direct comment on what I was praying about. That always feels like something real is happening there: personal, divine attention.

RABBI JILL HAMMER, PHD

Feel the Love

In listening after a prayer, a response from God might be a word or an image or a phrase or a feeling. How do you know it's not your projection? You can get a slap-in-the-face kind of response, which might be just what you need to hear, a swift kick in the butt. It could be really tough. You need to get over this or you need to move on. But if you get up from your prayer and feel uncompassionate toward yourself, that's a sign that it's not from the highest source. It's going to feel loving and engender self-love and self-compassion. If not, you have to be pretty suspicious of it.

RABBI TIRZAH FIRESTONE

Observe Your Body

There is no litmus paper to tell you God has just spoken to you. It's an act of faith. But I can tell you this. After a while there's a certain flow of endorphins that give you a sense that you didn't talk to the wall. You get more sensitive to that with time and with faith, but remember, the faith is built on reason, because reason says, if I'm aware, then God is aware.

RABBI ZALMAN M. SCHACHTER-SHALOMI

I would explain by way of analogy with people. Sometimes you're in a conversation with someone and you've hit something that you both connect to. You get excited and you feel it in your body, a sense of aliveness on the skin, tingling. It could be intellectual, but when emotional, there's a sense or feeling of a warming of the heart. I feel it as a desire of the heart to really expand beyond the body; there's an energy coming out from the heart. That's similar to the feeling that I have when I feel connected to God in prayer. It's an aliveness, an expansiveness, particularly for me, in the heart region. It also stimulates a lot of thinking in the brain because that's just where I go. But it's an overall sense of presence and also a presence filling the space around me.

DR. TAMAR FRANKIEL

I know, I sound like a broken record, but this is where body awareness really makes a difference. The body doesn't know how to lie, and it is a great source of wisdom to those who listen to what their bodies have to say.

The two biggest decisions in the last decade of my life should have been stressful. The first was deciding to leave Israel after fifteen years in Jerusalem. Unlike most of my friends who moved to Israel, I never had second thoughts. I couldn't even imagine leaving the home I loved until the unemployment ran out and I had to decide between my calling as an outdoor Jewish educator or staying in Israel. The second was the decision to propose to my wife, a first marriage at the age of fifty. Both decisions might have involved a fair amount of trauma.

But neither decision was difficult. I took them with little reflection and no hesitation. After a decade of practicing tai chi, several years of yoga, and hiking in the Judean Desert, I was used to paying attention to my body. Even though I had yet to meditate and really tune in, I listened when my body told me what to do. When I considered leaving Israel, instead of feeling contracted, I felt calm and relaxed. The unknown journey ahead was attracting me instead of making me afraid. I cashed out my pension and moved. A decade later, when I proposed to Jody, I was well attuned to my body's ways. Usually a difficult decision causes anxiety. Not this one. So far, at least, my body has not steered me wrong.

Rarely does my body instruct me so emphatically as in these two cases, but when it does, not only do I listen, I move forward with confidence. I don't particularly like the word *faith,* because in the American religious lexicon, it often implies a blind faith. The Hebrew word for faith in God, *emunah,* literally means "trust," and that's what I experience through my body.

God Answers Prayer Immediately

Rabbi Nehemia Polen makes an astounding claim. His prayers are answered immediately, every time. Notice that he, too, employs body awareness in praying.

I use an acronym to summarize my method of prayer, PRAY. The *P* is presence, meaning the first thing you have to do is know where you are. That could be meditation, or psalms, or even just being aware that I walked into a synagogue or into a beautiful field or here I am in my body. R is resonance, whether of the sound of the letters or of a *niggun* [wordless melody], being aware of yourself as a vocal emitter. Singers talk about their instrument—that's the voice. A is alignment, meaning align all the different levels: body, sound, and semantic meaning of the word; what it means to you; how it relates to you at this moment. And the Y is YES! You ask if prayer gets answered. This prayer gets answered every single time. When you do this, and surrender it, just let the whole thing go, the answer is yes. Immediately.

Yes, immediately. The Baal Shem Tov taught his students that every prayer is answered immediately. It's reported that his students raised their eyebrows, so it's not as if people are crazy or stupid, but he insisted, yes, every prayer is answered the instant it is uttered. That is the moment.

What we really want always is intimacy—with God, however I understand God; with other human beings; with the universe; with my own deep self. And when I do this, I feel that intimacy immediately, and that's "yes." That's "yes."

RABBI NEHEMIA POLEN, PhD

As preposterous as this claim is, I have to say, I experience the same thing. Through body awareness, rarely do I pray without entering into *mochin d'gadlut*, expanded consciousness. Regardless of whether a particular insight or message comes my way, just feeling that intimate connection with Divinity is already an answer to prayer.

Finally, we conclude with two teachings that speak about the tendency to doubt our own experience when it does not conform to the expectations of our culture.

Trust Your Experience

I sent a group out to do *hitbodedut* [freely speaking to God, see practice 12], and a woman who had studied theology came back looking quite stunned and reported that she had been completely knocked off balance. I asked her what happened and she said, "I don't know. I don't even have words for it. There's no place in my theology where this fits." All I could say to her in the few moments we had right then was, "Do you have any doubt that this experience was real?" She said,

"No, that was the most real thing I've ever experienced."
"Then that's what you need to hold on to and remember," I
told her. "This was the place that was most real, even if you
can't understand it, even if your mind can't grasp it. Don't
deny it. You may spend the rest of your life trying to figure out
what that was and give it language that's satisfying, but trust
that the experience was real."

DR. LINDA THAL

Trust Your Intuition

Theology is the afterthought of the believer. You never have
someone coming up with a good theology if he or she didn't
first have an experience. So it's very important to have an
experiential basis for things. Nobody can take that away from
you. Think about intuition. When people say, how do you
know? And you say, I know. And they say, but how do you
know? You're asking me for causes of knowing. But the cause
is in myself. Most people talk about knowledge as a definite
object. And for many things it is that way. Sensation brings us
to knowledge. Reason brings us to knowledge. Feeling brings
me to a certain kind of knowledge. But how does intuition
work? It is totally subjective. How do I know I'm alive? I know.

RABBI ZALMAN M. SCHACHTER-SHALOMI

PART II

Beginning to Pray

We now turn to what most people would consider the central paradigm of prayer: speaking to God. After some general advice from our teachers, we turn to two central models for the dialogue with Divinity: blessings and spontaneous prayer.

We'll also address an issue that makes prayer difficult for so many. If my belief in God is tentative, or if I perceive or conceive of God as All Being, the Universe, or an impersonal force or stream of energy, how can I address God like a person? Is it honest and truthful to say "You" to Divinity?

9

Advice for Beginners

Here our teachers speak directly to those starting out on the path of prayer. I've been davenning for forty-plus years, but I found fresh inspiration from their wisdom.

Follow Your Delight

Where's your delight? What do you love? Even if it's one prayer, one song, one word. This is the same advice I give as a movement teacher. We are so not used to letting delight or joy be a standard of what we might do in our lives. It's really radical to open my awareness to what feels good, and do it, and let it grow and develop.

RABBI DIANE ELLIOT

Let Nature Take Control

In a lot of ways, prayer is like sex. You want to think about it first; you want to make some good judgments about it. But at a certain point you want to let nature take control. In our culture, it's interesting that we use the same words—*private* or *privates*—to describe the parts of ourselves that are sexual and the parts of ourselves that are spiritual. We don't really want to talk about it a lot in polite society. There is a power to that privacy. Privacy gives us permission to not be our rational selves in these moments of intimacy. I don't want to know about your sex life and I don't want to know about your prayer life in their most intimate moments, because even to know about it is itself an act of intimacy. So if we could make our best prayer moments as wild and uninhibited as our best sexual moments, that would be a good step toward redemption.

JAY MICHAELSON

Let God In

There is no beginning or end as to where to start. The first step to entering into the world of prayer is the willingness to let God enter into your heart and soul. Praying asks of us to have the courage to say, "I no longer want to walk this world alone!"

REB MIMI FEIGELSON

Authenticity, Not Perfection

Culturally, we twenty-first-century American Jews suffer from an achievement complex, and consciously or unconsciously assume that there is a "right" way to pray, and assume, as well, that we don't know how to do it "right." (And God forbid we should be beginners or anything but "excellent" in our endeavors.) Prayer is a vast territory of possibility, modality, and nuance. Instead of aiming to pray "right," we need to strive to pray "authentically." Conditions for authentic prayer can be set, but each pray-er must make that discovery for herself.

RABBI NANCY FLAM

You Have to Do It

If a physician said to you, "You're deficient in iron; take a supplement," you wouldn't say, "No, I know the concept of iron; I don't actually have to take it." Your body would say, "I don't care what you think; take it." So why do we treat our spiritual lives differently?

RABBI SHAWN ZEVIT

Every Day

If you are a person who seriously wants to connect to God, I highly recommend that you pray every day. Just ten minutes a day, but every day. Listen and trust that HaShem, the great mystery, wants to speak to you and wants to hear you and wants to be heard by you. There is something on the other side that needs you, is invested in you, and wants you to go to the next level. I like to write my prayers in my journal. This has saved my life many times. When I begin to think that it's all hocus pocus and there's no meaning, when I get cynical or fearful, I look back on my journal and see that there's no way I could have written these words if it was just me. You really do penetrate into these deep places if you pray with all your heart and speak from a place of deep yearning.

RABBI TIRZAH FIRESTONE

Pray Through the Embarrassment

I remember hearing a story years ago about a student who asks a rabbi why he puts on *tefillin,* and the rabbi says, "You have to put on *tefillin* for a year in order for me to answer that question." And I think there's a lot of truth to that. The discussion of prayer is inadequate in the same way that the discussion of the taste of an orange is inadequate. The best advice to someone who wishes to understand prayer is to pray. I know that answer might not be helpful. What might be helpful is to tell people that they can pray through their embarrassment and they will actually come out the other side if they continue to pray. If you stop, it's a mistake, because in time, if you do it often enough, you will derive the experiential benefit. But you have to push through the barrier of your own discomfort with it.

RABBI DAVID J. WOLPE

Prepare for a Change

Really wanting to pray is a change in your life. It doesn't have to be an hour a day, but you have to want to change, and it's very hard to change without support—a partner, a teacher, a community. It needs to be an open process, not an elite club that knows what they're doing and excludes novices.

DR. TAMAR FRANKIEL

Find a Teacher and a Friend

The hardest thing in the world is to feel we are a cognitive minority of one. Many of us feel that way because we say, I have an experience of God or I'd like to feel God or I'd like to believe something, but the world is full of people, people of substance, psychologists, philosophers, scientists, our neighbor next door, who suspect that there's something wrong with us. So the words of our tradition are: Find a rabbi and a fellow student. The ultimate searches of meaning in life cannot be done alone; they need to be done with others. And if your friends will cast doubt on your search for meaning, find somebody else. Find a rabbi you can talk to, who has the experiences you want. And find yourself some friends. Find a community where this stuff goes on, a synagogue where these conversations occur.

RABBI LAWRENCE A. HOFFMAN, PHD

What to Do When You Don't Feel It

You can always want to want; you can yearn to yearn. Rabbi Nachman talks about this. You can make your lack of yearning an object of your yearning. It's really powerful. It's part of the process of dealing with "what is" instead of "what isn't." "What is" is that I feel dead. So work with that. Prayer is working with "what is."

RABBI DAVID INGBER

Uncover What Is Already There

The human heart is—in its native state—always attentive to love, gratitude, righteousness and justice, and the desire for peace and well-being for all. Prayer is the process and product of our endeavor to uncover what is already there. So, if you want to start praying, start speaking what you already know to be true in your heart. Articulate your full self.

RABBI JONATHAN P. SLATER

Start Where You Are

I give myself the space to identify which part of my heart most needs to express itself. Is it the part that is overwhelmed with yearning and longing, or is it the part overwhelmed with gratitude? Is it the part that is just shattered, or the part that is screaming in anger? What part of my heart needs to find expression *right now?*

RABBI SHARON BROUS

Pay Attention at the End of a Prayer

Isn't the point of prayer to open us up and give us a deeper sense of awareness? Then maybe what you do the second that you're done praying matters a lot more than at any other time because this is what you're taking from your prayer service.

RABBI ETHAN FRANZEL

It's In My Hands

I don't put responsibility on others. Prayer is an opportunity to be "with God." Sometimes there are stumbling blocks and sometimes they're on the *bima* [podium] or sitting next to me, but I have to take responsibility. It's in my hands.

CANTOR ELLEN DRESKIN

It's All Prayer

So many phenomena fall under the category of "prayer" that we are mistaken to characterize it as if it were one activity or experience. In my own life, I know instinctive beseeching prayer that comes from a place of helplessness, pain, and want, not unlike calling for Mommy. I know the kind of prayer Rebbe Nachman talks about, where my sole desire is to find a way back to some felt connection (any connection) to a sense of God's presence. I know talking-out-loud-at-the-kitchen-sink-while-washing-breakfast-dishes prayer, once my husband has gone to work and my teenagers have gone to school, subtly reinforcing through the performance of speech the conviction that God is real and present. I know prayer in shul with my community on Shabbat mornings, riding alone together on the currents of liturgy, as well as times at home myself with the morning liturgy. I know getting-up-in-the-morning prayer, saying traditional blessings to accompany each movement of waking, taking none of it for granted. I know prayer as the process of becoming so exquisitely still and receptive that the veils of separation lift. I know prayer as listening. Prayer comes in movement, in stillness, in song, in tears, in music, in silence, in words. The flavors are all different, but the taste is the same: conscious awareness of the One, however dim or bright.

RABBI NANCY FLAM

10

The Power of You

Martin Buber said, when we speak of God as You, I understand what we mean, but as soon as we talk about God as
He, She, or It, I don't understand and I don't believe. I feel the
same way. I think that it's not the second-person language
that gets us in trouble, it's the third person. This desire that
humans have to understand the universe is beautiful, but then
we impute all kinds of characteristics and actions to this primal need and create a God-concept—a third-person idea
instead of a second-person experience. God likes us but not
those other people; God is a He but He's not a She. These are
third-person terms, and anytime there's a move from first or
second person to third person, there's a move from an immediate experience, something that's right now happening in
your present awareness and understanding, to a concept and
an elaboration, and that's asking for trouble.

JAY MICHAELSON

For me, praying without saying "You" to God is like getting a
greeting card instead of a love letter. While third-person language might express truth with beautiful words, the language of "I
and You" gives voice to the direct experience of my heart in a relationship—my desire, my pain, my hopes.

But for those of us who don't believe in God as a person who makes personal decisions about people and events, praying to God directly seems disingenuous, if not dishonest. We understand why mystics meditate: to strip the illusion of separation and become one with God. But praying to a Person outside of themselves? Isn't that the dualism they decry?

> If we're fully enlightened and everything is perfect and every-thing is God, then yes, we should do away with second-person prayer language because we don't need it. But most of the time we need it. As soon as we say "You," there is a sense of immediacy. There is a real beauty to striving to say "You" to as much of life as possible.
> JAY MICHAELSON

Indeed, as we have already seen, our mystic and neo-mystic teach-ers find that personal prayer adds a critical layer to meditative prac-tices: love and devotion.

> I have a relationship with God as lover, with something that is real outside of me, but at the same time, it is real and I am a part of it. So when I pray, I choose the position of viewing it as outside of myself because that adds something to my experience. When I meditate, I choose the experience of knowing that I am part of this oneness, and that if I'm com-pletely present, I can let go of the boundaries between self and other. You ask, why not pray by making affirmations with-out addressing God? I wouldn't tell someone who enjoys affirmations, "Don't do affirmations; go talk to God instead," but there is an emotional connection achieved through the poetry of me and you that touches me very deeply. It is open-ing my heart to the other that has the potential for dramatic change.
> RABBI LAVEY YITZCHAK DERBY

The heart language of "I and You" allows us to express our yearning for connection with the Divine. There is a special quality to the dialogue when the other is God. I am devoted to my wife and family, but I serve them differently than I serve the transcendent. Expressing devotion to God allows us to articulate and internalize our highest desires.

> My Buddhism and Judaism complement one another. In the dharma, we want to see clearly and accept what is. We may not like it, and we may work to change it, but seeing things as they are is the first step toward liberation. "It is what it is." Judaism adds a devotional ingredient. The "Is" turns to You, to I—"I am what I am" [Exodus 3:14]. We personalize our interaction with the infinite.
>
> JAY MICHAELSON

Saying You comes from the heart and lets our yearning soar. Prayer would be diminished without it.

Still, prayer must be truthful to be effective. If God is All Being or an impersonal force and my speech to God is not reciprocated, is my prayer honest? If God as person is a projection on my part, am I addressing my own projection? This question is both pivotal and troubling for me.

As a leading proponent of Process Theology, which views God as manifesting in the evolutionary processes of the universe, Rabbi Bradley Shavit Artson must deal with the same issue.

> I live in a very personal way with a lot of impersonal things. When I go to the Pacific Ocean, I talk to her all the time. I don't expect the Pacific Ocean to be conscious of my conversation and I don't think the Pacific Ocean is listening to me, but she's definitely my mother, and I go into her as one of her sons. That has to do with me and my personality with her. I do that with mountains and trees, and I talk to all sorts of inanimate objects constantly because that's the only way I

know how to relate to everything. So on the one hand, I don't spend time worrying about whether God has personality or not, because I talk to everything, and the amazing thing is that if you talk to everything as though they have personalities, eventually you notice the personalities that they have.

RABBI BRADLEY SHAVIT ARTSON

Since I gave a great deal of care to my treatment of this question in *A Wild Faith: Jewish Ways into Wilderness, Wilderness Ways into Judaism* (Jewish Lights), I'd like to share it with you here.

Which metaphors shall I use for God, this more-than-a-person (indeed, more-than-anything-I-know) reality, which I perceive as a force possessing intelligence and will? ...

The Kabbalist's metaphor for the *shefa,* the River of Light, best models my experience of God. A river is always rushing toward me. Divinity is always coming my way. And how I stand in it influences the flow. So my experience of the river has a lot to do with my own willpower, decisions, and actions. I can swim upstream or float along.

What I can't control is the flow and course of the river. Sometimes the waters are still and I'm so busy watching television or cooking a meal, I can forget that I'm in it at all. At other times I go over a waterfall and I can't help but be aware of the river.

But the key point is that I experience a river personally. When I paddle this way or that, the river pushes me in response. It may send me along my course or divert me to a new direction I did not intend. But the river's response to my action is unique to me. It pushes me in this direction at this time, and no one else.

So, too, do I understand my relation to the River of Light. Because of my inability to live in receptive mode, often I am hardly aware of it. But when I enter I-Thou, the river "speaks" to me loud and clear. I have no idea what it will say.

Sometimes it may demand justice, sometimes I feel over-whelming love. Sometimes I am humbled and contrite, other times empowered and energized. The encounter with God is spontaneous and open-ended. Most important, it is always profound and meaningful in a personal way. God has "spo-ken" to me about my life in this moment in this place. I live in personal relationship with impersonal God.

The Kabbalists capture this when they say that the ten aspects or spheres of Divinity comprise what scholars call the "godhead," the totality of God's knowable self in the cosmos. It is as impersonal a name for God as it gets. Each sphere rep-resents different aspects of the Divine—mercy, judgment, beauty, love, strength, etc. Depending on what people think, say, and do, people interact with the sphere that their behav-ior has merited. From the impersonal godhead they have received a personalized rejoinder.

Prayer makes us conscious of the fact that we are always standing in the *shefa*. It moves me along the spiritual path, toward receptive mode. And when I say You to the sacred One—standing with senses open, fully aware of this precious world—I am likely to feel the press of holiness against me, a window of I-Thou in an I-It world. I receive a response to my thoughts, words, feelings, and fears in this moment of my life. God has answered my prayer.

11

Blessings

A blessing practice is a great way to start with prayer. Gratitude is a very important place to begin, because it opens the heart. It can become a practice, a process of noticing all the things we ordinarily miss or don't think about being grateful for. So often, the stories we tell ourselves are about what's lacking or what's not right in our lives.

DR. LINDA THAL

How do we begin to pray? We follow Dr. Linda Thal's advice and begin with blessings, for they are the quintessential form of gratitude prayer in Judaism.

I would have a big problem if I took *baruch ata* literally, speaking to something separate from me, who heals the sick, because I don't think that's how it works. But when I say, "Blessed are You who heals the sick," I translate it for myself as "I'm so grateful that there's healing in the world and that I can be a part of that." I'm grateful for the laws of nature; I am aware that redemption happens daily. Every time I say *baruch ata*, it's an expression of gratitude and it opens up doors, reminding me of the larger things that I'm supposed to be grateful for, lest I have forgotten.

CANTOR ELLEN DRESKIN

The standard blessing form in Jewish prayer, which begins "*Baruch ata* ... " is often translated as "Blessed be You God, Sovereign of the universe ... " and is followed by a phrase such as "who has brought us to this moment," or, "who hears prayer," or, "who commands us to light the Sabbath candles." The formula is ubiquitous and appears throughout Jewish liturgy, sometimes as stand-alone blessings, often as the beginning and ending of the Rabbinic prayers found in the Siddur.

Many find the words as meaningful today as they were when monarchs reigned across the planet. Others, like Cantor Ellen Dreskin above, translate the words away from their literal meaning when saying them. And still others prefer alternative formulas, such as "*Brucha at Yah, ruach ha-olam*" (Blessed be You God, Spirit of the universe).

In addition to expressing gratitude, blessings are a *kavvanah* tool, a way of setting an intention before performing a mitzvah, a religious commandment. And blessings cultivate awareness.

We're biting into a peach and we're driving or talking or reading and not noticing this tasty, gorgeous, juicy peach. A blessing puts the pause button on the chatter, the busyness of our lives, and allows us to be mindful. We have a custom in our house that when we're about to go on a hike, or we're coming back from a fight, we say a blessing, the *hatov v'hamateiv* [(Blessed be You ...) Source of goodness], or the *shehechianu* [who has brought us to this moment]. Just a pause to really be present to the joys of our lives.

RABBI TIRZAH FIRESTONE

Following Martin Buber, my own view of blessings is that they do even more than bring us into awareness of the present moment.

Blessings not only recognize the inherent holiness in most every thing and every event we encounter, they also *actualize* it. Holiness arises in the Between when we engage in I-Thou relation, and prayer can bring us there. Saying blessings spreads holiness in the world. (For more on this topic, see chapter 9 in my *A Wild Faith: Jewish Ways into Wilderness, Wilderness Ways into Judaism* [Jewish Lights].)

Many, many blessings from the Jewish tradition have been collected and codified in prayer books and other devotional literature. Observant Jews carry them around in their heads, and they are available when needed. There are standard blessings for seeing a beautiful mountain, a sunset, a rainbow, or a wise person. I call these prayers reaction blessings. First we see or hear something, then the blessing becomes our response. This can be very helpful. If we make it a habit to respond with the appropriate blessing, sometimes the blessing just pops out of our mouths when we are in "small mind" and reminds us that we are in the presence of a miracle that should not be taken for granted. Sometimes we are dumbstruck, such as when we hear that someone has died. The prescribed blessing gives us a way of verbalizing our befuddlement, without saying something we will later regret as inadequate, or worse, painful to the person who told us.

> Here's an example of how the liturgy really helps. The rabbis have a blessing for when you see a very unusual (that is, unattractive) person. They recognized that this person, too, is made in God's image. When I was in an airport last week and saw a very unusual and unattractive person, my first reaction was, "Oh my God, that's a really unattractive person." But I caught myself and said the *meshanei habriot* [who makes varied creatures[1]] blessing. I drew on the liturgy in a spontaneous way. The liturgy is so beautiful and rich and there's so much there, if we know how to access it. When possible, I go back to the liturgy as the starting place for my prayers.
>
> RABBI ZARI M. WEISS

The downside is that blessings can be said by rote, without any awareness at all. And sometimes, a formal blessing can just plain get in the way.

> The traditional prayers are meant to be a bridge, and often they are, but sometimes they are a stumbling block. If I'm walking down the trail and I see something wonderful, if I start thinking, "What's the right prayer for that?" it becomes a stumbling block. Where if I just say, "Wow, way to go, God. Nice sunset," it's praise and it's authentic and genuine and it does what it's supposed to do.
>
> RABBI JAMIE KORNGOLD

The Talmud has hundreds of blessings; clearly the rabbis had no problem with making up their own. In fact, in a passage that was later codified into Jewish law,[2] Rabbi Meir said, "A person is obliged to recite 100 blessings every day."[3] Long before the first prayer books existed, let alone the printing press, Jews were spontaneously offering blessings to raise their spiritual awareness and give thanks to God. And that's the point. Whether traditional or original, a blessing is meant to bring our hearts to the forefront, move us into *mochin d'gadlut* (expanded consciousness), and connect us to holiness in the world by bringing God into the equation.

12

Cultivating a Personal Prayer Voice

We need to illuminate for people that prayer is not only communal. We've sold them a line that you can't be a Jew by yourself, but, of course, that's ridiculous. In fact, if you can't be a Jew by yourself, then you can't build Jewish community. So, teaching people to wander off alone and to sit in silence, teaching them to daven by themselves, that's a gift. Because that will revitalize the praying they will do in community, too.

RABBI BRADLEY SHAVIT ARTSON

I get there's a dialectic between tradition and what works, but if I have to choose, I'd rather have people who are open to God in whatever way. And if it doesn't end up being in Jewish language, I'll feel saddened, but I'll also feel really excited that people are connecting with God. That's the challenge. I'd sacrifice the Hebrew content for God content; ideally I'd have them both.

RABBI DAVID INGBER

Finding my personal prayer voice was extraordinarily difficult and incredibly easy.

It was so difficult that I was well past ordination, into my forties, before I could say, "Please, God, may it be that … " The block was entirely mental.

Personal prayer is difficult because the public model of such prayer seems to make a mockery of it. How many times have we heard an arrogant, self-righteous televangelist speak as if God was in his pocket?

> American Jews are so turned off by what looks to them like the excesses of Christian fundamentalism and the politics of much of Christian fundamentalism that this kind of overtly spiritual God-talk makes them very nervous. And rightly so.
> RABBI BRADLEY SHAVIT ARTSON

Personal, spontaneous prayer was just not an option for me. Never mind the theological issues. My self-image as an educated, intelligent citizen of Western civilization made personal prayer distasteful.

But my internal resistance was like the Berlin Wall. It was rock solid for decades; once it began to crumble, it came down fast. The last brick fell at a Buddhist meditation retreat, where we engaged in the blessings practice presented later in this book (practice 7). Never had I connected words so strongly to my heart's desires. This was due partly to the wisdom of praying in this fashion. But another factor was also at play.

I spent hour after hour observing myself, examining thoughts and emotions. I watched my personality, and even my subconscious, interact with the world in great detail. It was a practice of cutting through delusions about who I am and what makes me tick.

The result was stunning. Like never before, I knew what I needed, really needed, deep down, where the neuroses and bedrock fears were shaping me. I prayed and prayed. Looking back, I think I know why. And that leads me to a theory of prayer that works, at least, for me.

When you know what you really need, truly and honestly, prayer comes easily, because it is the right prayer. The method is simple. Take some time to discover what you really need and what you really feel. Then put it into words (or movement or music or mental images), address it to God and let it go.

The word *discover* above is not accidental. We have myriad defense mechanisms to get us through the day, and they serve to cover up our deepest needs, lest we cease to function. The listening and mindfulness techniques covered in chapter 7 are important. As the old adage says: a wise person listens before she speaks.

Here is wisdom from our teachers on cultivating your personal prayer voice.

Starting to Pray

I learned to pray from M. Scott Beck, who wrote *The Road Less Travelled*. I had invited him to the 92nd Street Y when I was working there. I was to interview him on stage and we were waiting together. We got the five-minute warning, combed our hair, straightened our ties, and he turned and said to me, "Rabbi, bless us." The only thing that came to mind was *hamotzi lechem min ha'aretz* [the blessing over bread]. He was saying rabbi, pray, pray for us at this moment. Forget the script, what are your *kishkas* [guts] saying? What is your soul saying at this moment? And it absolutely transformed my prayer life. I started to pray spontaneous prayer. Now, I do it all the time.

RABBI LAVEY YITZCHAK DERBY

A woman came to me, she was having surgery, and she realized that what she really needed was to pray about it. She's an Orthodox woman who knows how to pray, but she felt she needed to say something particular about her situation. We sat down and I asked her what she needed to say. And this most beautiful, personal prayer came from the very same woman who felt she didn't have the words.

RABBI NAOMI LEVY

Start with *Hitbodedut*

A place to begin that is challenging but really works for some people is a *hitbodedut* practice [see practice 12], where we speak freely to God without stopping. It's very important to know that even Rabbi Nachman [the Hasidic rabbi and originator of this exercise] didn't always know what to say and he had a way of handling that. He would repeat *Ribono shel olam* [Sovereign of the universe] over and over until something new came up. You can just keep saying or writing, "I don't know what to say, I don't know what to say," until more comes. It's a way of bypassing the resistance.

DR. LINDA THAL

At the Western Wall

I thought I knew something about prayer, but I found out otherwise. I was at the Kotel [Western Wall], saying *tehillim* [psalms], and thinking that I was really praying. Then I saw a blind man being led down to the Kotel. He ran his fingers over the stones, feeling thousands of years of history. Then he kissed the Wall, and began talking to God. He spoke very rapidly, and I could not understand everything he said. Abruptly he stopped, paused momentarily, then said, "Oh, I told you about that yesterday," and resumed his communication. I realized that he was really communicating with God, and knew that He listened. I resumed saying *tehillim,* but with a much different *kavvanah.*

RABBI ABRAHAM TWERSKI, MD

Your Prayer

Prayer is not always ancient,
Most prayer hasn't even been written yet,
Your prayer hasn't been written yet....

RABBI ZOË KLEIN

PART III

Growing
and Healing
through Prayer

The tendency among Jews is to think of prayer as a synagogue activity. But most of life, including the very times when prayer might be most helpful to the individual, does not happen in a shul. I speak of the various crises we encounter in life, from illness to job loss, and the ongoing spiritual tasks in our lives: improving our characters and responding to others. In this section we ask, what role might prayer play in the trenches of life?

13

Teshuvah: Personal Change, Communal Responsibility

The Hebrew word *lehitpalel,* to pray, is a reflexive form of the root *p.l.l.,* which can also mean to arbitrate, judge, or intercede. A judge or umpire is *paleel* (Deuteronomy 32:31) and the office or quality of judgment is *pelilah* (Isaiah 16:3). So, when we pray, we judge ourselves. The values and aspirations of the prayer book, and the divine character reflected there, are the standards by which we judge. Embedded in the very word for prayer is the injunction to question ourselves; to judge ourselves; to use prayer as an opportunity to arbitrate and intercede in internal disputes, in conflicts with others, and in our relationship with God.

RABBI DEBRA ORENSTEIN

*T*eshuvah, usually translated as "repentance," literally means "turning," as in re-turning or realigning with God. It is a broader term than repentance, for it implies not only repenting from sin, but any act that inculcates proper values and demonstrates improved behavior. Turning to God is turning to godliness, to virtue, in all of its forms. The work of repentance, engaging the inner processes of self-change and growth, is the beginning. Embodying Jewish values—living a life of integrity, hearing the cries of pain and injustice around us, and acting in response—is the end. *Teshuvah* is the global process of becoming a *mensch* (Yiddush for "a good person").

While *teshuvah* is usually associated with the High Holidays, Jewish law asks us to do *teshuvah* throughout the year. Prayer can help in several ways.

Personal Growth

In my view, the most challenging part about personal change is the first step: getting honest and seeing ourselves as we really are. The defense mechanisms we need to make it through daily life are so strong and established that it takes real effort to break through the bricks and tear down the walls.

When a crisis hits and we become immobilized, we find ourselves at the psychotherapist or the Twelve-step program, trying to lift ourselves up. In both cases, the first step is to honestly admit where we are and truly to see the problem. Hopefully, we don't need a crisis to engage the process of *teshuvah*. Spiritual practice aims to keep us honest on an ongoing basis, to prevent us from sinking to the depths, and to keep us swimming toward the surface.

Perspective

Getting honest requires getting perspective. We need a break from the routine and a place outside of our everyday lives to examine ourselves with clarity. Prayer can provide that distance and prod us to look deeply at ourselves.

> I think that resistance, skepticism, and doubt are such enormous impediments for most liberal Jews. Some people find

that the practice of *hitbodedut* [see practice 12], of speaking freely to God, just really opens them up. That surprises them. It's often accompanied by tears, or great emotion. You keep going deeper and deeper. You often hit an insight or a feeling that hasn't surfaced before, at least in quite the same way. Very often, there's a yearning that all of us carry, a sense of incompleteness, the desire for closeness, or it may be a sorrow or disappointment or shame. Whatever it is, if you do a *hitbodedut* practice and stick with it over time, there is a strong likelihood that it will arise to consciousness, and thus there is the possibility of working on it in the company of God—or perhaps finally turning it over to God. [See practice 19.]

DR. LINDA THAL

Once again, prayer is a great gift when it reveals our selves to ourselves.

Prayer is effective in the way that having a good long cry is effective, or a belly laugh. We feel better. Prayer allows us the catharsis of knowing the emotional truth of this moment, knowing what you really feel, seeing your emotions and being with them, and accepting them.

RABBI LAVEY YITZCHAK DERBY

Setting the Intention

The next step is announcing the decision to change.

You can explicitly pray for these virtues and ask for help in cultivating them. Or, when you pray the liturgy, you notice that this is the way the liturgy describes what it means to be fully human, that these are the attributes for which we should strive, that these are the values that are important in life. These are likely to be things that we know in our minds, but when we're reading them in prayer, they may be absorbed in a different way, so that we come to know them in our heart and feel drawn to manifest them in our life. You may stop hearing them as the nagging parental voice we remember from our youth [and hear them] as a real prophetic call.

DR. LINDA THAL

Inculcating Virtue

If it were enough to simply figure out why we do what we do and think the thought, "I will change now," psychotherapy would have a better track record and we would all be better at improving our actions. The mysteries of the subconscious elude us. Many therapies concur with what spiritual traditions have long known. The irrational side of behavior must be addressed. This has less to do with good thinking, though that is important, and more to do with sensitizing us to the feel of our emotional states, and training our bodies and minds to behave differently.

Both personal and traditional prayer can help by allowing us to verbalize our intentions, thus internalizing them in our bodies. It is like planting a seed and watering it every day.

A significant part of prayer is being in that more contemplative state where you're overriding the judging, analyzing mind. So if you're chanting about a particular virtue, it has the potential to enter the unconscious or the subconscious. Liturgy also has the potential to speak to your conscious desires to be a certain way.

DR. LINDA THAL

I will take a line from the liturgy and repeat it over and over again, until I'm done. If I feel that I need to feel more compassion in my life, I might repeat a line, *chanun v'rachum Adonai* [compassionate and merciful is God], just to open my heart. I speak the words because they're coming from my heart, or I speak the words because I want to have an influence on my heart.

RABBI LAVEY YITZCHAK DERBY

Asking God for Help

Prayer is a form of affirmation. The previous stage can be understood as the important process of training the emotions through positive thinking. For those of us who relate to God as the Holy Other, who do not believe that God's actions in the world are purely internal to human beings, there is one more role for prayer in the process of *teshuvah*: explicitly asking God for help. While this is natural for the theological traditionalist, it also makes sense for a neo-mystic like myself. As discussed above, addressing God as "You" changes everything. In asking God for help, particularly in spontaneous, personal prayer, I reach into my heart. Just as asking for help from another person is often emotional and painful, for I must expose my own inadequacy, so too with prayer. Admitting that my power to act well is lacking humbles me. Precisely here, confronting my impotence and vulnerability, the potential for deep and lasting change arises. I need help.

I know enough about God to believe that God is capable of helping me. Prayer brings me into *mochin d'gadlut,* which brings out the best in me. Connecting to God through spiritual practice seems to me a very transparent and rational enterprise. But there is a mystery here. I don't really understand why I can't change or how God manages to tear down the walls around this stubborn heart. I only know that it has happened in the past. I have changed through the encounter with transcendence. I have felt the warmth of divine energy as love enters my life.

I know that if I want to feel that again, it helps to invite it in. I need to ask.

Here is an example of how chanting a Hebrew phrase can lead to lasting change.

I was preparing for Shabbat and I came across these words from Isaiah: "your service is fulfilled" [40:2]. I thought, these are great words to chant before Shabbat, as a way of letting go of the week. But as I was chanting, I felt the words so strongly. God was saying, "You've done enough, and you are enough. You've completely fulfilled your mission in this moment." It exposed a disease I didn't know that I had. I was holding on to a low-level anxiety, a voice saying, "You're never enough and you're never done. You always have to stay vigilant because something is going to fall through the cracks."

I experienced what it was like to know that I was completely finished, in this very moment, and then to take up the next moment from the place of joy rather than anxiety. I experienced it as switching fuel tanks, that before what fueled my work in the world was a little bit about anxiety and not getting things done, and now I felt what it was like to live from the pure joy of the work itself. Chanting that phrase gave me an experience, a new compass point, to guide my life. Because I had a moment where I felt what it was like to be enough.

RABBI SHEFA GOLD

Prayer and Recovery from Addiction

Perhaps the most difficult *teshuvah* is turning away from addiction to alcohol, drugs, or other vice. Rabbi and Dr. Abraham Twerski, founder and medical director emeritus of the Gateway Rehabilitation Center in Pittsburgh, reflects on prayer and recovery.

Prayer and the 12-Step Program
RABBI ABRAHAM TWERSKI, MD

Prayer is important in recovery from addiction. However, it is a special type of prayer.

The Talmud says that Moses gave us 613 mitzvot. David condensed the Torah into eleven (Psalm 15) Isaiah into six, Micah into three, and the prophet Habakuk into a single principle: "The right-eous person shall live with *emunah* (faith)." There is little point in discussing any aspect of prayer unless *emunah* is firmly estab-lished.

But true *emunah* is at a premium, and the reason may be found in the following anecdote.

At a meeting of Alcoholics Anonymous (AA), a man related that he was seven years sober. "I walked out on my first contact with AA. They were talking about having a Higher Power, and I was an avowed atheist. When I could not get sober, I returned and said that I want to join the program, but I don't want any of the God talk, and they said, "Okay." They told me I had to get a sponsor, which I did, and my sponsor told me I had to pray every day. I said, "Hold it! I was assured that I would not be bothered about God." My sponsor said, "Look here, you S.O.B. Do you want to get sober or stay drunk? If you want to get sober, you're going to pray every day."

"Well, I prayed every day, but I didn't pray to God because I didn't believe in God. But when I prayed, that reminded me that *I was not God.*"

This is an important observation. We are monotheistic. There cannot be two gods. As long as I believe that I am my own god, I have no room for another god.

This is clearly what Moses said (Deuteronomy 8:17–19): "You may say in your heart, 'My strength and the might of my hand made me all this wealth.' Then you shall remember that it is God who gave you strength to make wealth."

The first step in recovery from addiction and in the effort to achieve a relationship with God is humility, the realization that we are not God. Only then can we have *emunah*. Until then, our prayers may only help us realize that we are not God.

In step 7 of the AA program, we humbly ask God to remove our character defects. This is not the typical "Gimme" prayer: give me good health, give me a job, give me the winning lottery num-bers, and the like. Rather, it is a prayer asking, "Help me become a better person." This prayer is preceded by step 6, whereby we become "ready to remove all our character defects." This readiness consists of homework, of restraining our anger responses to provocations, of being considerate of others, of being meticulously honest. Only when we have done all we can do to overcome our character defects can we ask God to finish the job.

The prayer for step 11 extends the self-less concept. We "pray only for knowledge of His will for us and the power to carry that out."

The overriding characteristic of an addict is bottomless desire for self-gratification. Whether the addiction is to alcohol, drugs, sex, gambling, food, or anything else, nothing stands in the addict's way. The addict will push anyone and everyone out of the way—including spouse and children—to gratify the addictive drive. Recovery, therefore, requires a 180-degree reversal, to de-emphasize our wants and to make something else the goal in life—in this case, the will of God.

For prayer to be effective, it must be sincere and come from the heart. At an AA meeting in Jerusalem, a man who had not thought himself to be a believer related that when his drunkenness hit "rock-bottom," he found himself walking on the beach in Tel Aviv. "I had nowhere to go," he said. "My wife threw me out of the house. In desperation, I looked up to the sky and shouted, 'If You're up there, then help me!' and He helped me."

As I heard this, the verse in Psalms 145:18 went through my mind. "God is close to all who call upon Him—to all who call upon Him sincerely." That's the key word: *sincerely*.

Responsibility

The path that we walk is one of co-creative partnership with God. So prayer for me is really the process of keeping myself aware of that truth, conscious of my responsibility. And constantly bringing myself back into alignment with the divine purpose.

RABBI NADYA GROSS

Self-growth is the immediate goal in engaging the difficult process of *teshuvah*. But it is never an end unto itself. In Judaism, the purpose of self-change is not to reach a state of bliss in a monastery. Rather, we hope to remove the obstacles that prevent us from responding to others with compassion and leading a life of integrity and service. If we succeed in straightening out our personalities, we are less self-occupied, more transparent, and more open to the world around us.

> It's not just about my relationship with God. Yes, I want to feel good and connected and in alignment with my deeper self, but I also want to engage in soul refinement, to be a person who lives a life of compassion, integrity, truthfulness, the various *middot* [virtues] we name. The two go hand in hand and are inseparable. Where one starts varies with the individual, but to have a genuine flow of spirituality requires both.
> DR. LINDA THAL

Jewish liturgy never lets us forget that we are part of a larger whole. In every service we pray for justice and communal redemption. We are responsible for more than ourselves.

Prayer and Mussar

Started by Rabbi Israel Salanter, the Mussar (instruction, conduct) movement responded to both the rampant poverty and rapid assimilation of nineteenth-century Eastern European Jews by freshly reconnecting to the ethical and spiritual core of Judaism. Mussar teachings have been revived and popularized in the Jewish world in recent years, thanks in part to Rabbi Ira Stone. I asked him to comment on the role of prayer in Mussar.

> In our culture, we're concerned with the salvation of our own soul. In Mussar, we are concerned with the salvation of our own soul based on how well we respond to the needs of

another. In fact, there is a statement credited to Rabbi Salanter that says, my spiritual needs are the material needs of my neighbor.

Prayer is me overhearing my neighbor. And by the way, my being overheard by my neighbor. So to the extent that my needs are in fact real, it makes me recognize that I can't solve them without the response and the help of another. At the same time that I'm crying out, I'm also hearing the cry.

One of the reasons that not only communal prayer, but also fixed prayer, is so important in Judaism is that it serves to interrupt my absorption with myself. When I follow a traditional structure for prayer, that structure overrides my mood or my spiritual situation at the moment. I have no choice but to stop. The impact of interrupting my own self-importance is profoundly important. And the beauty of this sort of a system is that as I stop and interrupt myself, I automatically give myself space to hear the other. The two things work together. Praying three times a day with a minyan has these two aspects simultaneously built in.

The only icon of God in the world is the voice of the other person. If I'm really going to connect to God it requires that I hear the voice of the other.

RABBI IRA STONE

The Peace of Wholeness

Personal change and communal responsibility are seen as two parts of a whole and, when together, add up to more than the sum of the parts. Can we truly understand ourselves if we cannot listen well to others? Can we respond to others with compassion if we have no compassion for ourselves?

I think prayer helps cultivate an open heart because it helps us blur the lines between us. My father is an artist, and he used to teach me that the difference between a good painting and a great painting is always in the lines. In a great painting, the lines breathe. I think that when we pray, we allow our lines to breathe, so that you are a little bit me and I am a little bit you and we are all a little bit God and everything breathes everything else.

Rabbi Heschel once said, "Prayer may not save us, but it makes us worth saving." I believe that as a river smooths the most ragged rocks, prayer soothes and burnishes a being. To me people who pray regularly have a glisten and a shine that distinguishes them, almost imperceptibly, from others. They have a calm and a centeredness that always draws me near.

RABBI ZOË KLEIN

As a spiritual practice, prayer is best judged by the kind of personalities it helps to create.

People ask me, "What makes you the way you are?" How surprised they are when I say, "I have an active prayer life."

CANTOR ELLEN DRESKIN

14

Coping with Loss

I remember after the Asian Tsunami hearing someone say, "How can these people believe in God anymore? How can they even pray? They've lost everything, everyone, not even a photograph of their loved ones exists, everything is gone, and yet they pray!" And another responded, "They've lost everything, and now you want to take God away from them, too?" I was really struck by this answer. I have been through many troubling and trying times, and have accompanied people when their paths became burdensome and nearly unbearable, and I have noticed a difference between people who try to muster some relationship with God in crises and those who have always been in relationship with God. Those who have always been in relationship can lean more easily on God, and can speak more freely, expressing their hope as well as their anger. I have seen prayer help people overcome loss, deal with grief, change their direction, and recover, but usually it is in people who have become practiced in prayer through their own rituals and devotion to it. It is not usual that someone prays for the first time and their life is altered, although sometimes it can happen, rare as revelation.

RABBI ZOË KLEIN

Loss—whether a job or a relationship, a loved one or our own health—can engender crisis in our lives. It is precisely at such a time that we might expect spiritual practice to help us the most. But sometimes, even experienced spiritual practitioners are at a loss. I was praying the traditional liturgy every day when I was drafted into the Israeli army. During basic training, rising early to daven helped me to keep my sanity, even though it cut into the few hours we were given to sleep. I carried a Siddur in the cargo pocket of my uniform. But when my service started, at a West Bank prison for Palestinians during the first Intifada, I was too upset and depressed to take it out of my pocket.

> It would be nice if God would come down and explain to us why life is unfair and why innocent people suffer and why the world is filled with both great beauty and great pain, but so far God hasn't explained it. There are times when prayer does not solve the problem. There are times when I can't feel God. And I don't know what to pray and I don't sense God's presence. I just don't. I understand why people hang up the phone until they're ready to call again. That's part of my story.
> RABBI NAOMI LEVY

I would never judge one who told me that they couldn't pray, especially when facing significant pain or loss. And yet, I would recommend it. If we can gather the strength, spiritual practice from the midst of crisis is a unique opportunity to move down the spiritual path and mature as a human being.

I remember teaching a class on Job, and as people spoke, it became clear. Nobody took the class out of academic interest. Everyone was dealing with loss. Surprisingly, most people reported that their faith was strengthened by the experience. Finally, my friend Debbie Mell asked, "Does anyone get to God without a crisis, without suffering?"

I'm sure there are people who do, but it seems to me that more people discover God, rather than lose God, when they suffer.

As a liberal Jew, I am not surrounded by people who would blame God for a disease, let alone a divorce. So perhaps it is not surprising. But secular critics claim that people turn to God in times of crisis as a crutch. Are these people turning to God out of desperation?

Not from what I can tell, and not from my own experience. Neither the liberals nor the traditionalists I know think that God will solve their problems for them by waving a wand. Rather, when crisis hits, we are stripped of so much of who we are. The death of loved ones, illness, divorce, the loss of a job: suddenly we can no longer live the way we were just a short time before. The future is unknown. Against our will, the psychological safety net, and sometimes our physical security as well, have been torn from us. Our expectations about how the world works are no longer valid. Most painful of all, our self-image has shattered. We are vulnerable, exposed, and searching for a new path.

Why don't people change? It is often too difficult to risk letting go of the patterns and defense mechanisms, psychological and physical, that keep us safe. Better to stick with some bad habits than suffer uncertainty. But in times of crisis, the familiar patterns are taken from us whether we like it or not. If we can be with the pain without losing ourselves—if we can get some perspective—opportunity knocks. We are given the possibility of changing for the better. For when we are searching, we are more receptive to new ways of living in the world. And when we are vulnerable and exposed, we might find ourselves willing to hear voices we previously blocked out. We might receive the support of sources we refused to consider in the past. We might discover God.

> In emotional moments, I'm convinced that people pray harder not because they need to ask God stuff that they didn't ask before, but because it opens a part of you that otherwise is closed. It's not that there are no atheists in foxholes, it's that you can pray differently in a foxhole, because there is more of you available to you.
> RABBI DAVID J. WOLPE

Here is a series of comments from our teachers on prayer and coping with loss.

Prayer Shifts the Energy

Once I had a bad diagnosis and had to get a biopsy and was really afraid. I knew so many people who had been down this path and I was wondering if my life was over. It felt like this big downward vortex, like I was spinning down into the drain, into doubt and fear. That life had no meaning, was really just random. I poured all my pleas and prayers down into the vortex. That was the image. It's kind of crazy. The direction of the vortex turned upward. I began to feel okay. Maybe things won't turn out well, but I'm putting myself in God's hands. I'm going to be okay. For me, the connection is critical. It's really like putting myself on an axis, à la Jung, to the Great Self. If you do that, there's an energetic shift from downward to upward.

RABBI TIRZAH FIRESTONE

Not to Be Left Alone

I realize that in moments of crisis in my life, I've never expected prayer to get rid of the problem. When I thought that I was going to lose my wife and my twins in a really chilling moment of her pregnancy, I prayed a lot. I cried, I pounded the wall, I was talking to God out loud. Two of the nurses walked by and one of them said, "I'm not worried about the mom, but I'm worried about the dad." And I turned to her and said, "I'm doing exactly what I'm supposed to be doing right now." In that moment of praying, I wasn't alone. I felt absolutely that the Divine was with me. I had no expectation of changing the outcome. That was medical, what the doctors do; that was biological. I didn't expect a suspension of the rules. I just expected not to be left alone. And that's what I turn to prayer for. It's enough.

RABBI BRADLEY SHAVIT ARTSON

What Is Healing?

When we ask for *refuah shleimah,* a complete healing, a completion of the person, sometimes they need to get through something to get to some end result. That might mean healing, that might mean a new way of living, that might mean the end of their lives. I don't know what that is. But whatever I can do to help them, I've just given myself a better chance of doing it.

RABBI ETHAN FRANZEL

Opening to the Divine

A friend came to me for counseling during a long period of unemployment. He didn't have a spiritual practice of any kind. He felt so anxious—unsure what the future would bring. I thought of the prayer from the morning blessings, "Praised are you God ... who makes firm our steps." I asked if he had a sense of how God has guided him to this point, and continues to guide him forward. I invited him to say the line, to rest in it. In that moment, he suddenly dropped into a place of groundedness. It was profound. He didn't just say the words. He really put himself into them. Suddenly, he felt a sense of trust, that somehow, God was guiding his footsteps. He just said, "Wow."

RABBI ZARI M. WEISS

Seeking Connection

I recently visited a woman in the hospital who was diagnosed with cancer—a tragic case, where by the time they discovered the disease, it was too late to treat it. We chatted and then I offered to say a prayer with her. She said, "No, I don't believe in that." I said, "Fine," and we chatted about something else and then she said, "You know, I've changed my mind. I want that prayer. I want all the prayers I can have." When in a hospital, people sometimes want to pray the *Shema.* It's strange to say the least, as that's the prayer the tradition would have you say just before you die, but people don't know that, and they want to link with the Jewish prayer they know best.

RABBI KAREN FOX, DD

Prayer and Healing

Can God directly bring about healing? Here are three positive responses, one from the place of a traditional theology, two from a mystical perspective.

> We've all prayed for people who have gotten better and for other people who died. The story of Hezekiah, who prayed that he'd get better and God allowed him to live longer, in some ways, is a very troubling story; why did God need prayer to change Hezekiah's destiny? There are other times when God waits for the Israelites to call on the Divine before God is ready to start the process of getting them out of Egypt ... but I do think that if God either isn't sure whether somebody's time has come or is willing to give them more time depending on who intercedes, I do think that prayer matters. That's a simplistic way of phrasing what goes on, as it were, in God's mind, but I think it does and I think that prayer can strengthen the patient's own resolve and contribute to their healing.
>
> RABBI RICHARD N. LEVY, DD

> If I bring consciousness to the need for healing for someone, I'm making more healing consciousness in the universe, and consciousness affects physicality. There is some efficacy in prayer. We direct God's intention since God is not separate from divinity in us.
>
> RABBI JEFF ROTH

> Often people get angry at their illness or at themselves with illness. Prayer can help you forgive, to make a peace treaty

with yourself, to not be at war with yourself, which does have physical effects.

RABBI DAVID INGBER

Anne Brener, rabbi, therapist, and best-selling author of *Mourning and Mitzvah: A Guided Journal for Walking the Mourner's Path through Grief to Healing* (Jewish Lights), shares her thoughts on the role of prayer in coping with loss.

Prayer and Loss: Building a Temple of Tears
RABBI ANNE BRENER, LCSW

In a cabinet in the foyer of my synagogue is a small glass bottle with two openings. It is an object from around the year 100 CE that caught and held the tears of those who mourned the destruction of the Temple. According to a legend, it was believed that when the bottle was filled, the Messiah would come. This extraordinary ritual object is from a time when the Jewish worship system transformed from sacrifice to prayer, as the ritual practices of the Jewish people were reinvented following the traumatic loss of the Temple and exile from the Promised Land. The experience of the Jewish people provides a precedent for those who suffer. For when our lives are shattered through the experience of loss, we must reinvent our own belief system and create new tools for aligning ourselves with meaning and peace. Very often, we need to begin with our own tears.

"Prayer of the heart" is where we begin when we feel bereft, not only of whom or what we have lost, but also the sources of faith and support that may have sustained us in the past. Our grief may be the result of the death of someone we treasured. It could be caused by illness, divorce, job loss, communal catastrophe, or any other life-changing trauma that devastates us and forces us to re-examine our basic assumptions. Whatever the cause, we must begin where we are and find the sounds, words, or physical expressions that connect us to our deepest pain.

We might think of prayer as a collection of written passages, gathered in a prayer book written many years ago by people whose lives have little relevance to our own. When we open the prayer book in a time of crisis, the words may ring hollow. Perhaps our loss provokes a spiritual crisis. If we are people of faith, we may feel betrayed. The theological underpinnings of our lives may feel like a temple in ruins. And if we are people who have not relied on God or prayer in the past, our earlier doubts seem validated, provoking deeper cynicism and alienation.

Perhaps we have understood prayer as a way of asking God to fulfill our yearnings. Now, with our hopes devastated, it feels futile to reach out to that punishing deity. At our lowest moments, we often feel far away from the force that runs the universe. Any assumptions we had about God's benevolence or the efficacy of turning to God when we suffer may have been swept away in frustration and disillusionment.

Often prayer is a way of expressing gratitude and offering praise to God. But gratitude and adoration are hardly what we feel after a loss. We are much more likely to feel anger, an emotion that we hardly think of as an acceptable form of prayer.

It is necessary to expand our understanding of prayer beyond the limits of these definitions. If prayer is going to help us when we are suffering, we must make no assumptions about the benevolence of the Force that Runs the Universe or Its expectations of the way in which It wants to be addressed. We must also stop thinking of prayer as something fixed in a book and existing outside of ourselves. To reconstruct our understanding of prayer, we have to look to our own feelings for the source of our prayers. Conceiving of prayer as the spontaneous outpouring of the heart makes room for the full range of our feelings, running the gamut from tears to rage. We go to the most visceral reaction to our loss and begin with the pains in the stomach and in the heart. We give voice to the sounds, words, and expressions that articulate our wounds.

That such expressions are, indeed, prayer, is validated in ancient Jewish literature. Rabbi Johanan (Midrash Deuteronomy

Rabba, Parshat Vaethchanan) described prayer with a list of ten synonyms, many expressing the emotional state of the Hebrews trapped in the depths of slavery: cry, lament, groan, sing, encounter, trouble, call, fall, pray, and supplicate.

When we take leave of the intellectual view of prayer and seek guidance from Rabbi Johanan, we access the possibility of healing change. Prayer becomes a process independent of any belief system, even of any expectation of outcome. It becomes the wings for our yearning for healing. They fly beneath the radar of our certainty that we cannot move beyond our pain and bring us to a place not yet imagined. This change begins with the cry of our hearts. Prayer focuses and amplifies our feelings and these, in turn, bring transformation.

Transformation may look very different than expected. Sometimes prayer brings deeper feelings. Sometimes it brings relief. The process can also be calming, as the repetition of sounds and the movement of prayer create a "relaxation response," reducing stress and producing tranquility. Certainly this is healing.

Our understanding of healing may change in other ways, as well. Initially, when we suffer, we can only imagine healing in terms of "cure." If we are sick, we think of healing as the cessation of our symptoms or a return to the way we were. We want our old lives back. We want our family to function as it did in the past. We want the people who have left us back in our arms. Even though this conception of healing is not congruent with what is possible, any other form of healing is unimaginable.

But when we seek healing through prayer, we aim toward the inconceivable. We suspend the intellect and call out that holy phrase, "I Don't Know." We reach beyond the limits of our understanding and glimpse an unknown picture of the world. We open to the possibility of reframing our suffering. Through the use of prayer, we step through the new frame and into the unknown.

Judaism's most well-known prayer for healing, the *Mi Sheberach,* asks for a *refuah shleimah* (complete healing). This is a healing of both body *and* soul. We might understand that *refuat ha-guf* (healing of the body) and *refuat ha-nefesh* (healing of the soul) are at once distinct and interrelated. This awareness challenges our notion that healing and cure are synonymous. There are times when the symptoms of illness leave the body but the soul continues to ache, and there are times when the body does not get better but the soul finds transformation and healing. In addition, there are times when *refuah shleimah* must include the difficult truth that the healing may never come. The loved one will not return, the illness will not improve. That for which we yearn is not a possibility. But this understanding may also be a form of healing, as we come to terms with the painful truth. The *Mi Sheberach* teaches us that even when a complete healing is unachievable, healing is still possible. This shift in understanding is a healing in itself.

Coping with loss is never easy. In shifting our understanding of both prayer and healing, we claim prayer as our own and unlock its potential for healing.

Practices 16–19, the first three by Rabbi Anne Brener, put the above ideas into action.

Mourning and Death

Prayer can also play a central role in coping with irrevocable loss, with death. I'll never forget a woman who spoke to me after I gave a guest sermon about prayer. In her early thirties, she was already a widow. The second paragraph of the *Amidah* praises God for "healing the sick, freeing the captive, and keeping faith with those who sleep in the dust." That line, she said, saved her. Every Shabbat she came to synagogue to connect to God who stays with those who sleep in the dust.

After my mother's recent death, I followed the laws of mourning and attended a daily minyan to say *Kaddish,* the Jewish prayer uttered in memory of the departed. The wisdom of the tradition was brilliant. Every day I spent a few minutes connecting with my mother. In fact, I was devastated when the year of mourning was over and I had to stop. I knew I would no longer keep the connection fresh and I felt her loss all over again. But the Jewish liturgical tradition was speaking to me. It's been a year. It's time to move on.

Prayer as Preparation for Ultimate Truth

Upon hearing about a death, the tradition bids us to say the blessing *baruch dayan emet*, "blessed be the true judge," or "judge of truth." I don't believe in a "judge" who issues decrees, but I do relate to God as judge in a broader sense. It is the judgment of the universe that we shall die. Living is not possible without death. The spiritual question becomes, "Can I put my personal encounter with death in a cosmic context?" And I particularly relate to *emet*, truth, which here means genuine or authentic. Another meaning for *emet* in the Hebrew Bible is loyal or faithful. In this moment of ultimate contraction, can I remain authentic? Can I respond from an open heart? Can I remain loyal and genuine to all that I have gleaned in my relation to transcendence—to my values, to my heart, to God?

> A nineteen-year-old Israeli soldier was on his way home to see his family in the summer of 1994 when he was kidnapped by members of Hamas. For several days his family and the country held their breath as they searched for him, desperate for a sign that he was alive. Finally, in the middle of the night, there was a knock at the family's door. The soldier's father opened the door and saw three generals standing before him, the requisite number for a *beit din*—a Jewish legal court. He immediately knew what this meant. But before they could even tell him that they had found the body of his beloved son, his "tall blue-eyed, golden-haired son who was always smiling with the innocence of a child and the understanding of an adult," he had the following thought: *thank you, God, for blessing me with nineteen years with this angel on Earth.* His

beloved son was murdered by terrorists, and his first thought was an expression of gratitude for the blessing of his life.

Years later, the father explained: "I understood in that instant why I had been praying three times a day my whole life. It was all preparation for that moment." Over the course of a lifetime he had built a consciousness that allowed him to grieve with gratitude.

What made it possible for that father to recognize, in the moment of his son's death, the great blessing of his life? He had spent a lifetime cultivating a humble awareness of the gift of life, of the majesty of the world, of the presence and possibility of love. It doesn't mean that loss isn't excruciating, it means that a life of humble gratitude places loss in a context of meaning. It means that even in the darkest and busiest moments, our hearts are open to beauty and possibility. This is the essence of prayer.

RABBI SHARON BROUS

PART IV

Embracing Traditional Jewish Prayer

We turn to what many consider the essential element of Jewish prayer: the Siddur and the synagogue service. Unlike other resources on the subject, this book's primary goal is not to provide the information you need to learn the traditional Jewish prayer service. Rather, our purpose is to provide inspiration and a conceptual approach to learn from the many books on Jewish liturgy in a productive way.

We begin, as always, with the most basic question. Why might it be a good idea to pray in traditional Jewish style? We then turn to learning the skills to do so in chapters 16 and 17. In chapter 18, "Best Practices," we approach our teachers as role models to learn from their experience as davenners. We then ask about the relationship of traditional prayer to the personal prayer skills we have cultivated in *Making Prayer Real*. Finally, we ask our teachers for advice on how to begin.

15

The Spiritual Dynamics of the Siddur

The prayers are there to open the blinds on different windows, to look out at different aspects of self and beingness, to see all the different intentions and possibilities and awarenesses that can be and should be informing our lives. They're all present in our traditional prayers. It's for us to discover them, and we don't discover them by just saying the words every day. We discover them by looking at them deeply.

RABBI NADYA GROSS

Davenning is a very powerful practice, but people mistakenly scorn it. They think it's like you speak to a Big Man in the sky. That's a superficial understanding of it. It's much deeper. Prayer can take you to the goal, to God-consciousness.

MAGGID YITZHAK BUXBAUM

Many of us know what synagogue services look like when they don't work for us. What does Jewish liturgy bring to the table, whether public or private, when it is working? Why study the Siddur? Why use it to pray?

We have organized our teachers' responses into three categories: the benefits of praying from within a tradition, from within a disciplined practice, and from within a community.

Praying within a Tradition

Prayers, like poetry, are allusive. What makes the Siddur so alive after a thousand years is that there are so many things that connect to it. When there's a thunderstorm, there's a *bracha* [blessing]; where there's pain in your life, there's the psalms. And go the other way. Look at the *bracha* for the body, you learn about the body. The Siddur alludes to the universe and the universe alludes to the Siddur; the Siddur alludes to the rest of Jewish practice and all of Jewish practice alludes to the Siddur. It's like a hologram, a web of connections.

DR. TAMAR FRANKIEL

We contemporary Westerners have a good sense of individual potential and creativity. Our culture is forward looking, and due to the needs of consumer capitalism, the media always lauds the new and the novel. But in any artistic practice, we stand on the shoulders of generations gone by. Can you imagine a great writer who is not a great reader? My jazz musician friends learned to read music and studied the great improvisations of jazz tradition note by note. Great artists don't circumvent tradition; they master it, and even if their creativity leads them to rebel, they stand on the accomplishments of the past. So, too, with prayer.

Isaac Bashevis Singer is reputed to have said, "We Jews have many faults. Amnesia is not among them." That's a great citation because, in fact, it's true. We remember the past and have, therefore, a great deal of depth to bring to bear on any given situation. And our liturgy brings that depth to us and invites us into the past through the present and then back to the present again.

RABBI LAWRENCE A. HOFFMAN, PHD

For me, the depth has emotional ramifications. Quite apart from the spiritual content, I find it amazing, and powerful, that I am saying words said by my ancestors in the Temple, in Babylonia, in Yemen, in Europe, for millennia.

> I think that it's helpful to know that millions of people over thousands of years have used these same forms. Your community is not only contemporary. Your community is through time. You are part of a large, extended group of people. And since prayer in Judaism is communal, the larger your community, the more powerful your sense of connecting not just to God but also to others.
>
> RABBI DAVID J. WOLPE

Discovering Ourselves through Tradition

> Our experiences are unique to us, but those who came before us faced similar challenges. We're not the first to fall in love, to experience failure, to suffer loss, to long for the Divine Presence. By reading a psalm, I have the potential both to be validated as a wholly unique individual and also to find my struggles given expression through the lens of those who came before, and that is an empowering and humbling and inspiring experience all at the same time.
>
> RABBI ELLIOT J. COSGROVE, PHD

Just as we learn some of life's most profound truths from novels, plays, and poems, we learn from past literary works like the Siddur. When a tradition works, it is provocative, sometimes shocking. It exposes us to aspects of life that we might have missed.

> I love literature, and that is a door in. I don't get alienated by distance; I get curious. That's the value of study. Did the rabbis write something purposely alienating? From their perspective it was true, so we can ask, what was that?
>
> DR. TAMAR FRANKIEL

I love the words of the Siddur. I don't think they're frivolous or willy-nilly or one person liked them and now we're all stuck with them. I really respect the thought that was put into it. I look for those words to bring me either challenge or comfort and they haven't let me down yet. I'm always finding new stuff. And I'm always looking for new stuff. If a prayer seems tired to me, then I better look harder at it.

CANTOR ELLEN DRESKIN

It's like [Bob] Dylan's "Knockin' on Heaven's Door"—one of my favorites from Woodstock. Well, I wasn't at Woodstock and I've never been in a hangman's noose waiting for the trap door to fall out, so I can't sing that song? No, we just jump in because it touches us. So part of Jewish prayer is allowing ourselves to say, "These are words of my people, and I'm connecting to them." People who weren't at Woodstock claim it as their music, their generation, as if they were there. I can sing the words of my ancestors and claim Sinai.

RABBI SHAWN ZEVIT

The Tradition's Words, Our Words

Sometimes the virtue of Jewish liturgical tradition is simply its availability to us when we can't find our own words of prayer.

There are so many times that words fall short, and I don't even know how to articulate what I so deeply yearn to express. I find that returning to the Siddur offers me security when my spiritual stepping is questionable.

REB MIMI FEIGELSON

Sometimes you're just too strung out to come up with your own personal prayers. Having the text in front of you kind of takes you by the hand and walks you over to something that matters more than whatever is getting you down.

JAY MICHAELSON

The optimal situation is when the border between our words and the words of the tradition dissolves.

> Sometimes, often, something happens, and words come up to express my emotions. So an important question to ask is, at what speed of retrieval are words of Torah accessible to a person? That's important. Someone may find that what comes is Whitman, or the Beatles, which happens to me a lot also. I wasn't pressing for words, but the words came. The words come from the level that they have been internalized. I've lucked out that what I've internalized is much of the basic words of Torah and prayer. I know them. So they are easily accessible on the level of emotion and intuition, not just knowledge and information. We're in a world loaded with so much data; there has to be some body of words that are meaningful to you and have settled in you and are easily accessible when you want to alter your state, to be more reflective and expressive. When you get to know these words and befriend them, it's not them and you; it's yours.
>
> MELILA HELLNER-ESHED, PHD

Praying within a Disciplined, Spiritual Practice

One key in transforming our prayer lives is to give up the notion of prayer as a leisure-time activity and embrace it as an ongoing, spiritual practice.

> One place to begin is to reconceive of prayer as a discipline rather than an obligation. Prayer as obligation can lead too easily to speed-davenning just to get it done. Prayer as discipline acknowledges that there will be times when the act of prayer has no real meaning to the worshiper. Yet it is still important to pray in order to maintain the discipline of prayer. The difference, then, is that you have not fulfilled an obligation in this rote prayer. You understand that this act of prayer

was unsuccessful, but it is important to keep on praying to increase your prayer skills. It also lays the groundwork for the future potential of your prayer experience. Being unsuccessful is a goad to try harder next time rather than being satisfied with having fulfilled the mitzvah in a system that sees prayer as an obligation.[1]

RABBI MICHAEL STRASSFELD

Prayer becomes productive when it is a practice, grounded in discipline and regularity.

What is the structure that allows you to express your longing, your thanks, your wow, your reflection? I find that prayer, the structure of it and our own particular Jewish nuances of it, is an optimal part of the living diet for well-being. In the Jewish modalities of prayer, those very longings, those human dimensions are addressed, and they're also addressed because they have layers of Jewish Peoplehood and our experience over four millennia, as well as the universal human aspects.

RABBI SHAWN ZEVIT

My discipline comes mostly from an inner urgency for regularity, for having a special time to connect. I need a distancing from the everyday stuff and a methodology for sensing what I sensed as a child. It's a source of joy, so I want to do it. So it doesn't feel like an externally imposed discipline, though I do have a bit of that.

RABBI DIANE ELLIOT

Once, after I complained about the difficulty of establishing a daily spiritual practice, my teacher, Rabbi Jonathan Omer-Man, shared an important insight. When discipline is most successful, it is not imposed; it arises. Discipline creates space for play—serious, but fun as well. When it's going well, spiritual practice feels light, not heavy. As in any good relationship, commitment gives birth to spontaneity.

Like date night with my beloved, I have to consciously choose to make my relationship with God a priority.

RABBI SHAWN ZEVIT

Daily Wonder

To the prophets, wonder is *a form of thinking* ... it is an attitude that never ceases [emphasis in the original].[2]

ABRAHAM JOSHUA HESCHEL

These words have profoundly affected me. Usually we think of wonder or awe as something that happens to us in response to an event, perhaps a sunset or an intimate moment with a loved one. Heschel turns this understanding on its head. Wonder can be an attitude, a way of being in the world. Once we know what it feels like to experience awe and wonder, we can internalize it and turn it into a virtue. We can bring "eyes of wonder" to everything we experience in life. Consciously bringing wonder and awe from our hearts to the world is critical if we are to experience God in our lives.

Awe precedes faith; it is *at the root of faith.* We must grow in awe in order to reach faith. We must be guided by awe to be worthy of faith. Awe, rather than faith, is the cardinal attitude of the religious Jew [emphasis in the original].[3]

ABRAHAM JOSHUA HESCHEL

For Heschel, cultivating wonder and awe as virtues is an essential goal of Judaism as a spiritual practice.

Every evening we recite [from the Siddur]: "He creates light and makes the dark." Twice a day we say: "He is One." What is the meaning of such repetition? A scientific theory, once it is announced and accepted, does not have to be repeated twice a day. The insights of wonder must be constantly kept alive. Since there is a need for daily wonder, there is a need for daily worship.[4]

ABRAHAM JOSHUA HESCHEL

In the larger context of a spiritual practice, Rabbi Marcia Prager teaches, prayer and religious ritual aim to keep wonder and awe alive.

> People usually come to consult with me because of a circumstance of life for which they need a rabbi. Frequently someone comes in, sits down in my study and says: "Rabbi, before I begin, I just want you to know, I'm not a religious person." Yet, after a pregnant pause, so often that person will then add, " ... but I'm very spiritual." I smile a loving, appreciative smile. Then I ask a question. I ask, "Can you tell me about a spiritual experience you had that was important to you, what happened, and what you learned?"
>
> I am gifted with such a stunning array of responses. Moments of wonder, moments of awe! "I was on the mountaintop when the sun was rising and ... " "I was at the beach staring out at the ocean, gazing into that place where the expansive sea and sky touch, and suddenly ... " Sometimes people describe an experience unfolding in a moment of interpersonal intimacy, such as falling in love, or the birth of a child. "When my newborn opened her eyes for the very first time, our eyes met and through that gaze I saw the whole universe born in an instant!" And then, "Suddenly, I realized that there is meaning and purpose in existence, far beyond what I previously imagined," or "Suddenly, I became aware that there is something larger, that I am part of it, that everything is connected! Wow!"
>
> It's the "suddenly" that is like a finger pointing to the essential point of it all. "Suddenly, it all made sense!" "Suddenly, I was flooded with awe and inexpressible joy." "All of a sudden, I tasted awe and wonder, meaning and pur-

pose. I tasted eternity, and now I want to know—how do I get back there?" "Suddenly, I tapped into the very wellspring of being, but then just as suddenly, it was gone!"

Life brings us moments of transcendence. Doors open to wonder and awe. But as memorable as the "wow" may be, it can still be hard to live every day like that. I long to bring some of that peak experience home with me into my daily life! I want to know how to reconnect with that "suddenly ... wow ... " when I'm tired or lonely or frustrated or bored or pressured or car-pooling or paying the bills again, or in the aisle at the supermarket. Where is it?

You probably know that I'm a big fan of the inner meaning of words. Do you know where the word *religion* comes from? Think about a ligament. A ligament connects muscles and bones. *Lig* means "to connect." To "re-lig" is to connect again. So what is the function of religion? To help us reconnect again and again with the One Sourcing and Sustaining Power of the Universe we call God. Religion offers synergistically interactive practices that help us reconnect. This is what every religion is supposed to do. In Judaism we call spiritual practices mitzvot. The Hebrew root *Tz-V* means "imperative," so I sometimes translate *mitzvot* as "spiritual imperatives." But, you know, in Aramaic the same root means "connect"! So the rabbis taught that mitzvot are about the imperative, the necessity of staying connected! Our Jewish practices are a spiritual toolbox for reconnecting, so that awe, joy, power, meaning, purpose flow unimpeded into our daily lives.

RABBI MARCIA PRAGER

A Cumulative Practice

As for repetition, anything I do well in this world, I do frequently. Things I don't do well, I don't do frequently. It's about the repetition.

RABBI ELLIOT J. COSGROVE, PhD

I think the tradition is actually brilliant, in that forcing me to use the Siddur three times a day means that I turn to it in checklist mode and then in the middle of it I get swept away. Sometimes, not always. But there isn't a day that goes by that at some point in some *tefillah* [prayer], something in the Siddur doesn't knock me over, and that wouldn't happen if I weren't davenning regularly.

RABBI BRADLEY SHAVIT ARTSON

I can go on a hike and get a wow, but my daily minutes on an exercise bike are not a wow. I do get some wows from prayer, but I don't expect them on a given day, and when I get the wow, it's only because I've built a foundation that the wow moments can stand on.

RABBI ELIE KAPLAN SPITZ

Not only in the gym does repetition and practice build strength. In spiritual practice, in daily davenning, we are acquiring and honing a set of skills. Prayer works when it is cumulative.

When worship is entertainment, as it may be in some "Friday Night Live" or "Synaplex" experiences, our expectation to be entertained obfuscates deeper spiritual needs. Worship cannot be only for the happy person. Prayer becomes more powerful over time; its meaning is cumulative through the experience of it, whether we are feeling sorrow or joy, doubt or certainty. The more we participate, the more we will "own" the experience and receive what we need.

RABBI ELYSE FRISHMAN

It seems like an oxymoron. Scheduling heartfelt prayer for Shabbat morning is like saying, "I will be moved by the victims of war in Africa this Tuesday at 7 a.m." But look at any successful practitioner of their art. Whether musicians, dancers, or athletes, they practice, practice, and practice some more. The writer doesn't know ahead of time if today's creative effort is destined for publication or yet another contribution to the circular file. What a writer does know is that she must write daily.

Even in matters of the heart, we do better with practice, for as we have learned, there are skills involved in opening the heart. Of course, we can never schedule the encounter with God. Even if we do our part, we cannot control what God might send our way. What we do know, however, is that the more we practice, the more productive our practice becomes. We become quicker and more efficient at emptying our minds and listening—to the needs of those around us, to our own hearts, and to God. We grow accustomed to putting our emotions into words. We don't know what any given day of davenning will bring. But we can get better, and watch ourselves get better, at creating the conditions for heartfelt prayer.

> When spontaneous prayer is part of a cumulative, consistent, disciplined practice, it works. When I choose in a moment of extreme pain to do something I've never done before, it doesn't help me or anybody. I'm just grasping at straws. But when I continue a long chain of practices, I'm tapping into all the experiences I've had previously.
> RABBI ETHAN FRANZEL

Praying within a Community

> I think there is something very powerful about recognizing this kind of holy network between human beings, who are praying from very different places but saying the same words and singing the same melodies. Some are crying out in pain and some in joy and gratitude. A rich and textured encounter is happening. I think of it as invisible threads connecting everyone in the room and lifting everyone higher.
> RABBI SHARON BROUS

I have sat silently with a hundred people in a meditation hall so quiet you could hear the proverbial pin drop. It is both amazing and profound. Sharing space and intention with a community of people empowers the individual, even when they don't say a word to each other!

The Spiritual Uplift of Praying with Others

In my minyan, everyone really knows how to pray. Channels of blessing open up and you can actually feel the flow, communally, of an expanded awareness, where you would look at somebody across the room and see a being in God's image. You can't dislike someone in that state. Lovingkindness is the norm.

RABBI DIANE ELLIOT

There has been a paradigm shift. Before, we were always thinking of these things as a solo item. My soul, separate from everything else, is connected with God. But nobody is separate from anything else because my body, from mitochondria on, is a community. And I'm a member of a community. That's why communal prayer is so important. In the community, we create a God-field that is much stronger than the God-field that I can create as an individual.

RABBI ZALMAN M. SCHACHTER-SHALOMI

Praying with others gives us a different perspective on prayer, one that decenters the individual worshiper.

Personally, I respond better to communal worship. I think it packs a bigger punch. I find that when it's just me, I tend to concentrate on just me, and I don't think that's the point. My spontaneous prayers are in the first person singular, and I think there's a reason why Jewish prayer, for the most part, is in the first person plural. It's about something bigger than us.

CANTOR ELLEN DRESKIN

For me, God is not a person, but rather a sense of connected-ness, and I am more in touch with that connectedness when I get out of my own personal dramas, when I'm not the cen-ter of the world. Most of the time I am. The *Shema,* when it really works, reminds me that everything is really God—not me, but God. The reason communal prayer is important is that it happens in community.

RABBI LAURA GELLER

The Virtues of Genuine Community

There's a study that was done about how high school students who regularly eat with their families excelled in high school. It was the one key variable. It's probably twenty-five years old, but it's been duplicated. My kids were young when this study appeared, and I thought, "Nothing very profound hap-pens at my dinner table." But then I thought about it. We con-veyed to our children that eating as a family was an important priority. There are times when there is a surprise in the con-versation. When someone does have a need to talk about a problem or express themselves, we're there. The advantage is their sense of belonging, a sense of identity and care, and the opportunity to process, an ease of processing out of the famil-iarity with the setting. The same thing for my prayer life. It defines me, and gives me a sense of place. I don't think a lot about it, yet it is at the core of who I am.

RABBI ELIE KAPLAN SPITZ

In a society where individualism is lauded and genuine community has receded, communal prayer is an exemplar of social ethics.

The remarkable experience of sharing Shabbat worship is that when we join together, our disagreements are irrelevant. Whatever tensions we've had during the week melt away in the spirit of harmony. Every person is welcome. Every person must *feel* welcome. Our differences disappear because we want this for one another. This deepens our understanding of the "other" and strengthens our community.

RABBI ELYSE FRISHMAN

More than Liturgy

The Torah learning is way better when I'm in community than when I'm doing it on my own. That's a big part of it. A lot of people come to our minyan, not so much because of the prayer experience but because of the learning that is embedded in the prayer experience, which is, you might argue, a different version of prayer.

RABBI LAURA GELLER

Joining together for Jewish communal prayer opens up opportunities for other communal activities, such as social justice projects and study. In the broader sense that we have considered prayer in this book, these, too, are part of the life of a prayer-person.

For me, study and prayer are almost the same thing. When I study the liturgy or study in a praying community, that, for me, is prayer. I think the Siddur is an incredibly rich treasury of theology. The heart of the entire experience for me, at least on Shabbat, is the Torah reading, which is a glorious experience for me. I want a full Torah reading with an impeccable reader. That, for me, is the re-creation of Sinai. I hear the voice of God coming down from the mountaintop and giving these words, and I'm at the foot of the mountain, listening.

RABBI NEIL GILLMAN, PHD

16

Learning the Siddur

One of the reasons people have problems with the prayer book is because it's a classic. No one would expect Shakespeare to be immediately profound if you've never studied Shakespeare. People take classes on just the tragedies, or just the sonnets, and they'll study them with a scholar, because they are convinced that there's worth to Shakespeare and you need to put in some learning in order to meet Shakespeare on Shakespeare's level. The Siddur is a classic. It can't reward simply opening the book and reading, because it is too embedded in layers of Torah and Bible and poetry and rabbinics. It takes studying.

RABBI BRADLEY SHAVIT ARTSON

If you don't know it, you can't possibly know how it relates to your life, and you'll be put off by it, bored by it, even offended by it. Here's an example, the *unetaneh tokef* prayer on Rosh HaShanah, "who will live and who will die." This is not an easy prayer to handle—some congregations purposely omit it—why, in fact, would anyone say it? On the face of it, it is infuriating. But what gives the prayer special power is the legend that it was composed by a medieval martyr named Rabbi Amnon. There was no Rabbi Amnon, however; he never existed. But Amnon has the same root as *emunah,* faith. It's a myth about "Rabbi Faithful" and reflects the Jewish plight in the Middle Ages during the Crusades. How do we face the reality of being powerless over our own lives? People suffering today face this issue all the time, when feeling alone and isolated by illness, for example. What do we do when we suffer? How do we remain faithful, not through martyrdom, certainly, but in our own way? Here is a prayer whose metaphoric depth invites you into the depth of your own life. To understand the prayer is to be invited into the depth of your own life.

RABBI LAWRENCE A. HOFFMAN, PHD

There are many ways to study any subject matter, and the Siddur is no exception. Considering that most adult learners have time limitations, how to approach the Siddur wisely is a very important question. I turned to Covenant Award–winning Jewish educator and Torah Aura Productions founder, Joel Lurie Grishaver, for guidance.

The Siddur According to Gris

Here are Joel Lurie Grishaver's keys to making sense of traditional Jewish liturgy.

1. Learn enough of the Hebrew language and its structure to know approximate meanings.

Hebrew is such a logical language that the knowledge of just a few roots and how to find them makes the meanings of traditional prayers accessible. Chapter 17 explains why and how.

2. Learn the basic structures of Jewish liturgy.

There are a few basic forms to Jewish liturgy. Knowing them helps you to feel at home in the Siddur.

It's important to know why the liturgy goes from prayer to prayer, and it's not a bunch of prayers thrown down the stairs, whichever landed the furthest goes first. In other words, structure matters. Along with that, I always want kids to tell me not that we have sixteen pages to go, but that we have the *Aleynu,* the *Kaddish,* and the closing hymn. Knowing where you are is really important, so that when you get lost, you know how to get back.

JOEL LURIE GRISHAVER

The blessing formula of *baruch ata* appears throughout, both independently and as the *chatimah,* or seal, of many Rabbinic prayers. This seal is the thematic headline of the prayer. Knowing the end helps you understand the beginning and the middle.

Each prayer is a literary work that contains a narrative arc. In other words, each prayer is a story. Two stories, actually. If you look at each prayer as an independent unit, it has a beginning, a middle, and an end (more on this in practice 24). And if you look at the prayers as a whole, the movement from one prayer to another also tells a story. For instance, the two prayers following the *Barchu* and preceding the *Shema* tell of God's creative powers. The first recounts and praises God's role in the creation of the universe. The second rehearses God's gifts to the Jewish People. The movement from the universal to the particular is, of course, intentional. The prayer before the *Shema* ends with God's love for us. The first prayer after the *Shema* rehearses the commandment to love God. The placement of these prayers conveys a message: God's love for us should be reciprocated with our love for God. Like any literary work, each selection of a given word or a biblical quote could have been otherwise. It helps to follow the authors' intentions.

3. Learn the overall structure of the service.

There are just a few major liturgical units in the Siddur, and they repeat. All appear in the morning service, when we are presumed to have more time to pray, and the fewest appear in the afternoon service. In the middle of the work day, only the *Amidah* is said, bracketed by a psalm and the closing prayers. Here are the three most prominent units.

> *Pesukei d'Zimra* (morning), "Verses of Song," are prayers of praise and gratitude, mostly from the Psalms.
>
> The *Shema* and Her Blessings (morning, evening), "Listen!" include the two blessings before and the three blessings after the *Shema,* beginning immediately after the *Barchu.* These are declarations, aimed at the person praying, to rehearse the God/world/Jewish People/individual Jew relations that delineate our role and purpose in life.
>
> The *Amidah* (morning, afternoon, evening), "Standing," is a series of blessings said in a whisper while standing. It is also called the *Sh'moneh Esrai,* "Eighteen," the original number of blessings (today there are nineteen), or simply *ha-Tefillah,* "The Prayer." Never skipped, this is the central prayer unit of a Jewish service. In between opening and closing blessings, there are petitionary prayers directed to God (except on Shabbat and holidays). This is also the place in the service for personal prayer.

Other units include the closing blessings (*Aleynu* and *Kaddish*); *Birchot ha-Shachar,* "Morning Blessings," a section of prayers to greet the day; Torah reading, added on Mondays, Thursdays, holidays, and Shabbat; the group of prayers (featuring the *Mi Chamocha*) connecting the *Shema* and the *Amidah* sections; and *Tachanun* penitential prayers, also on Mondays and Thursdays. There are various additions on Shabbat and holidays.

Each service is part of a master narrative, and knowing it makes a difference. In *Pesukei d'Zimra,* the liturgy starts with thanks and praise, the kind of prayers that move us from small to expanded consciousness, that banish anger and take us out of the stress and busyness of our work lives. With the *Shema,* we are reminded of our place in the world, of God's loving gifts and our responsibilities, and then in the *Mi Chamocha,* the promise of redemption. Finally, in this centered and humble place, we speak our most intimate words before God during the *Amidah,* both communal requests and the personal words of the heart.

4. Know the narrative context of the traditional prayers.

Some would say that the key to understanding a given prayer is to understand its theology. When you say it, you are affirming belief in X. I happen to believe that prayer is about narrative theology. If you look into Rabbinic literature, also Hasidic and folk sources, when they explain a prayer, they do so by telling you the story of the first time the prayer was said. The most famous example, probably, is Jacob dying and fearing that his children, particularly Joseph, will abandon God. And they say to him, "*Shema Yisrael*, listen Israel,[1] the Lord is our God, the Lord is one." And he replies, "Blessed is the One, the glory whose kingdom is renowned forever," in his dying whisper. This explains the dynamic of how we say it in synagogue and where it comes from.

JOEL LURIE GRISHAVER

By providing a context, the Rabbis give us an example for the intention and sincerity of praying the *Shema.*

My favorite example involves the words we are asked to recite just before the *Amidah: "Adonai sefatai tiftach, ufee yageed tehillatecha"* (Please, God, open my lips that my mouth will tell your praise). These words from Psalm 51 were spoken by King David after he sent Uriah on a suicide mission so that he could marry Uriah's beautiful wife, Batsheva (2 Samuel 11–12). The prophet Nathan appears in the royal court and tells King David of a poor man with a single ewe lamb. The poor man's rich neighbor has stolen the lamb from him to entertain a guest rather than offer hospitality from his own flock. David is outraged. Who is this man? Let him be brought to justice! And in one of the great moments of prophetic literature, Nathan replies, "You are the man!" David does not respond like a typical king. Instead of sending assassins to kill Nathan, he admits his guilt and begs for forgiveness from God. According to the Midrash, it is here that David says, "Please, God, open my lips.… " This is the model for how are we are to come before God during the *Amidah*—with urgency, trembling with awe, contrite for our failings, sincerely wanting to be better, recognizing the need for God's grace.

> So when I come to a piece of liturgy, it has a narrative context. This moment is supposed to be like that. This is supposed to remind me of my life's overlap with the story of X. The best way I can put it is, it's a lot like being inside the Actor's Studio and using the Method. The prayer represents the script, the Rabbinic tradition the backstory, and the search for *kavvanah* is looking for my sense memory that matches up with that moment.
> JOEL LURIE GRISHAVER

5. Delve into the arts.

It's hard to be an artist of prayer if there is no art in the rest of your life. Praying the liturgy is a rehearsal of spiritual themes such as gratitude, liberation, redemption, and revelation. Prayer cannot connect them to your life if you are not aware of how they operate outside of the synagogue.

> So if you don't work on creation in your life, if you don't see sunrises or try to paint or write about them or struggle with the fusion of internalizing external images, without artistic/ thematic practice in the arts, it's hard to get to the themes the Siddur revolves around. So I think you need practice in the arts, practice in expression of the places the liturgy goes to, which is different than praying it or studying it in a linear kind of way.
> JOEL LURIE GRISHAVER

Some final words from Gris:

> At the *Mi Chamocha* prayer [celebrating the Exodus from Egypt], I might ask, "What moments of servitude represent my

slavery in Egypt?" and then you add what comes up that day. It's not like you lock on to an archetypal moment, and that's the last time you work through the question. It's not the moment my fourth-grade teacher locked me in a closet and that's it. Rather, it's ongoing, struggles against addictions, say. Not Twelve-step grade addictions, but addictions nonetheless—decisions I regularly make wrong, things I'm in servitude to. One day it's about losing my temper, another it's about eating too much, or being confronted with a political situation [where] I feel I didn't do enough. So the *Mi Chamocha* becomes my time to think about slavery and redemption every week. Knowing the master narrative opens it all up. The liturgy is trying to be a theology of moments, of encounters, of particular kinds of experiences with God, which are also particular kinds of experiences with the self.

Some places are your places. When you go to Joshua Tree [National Park], you have your places there, or you go to the ocean. You know that when you go to that place, you're going to feel approximately X because that place has a history of feeling approximately X for you. But each time you get there, it's going to be X-plus, or X-minus. It's going to be that general vector, but it's going to be of the moment. So it's not like I sit there in services and say, "Now I'm approaching the *Mi Chamocha;* what's my meaning of it today?" I don't do any of that intellectualization. I say the words. And I prefer to sing the words. It takes me where it takes me. And sometimes I get lost in it and wake up when I'm told to stand up for the *Amidah,* and sometimes I just do a very surface gloss. I can't tell you when the individual gates will open. But I can tell you that the journey, repeatedly, leads to a pattern of opening gates.

There is the Jewish tradition and everything it represents writ large, literature and imagery and wordage and everything else, and there is personal experience, and the purpose of prayer is to overlap the two.

There is much to gain, then, from studying the Siddur. But this requires an investment of time before services.

> Studying prayer can and will deepen your prayer life. It is nothing less than enlightening to understand the flow of the service, the thematic connections among the prayers, the biblical quotations and allusions, a prayer's history and context, and the meaning of key root words. But I highly recommend learning about prayers *apart* and *away from* the minyan. You want to experience ritual and prayer as living practices. That means being led and moved and inspired. To be dissected, a prayer, like a frog, must be killed first.
>
> Rabbi Debra Orenstein

Above, Joel Lurie Grishaver offers suggestions for approaching the Siddur, some of which are demonstrated by our teachers in the Best Practices section and in the next chapter. For learning the narrative context of many traditional prayers, see his forthcoming *Stories We Pray* (Los Angeles: Torah Aura Productions). See the annotated Resources section for numerous books and websites on learning the Siddur.

Practices 21–24 help to uncover the spiritual dynamics of the Siddur. Various study aids are available to you at www.MakingPrayerReal.com.

Finding a local class is always a good idea. You'll likely find one at a local synagogue, Jewish Community Center, or college of Jewish studies.

Above, I presented a basic understanding of the flow of the Jewish prayer service from prayer to prayer. Here is an alternative narrative that is popular among those who come to the liturgy from a mystical perspective, written by the cofounder of Elat Chayyim: The Jewish Spiritual Retreat Center and founding director of the Awakened Heart Project for Contemplative Judaism, Rabbi Jeff Roth.

The Prayer Experience as a Pathway to Awareness of the Divine Presence

RABBI JEFF ROTH

I approach prayer as a vehicle for increasing awareness of the Divine Presence as it manifests within me and in the world. The traditional prayer service can support this inner work of attunement to the Presence. When we bring our full selves to the words, the prayers become indicators of what we might cultivate in our hearts and minds. For me, the most helpful template for eliciting the meaning of the service is the mystical model, based on "the four worlds."

The Jewish mystical tradition takes the name of God very seriously, seeing within it the secrets of the divine nature. In the Jewish tradition, the most holy name for God is the Tetragrammaton, the four-letter name *Yud, Hay, Vav, Hay*. The three-letter Hebrew root is *Hay, Vav, Hay,* the verb "to be." Our name for God is "Being." And since this name has four letters, the Jewish mystics understand that Divine Being has a basic fourfold nature, four "worlds" that together comprise reality. Viewed from a mystical perspective, the deep structure of the morning prayer service is a reflection of this understanding. The prayers can take us on a journey through the four worlds. Beginning with a sense of ourselves as individual "Beings," we move through stages to the oneness of "Being."

What we experience as physicality is the first world; it is the "embodied" aspect of Being. This world is characterized by the greatest sense of separateness, or as Martin Buber might say, this is the world of alienation and isolation. We experience reality as a subjective self, existing in apparent separation from all other objects in the universe. In the first section of the service, *Birchot ha-Shachar* (Morning Blessings), we acknowledge the fact that we wake up each morning in our own bodies, and this very body is a manifestation of the Divine Presence. The beginning prayers express appreciation for being physically alive. And the language of those prayers reflects this sense of a separate "I" having the experience. *"Modeh ani"* (I am thankful) are the opening words. *"Elohai neshama she-natatah be tehora he,"* means, "My God, the soul that you have given to me is pure." It is not till much later, in the third world of the prayers, that the language shifts to *Eloheinu,* "Our God."

Yet even this world of relative loneliness can be seen as part of the divine process unfolding in our lives. When we pray, "How good are your tents, O Jacob, your *mishkan* [the sacred traveling tent that accompanied the Jews in the wilderness], O Israel?" we are called to recognize that this tent, the body we inhabit, is a good place to reside. If we wrestle with what it means to be human, as Jacob did at the river Jabbok (Genesis 32:23), we, too, will receive our own divine name, just as Jacob became Yisrael (the God wrestler). We see our own body as a *mishkan* for the Divine Presence. In fact, because of the perceived separateness inherent in "embodying," the yearning for union with the Divine arises, propelling us forward on the spiritual journey.

In the second world, the world of "connecting/forming/feeling," we are called to recognize and make connections between the apparently separate objects of physicality. This world of prayer is defined by the letter Vav in the divine name. *Vav* in Hebrew is also a word, meaning "and," as well as "hook." A hook takes two disparate objects and links them together. They are no longer completely separate entities, but neither are they (yet) merged into one identity. In this part of the prayers, we pay attention to the world beyond "me" and look for the feelings of connection. The word *halleluyah* (praise God) symbolizes what it feels like to move out of alienation and into connection with other "beings." Thank God I don't feel so alone. The psalms in this section of the service record the moments when our ancestors felt connected to God. I am called to recognize the many paths of Divine-human relationship. I like to add my own verses of praise for the ways I feel connected in the present moment. "Connecting" takes me out of loneliness; it is an experience of the Divine.

The third section of the prayers begins with the call to public worship. The leader calls out the *Barchu,* "Let us bless Being, which is to be blessed." And all present respond, "Bless Being, which is blessed at all times." These words are only used in prayer when a community, a minyan of ten or more, has gathered for the service. Praying them indicates to my mind that I am now part of a bigger whole, and ultimately part of a bigger oneness, the "Oneness of Being." This is the world of "conceiving," which has the dual meaning of birthing and receiving mental concepts. In the prayers of this section, I attune myself to concepts that see the universe as a singularity. The separate objects of the first world, through the process of connecting one by one in the second world, are now linked together in a single interactive way. God is the cohesive patterning of all that is. From this place, I recite the words of the *Shema.*

> **Shema**—pay attention
>
> **Yisrael**—the community of all those engaged in the struggle to know God
>
> **YHVH**—"The Oneness of Being"
>
> **Eloheinu**—is our God
>
> **YHVH**—"The Oneness of Being"
>
> **Echad**—is the Only Thing that Is

This is the peak experience of nonseparateness that is available to our rational minds. In this picture of reality, there are still myriad apparently distinct objects, but they are all interactively linked in oneness.

Finally, the last section of the morning service is the silent standing prayer, the *Amidah.* While it contains traditional language, that it is a silent prayer hints to me that there is a fourth world beyond words. It is difficult to imagine a world outside of conceptual thinking, because the imagination itself uses conceptual thinking. Nevertheless, there is ultimately only one "I" having the experience of "Being" itself without any separateness whatsoever.

While this is a mystical experience, not available to the rational mind, it is available to all human "Beings." In my experience, meditation is a more likely vehicle for approaching this world. But I believe it is the essence of what I am called to in this section of the prayers.

Taken in this way, the morning prayers as a whole help me reclaim my life, moment by moment, as a manifestation of the Divine.

17

Overcoming the Hebrew Barrier

I have become passionate about the Hebrew words. Beyond the meaning, I'm shaping my body differently to form the different sounds. "Aah" or "Eee" or "Ooh" have a very different vibratory sense. The pure emotion comes through the vowels. The meaning is created by the consonants, which are stops. The stops come from different parts of the mouth and also feel different from one another. So just doing Hebrew sounds shapes my body differently. That's why different languages are almost like a different dance, and people change personalities when they go from one language to another.

RABBI DIANE ELLIOT

Frequently, I find myself running into people who claim to be in recovery from Hebrew school, sometimes after forty years! But even if a person overcomes his or her childhood trauma, is it realistic to expect a busy adult to learn Hebrew? Rabbi, scribe, and author of several adult Hebrew textbooks, Linda Motzkin reflects on our question.

Is Learning Hebrew Really Possible?

RABBI LINDA MOTZKIN

Yes, it's true. You are too old and you don't have enough time to become fluent in Hebrew. If you are beyond your teens, you have already missed your prime years for learning a foreign language, and it will only become more difficult to memorize and retain information with each passing year. And if you are a typical adult living in today's world, you are already juggling multiple personal and professional commitments, leaving little time for language study. The good news, however, is that you don't need to become fluent in Hebrew in order to get a lot more out of your prayer experience. A little Hebrew knowledge can go a long way.

It's important to be clear about your goals. Prayer book Hebrew is not modern conversational Hebrew. If you are planning on spending time in Israel and want to be able to carry on a conversation and interact in a Hebrew-speaking environment, then you want to learn modern Hebrew and you do want to achieve a degree of fluency. The best way to do this is to enroll in an ulpan—a Hebrew language immersion program—in Israel; second best is to take a modern Hebrew course at a college or university. Both require the dedication of significant time and effort.

But if you live outside the Land of Israel and your primary interest in learning Hebrew is to access the language of Jewish spiritual life, the language of the Torah, sacred texts, and the prayer book, then you want to study classical Hebrew. And you do not need to attain the same degree of fluency, because you will not be *producing* Hebrew. You will not be writing the Bible or prayer book but seeking to understand what is already written. Your goal is a more passive knowledge of the language—the ability to recognize in context words and grammatical structures that you might never be able to generate on your own.

This goal can be achieved through a series of modest steps, each of which can open up a little bit more of the Hebrew prayer experience for you. The first step is to learn the letters and vowels of the Hebrew alphabet so that you can sound out Hebrew words. Unlike English, which has bizarre spellings such as *cough* to represent the pronunciation "kof," Hebrew is written phonetically. In order to be able to sound out Hebrew words, you need to learn twenty-two letters, seven of which have a second variant shape and/or pronunciation, and another dozen or so vowel markings. Learning just these phonetic symbols, even without knowing what any of the words mean, can enable you to participate a bit more fully in communal prayer settings, simply by being able to follow along in the Hebrew as prayers are said aloud.

Once you have the ability to sound out Hebrew words, you can then work on understanding the language. By learning some key vocabulary and grammatical structures, you can appreciate a lot of Hebrew elements that are lost in translation, and deepen and enrich your understanding of prayer book and Torah passages.

For example, most Hebrew words are built around a three-letter root to which vowels, prefixes, and suffixes are added. The words *va-yi-na-fash* and *naf-she-cha* don't appear to have any connection when spelled in English letters. But written in Hebrew, נַפְשֶׁךָ and וַיִּנָּפַשׁ it is easy to see that both contain the root letters n-f-sh, נ־פ־שׁ. *Va-yi-na-fash*—the word that describes God's sole action on Shabbat (aside from ceasing work), is derived from the same root as *naf-she-cha*—the word meaning "your soul." What English translation can adequately convey the idea that Shabbat rest is a soul action? Learning a few key roots can enable you to make connections between Hebrew words and concepts that aren't readily apparent in the English translation or transliteration.

Classical Hebrew also has a much more limited vocabulary than English. This means that learning a few dozen words can open up many prayer book passages, as the same words tend to reappear in the liturgy. It also means that a single word in Hebrew can have multiple English meanings. To return to the word *naf-she-cha,* translated above as "your soul," it also could legitimately be translated as "your being," "your living essence," "your life-force," and "your breath." Every translation is an act of interpretation; the

translator picks the single English word that he or she thinks best
fits the context, and in the process limits the possibility of reading
any other meaning into the Hebrew. In the passage exhorting you
to "love God with all your heart and all *naf-she-cha*," is this your
soul? your life-force? your breath? all possibilities combined? You
can understand why there is such a rich Jewish tradition of textual
commentary, with layer upon layer of probing and analyzing the
meaning of our sacred scriptures, because the very nature of the
Hebrew language legitimately allows for multiple understandings
of a text.

A third feature of classical Hebrew, mentioned above, is that
prefixes and suffixes are attached to words. While many Hebrew
textbooks teach full paradigms of conjugations, it is possible to
learn just the few most commonly recurring prefix and suffix letters. To return again to the example of *naf-she-cha:* the suffix *cha*
ךָ means "you" or "your," hence the translation "*your* soul." But it
also indicates something that cannot be conveyed in the English
translation—that "you" are a single, discrete individual, not part of
a collective or group. (Hebrew has a different way of expressing
"you" or "your" when signifying a group.) The passage exhorting
you to love God with all *naf-she-cha* נַפְשֶׁךָ takes on an extra
dimension when you notice that it is addressed to you individually,
as your personal endeavor, in contrast with following passages that
are addressed to the community as a whole.

So how do you begin learning such tidbits of classical
Hebrew? The materials for learning exist; some good resources are
listed in the Resources section at the end of this book. More important, however, is how to use those resources. Some find it easier
than others to learn alone; for many, it is difficult to study Hebrew
without a class or a partner. The traditional Jewish model for learning is in *chevruta,* with a companion, not in isolation. If you have
access to a synagogue, Jewish community center or *havurah,*
inquire whether they offer any adult *classical* Hebrew classes. If
not, suggest that they consider offering one. Or find a study partner. Ask a synagogue to include in their e-mail announcements that

someone is looking for a partner to learn Hebrew. Your study partner does not need to live nearby; you can have a weekly phone session with someone from across the country.

The greatest barrier is the assumption that it's too hard, you're too old, and you don't have the time. It's not and you're not and you do, if you decide to make a bit of time. The important thing is to begin.

Got Motivation?

When I interviewed best-selling author Rabbi Lawrence Kushner, famous for his contemporary take on Jewish mystical thought, I didn't expect that much of our discussion would focus on his passion for Hebrew.

> I hear people say Hebrew is a barrier, or it's not welcoming, and I say phooey! A book isn't welcoming or not welcoming; a group of people are welcoming or not welcoming.
>
> In my former congregation in suburban Boston, we prayed the same service every week at the same time for thirty years and people came to know the whole service by heart. We have a lot of data from over fifteen hundred years that's incontrovertible: the more you pray, the more likely you are to pray in Hebrew.
>
> On the scale of linguistic difficulty from one to ten, of which Finnish or Turkish is a ten, and pig latin is a one, English is a seven and Hebrew is a three. There are five times more words in the English dictionary than the Hebrew dictionary. Once you get over the hump of the funny letters going in the other direction, you've got an easy language on your hands. And I think what rabbis ought to say is, "Cut the complaining and learn the fricking language already."
>
> If you found out that you were going to Portugal in six months for half a year, the first thing you'd do is buy the

Rosetta Stone software. At the end of six months, would you be able to give a lecture to the Portuguese Academy for Arts and Sciences? No. But would you be able to get around on the street? Yes. So I want to say to Jews, come on! You could memorize the Greek alphabet and swallow a goldfish to pledge a sorority; what's so hard about doing it with Hebrew?

We announced here at Congregation Emanu-El in San Francisco that we're going to do a class in how to read the Hebrew Bible in Hebrew. We're going to go word by word with verses from the weekly portion and analyze them from the viewpoint of syntax and grammar with a little theology. Thirty sessions; the whole year. Students would have to buy an Alcalay dictionary for 120 dollars, a Hebrew Bible without English, a grammar book—200 dollars, all told. We figured we'd get maybe a dozen people. One hundred fifteen people signed up. I think that if we tell Jews, "We're going to cut the Mickey Mouse and just do it. We're going to stop treating you like dummies," they'll respond. Reform Judaism, alas, is close to going down in history as the preschool of Judaism. It's one thing to have a low entry threshold; it's another to dumb it so down there's nothing left.

RABBI LAWRENCE KUSHNER

18

Best Practices

Here is one of my favorite teachings from Rabbi Zalman Schachter-Shalomi. The Siddur is like freeze-dried coffee. If you try to eat it straight, it's a very unpleasant experience. If you pour some hot water on, it can taste pretty good. We turn, now, to the specific techniques that our teachers employ for davenning from the Siddur. This is the hot water.

Mantra and Memorization

Our teachers agree that praying the Siddur is not, primarily, an intellectual experience. One powerful (and classical) way to pray is to use the Hebrew as a mantra. For Rabbi Lawrence Kushner, this is the preferred approach to davenning.

> It doesn't matter so much what you know; it matters that you got something memorized. And that enables you to do your prayer work. We are mistaken by reading and trying to understand the literal content of the words on the prayer book page. I don't think they were ever meant to be read literally. I think they were meant to create an effect. My favorite example is the long stream of "yits" in the *Kaddish: v'yitpa'ar v'yitromam v'yitnaseh v'yithadar.* They all mean the same

thing. They couldn't be language that's meant to communicate anything other than, "Put your brain in another mode." I
believe that's true about the whole Siddur.

RABBI LAWRENCE KUSHNER

This is particularly important for traditionally observant Jews, as it
is one of the few ways to redeem speed-davenning. But most don't
take advantage of the opportunity. The mind wanders endlessly if
we don't employ one meditative technique or another to maintain
focus. I prefer keeping part of my awareness on the body (see
practices 5 and 6). Some davenners actively direct their thoughts to
holy subjects while praying, particularly through visualization (see
below). Kabbalistic prayer books provide formulas, usually involv-
ing the names of God, to "speak" in thought while the mouth prays
the traditional liturgy.

My theory of prayer is that you use the mind to trigger the heart,
which opens up the soul. We're not using the words only for
their meaning. We're using the words, the Hebrew, for their
affective purpose, to change the state of mind for the purpose.

RABBI ETHAN FRANZEL

But even for "mantra davenners," the choice of words matters. It is
hard to pray regularly, in Hebrew or any language, from a phone
book. Even if they are largely ignored, the meanings of the words
are important for everyone at one point or another.

To have an in-depth relationship with a prayer, you need to
understand it. If you say "Modeh ani," and you don't know it
means, "I am thankful," it may take you somewhere, but not
necessarily to thankfulness.

RABBI JEFF ROTH

Once again, we return to a pivotal problem in the life of a prayer-
person—connecting heart to words.

Putting Heart into the Words of the Siddur

In chapter 5, we considered the problem of how to put heart into our own words. Here we consider the difficult question of how to put heart into someone else's words, the words of the Jewish liturgical tradition.

Reading words on a page in order to pray is different from ordinary reading.

> If I tell you to read the *Amidah* silently, you'll read it like Evelyn Wood speed-reading dynamics at two thousand words a minute with 90 percent comprehension. What you will discover after a page or two is that you're reading to get information and there's no new information in the Siddur. So the first thing you have to say to people is that reading prayers is not reading to get information.
>
> RABBI LAWRENCE KUSHNER

Rather, an entirely different kind of reading is required. The movement from outside in, the transfer of cognitive meanings from the page to our minds, is important. Prayers for peace or redemption or gratitude must be understood as such if they are going to move us toward their intended targets. But this is just the beginning of the story. (Too often, prayer is unsatisfying because it is the end.)

The printed words succeed as prayer when they evoke our inner desires and then move those yearnings outward—to other beings, to the world, to God. Liturgical prayer, then, is meant to be a dialogue. The reading needs to be reflexive; the meanings of the words run simultaneously in different directions. When I pray "Grant us peace ... " the same words that are meant to arouse the desire for peace in my heart also carry my prayer for peace out into the world.

While this sounds more complicated than it really is, it is critical to acknowledge that the dialogical nature of traditional prayer makes demands on us. We must bring effort, intention, and a set of attitudes to the task. If we are disinterested rather than curious, if we are distracted rather than attentive, if we read with our minds to the exclusion of our hearts, the Siddur cannot do its job and work its magic. Reading a prayer requires deep listening—to the words and to our hearts. This, too, is a skill we learn over time as part of a prayer practice.

Earlier we discussed chant and other meditative techniques for working with Hebrew phrases. We also learned in chapter 13 that sometimes there is no difference between our words and the tradition's words. Here are more techniques for making the tradition's words our own.

Read It as Poetry

People don't know how to use poetry, so they approach the Siddur as though it's a shopping list. So either you bought the tomatoes or you didn't. Either you like red peppers or you don't. If you read the prayer book as if it's a list of facts, then it's really, really, really problematic. But if you read it as poetry, I think it's provocative and profound and connecting.

RABBI BRADLEY SHAVIT ARTSON

Linger with a Phrase That Touches You

Over and over again, our teachers repeated a simple, basic technique. Don't rush, and when a word or phrase grabs your attention, stay with it.

Find a prayer that really opens your heart. It may be just one line from a prayer. And give yourself permission to dwell on that prayer. Don't feel like volume is so important; feel like depth is important. It's not getting through the prayer book. It's not even getting through the prayer. You're looking for the words that are going to spring the hatch on your heart.

RABBI TIRZAH FIRESTONE

I move through the prayers like mantras until one of them hooks me, and when it does, I linger there. I remember what Simon Greenberg used to say, that he would allow himself to find, each day, something in the prayers that meant something to him, and he didn't care if he didn't get to the end. Like the old story of the man who says to the rabbi, "I've been through the Talmud three times," and the rabbi says, "How much of the Talmud has been through you?" The same thing with prayers.
RABBI DAVID J. WOLPE

So I have this map, the prayer book, and I might choose one day to just go to one little spot on the map and hang out there, and other days, I want to go through the whole trajectory, usually depending on how much time I have.
RABBI DIANE ELLIOT

I learned an important practice from Rabbi Karen Fox. The prelude to the *Amidah,* as we learned in the previous chapter, is a line from Psalms, *Adonai sefatai tiftach,* "Please God, open my lips...." I repeat it, one time or ten, until I am focused and ready to continue. Only then do I start the *Amidah.* Here is another practice from Rabbi Fox.

Sometimes during the *Amidah,* I'll just take *shema koleinu,* [hear our voice], and repeat it over and over, until my prayer is done. What made me angry was that I couldn't find enough time in the service. Now I take the time.
RABBI KAREN FOX, DD

For most people, it helps to *do* less and *be* more. The very experience of staying present, open, and attentive is a kind of prayer. Sit quietly and enjoy God's presence. Connect with a single word. *Shema* (listen) from the *Shema Yisrael* declaration, *Modeh* (I am grateful) from the *Modeh Ani* prayer, or *Nishmat* from *Nishmat Kol Chai* (soul/breath of all life) are all good starting points. The essential prayer of those wishing to pray is: "May my prayer be enough." The unspoken prayer behind it is: "May my *being* be enough." By God's grace, it is.

RABBI DEBRA ORENSTEIN

Focus on the Words

Ultimately, however, there is no avoiding the simplest method of all, bringing our hearts to bear on the words in the Siddur by taking them seriously.

> Praying goes particularly well for me when I am not just trying to rush and keep up with the pace of the people praying around me. Rather, when I slow down and look at the Siddur before me almost the same way you look at an optical chart at the optometrist, when you relax your eyes and try to see which word or symbol hovers just over the page. Often a word seems to hover based on whatever I am experiencing in my life at the time. The Hebrew word for "purity" might stand out, or the word for "peace." I then concentrate on this word, on this concept that is reaching out to me. Even as my lips are singing prayers, my heart and mind are savoring this word until it adheres itself to me, weaves its way into me and becomes a part of me.
>
> RABBI ZOË KLEIN

> When I say *modah* (thankful), I connect with my sense of gratitude, then *ani* (I), my sense of selfhood, *I'm* the one that's saying this prayer. Then *lefanecha* (before You), and suddenly, it's not about me, it's about You, God, the One in whose Presence I am. And so on. I'll go through each prayer like that and that's how my heart is able to connect. It's coming from inside me. It's not intellectual. I embody the prayer. I allow myself to say, then really experience, gratitude.
>
> RABBI ZARI M. WEISS

Interpret the Prayers

Another simple but effective form of hot water is to bring your curiosity to the words. What do they mean *for me, here* and *now?*

> On the Shabbat after [Hurricane] Katrina, as we began the service as usual with *mah tovu* [How goodly are you tents, O Jacob; Numbers 24:5]. I pointed out the imagery of the tents of Israel and our dwelling places and the pictures we had all seen of those with no homes. The language of home, of caring, of embarrassment strewn throughout the liturgy had a new context and gave those assembled a liturgical framework to acknowledge their feelings from watching the pictures from New Orleans all week.[1]
> RABBI MICHAEL STRASSFELD

> I pause at the places that are fruitful. One place I usually stop is *yotzer or u'vorei choshech oseh shalom uvorei et hakol* [who fashions light and creates darkness, who makes peace and creates all]. For me, that prayer is a meditation on the cycles of the seasons, which are an important spiritual practice for me. The prayer is also a meditation about the things I understand and the things I don't understand, about life as wonder and life as painful. I'm also aware that that's a prayer that the rabbis changed to fit their own ideas. [The original verse from Isaiah 45:7 reads, "who fashions light and creates darkness, who makes peace and creates *evil*."] So for me, the prayer also becomes a meditation on the changing ways we look at God.
> RABBI JILL HAMMER, PhD

> *Aleynu leshabeach* [it is upon us to praise], I love those two words. I have an obligation to praise. If I don't, if I'm not grateful, I'm being small minded.
> CANTOR ELLEN DRESKIN

My favorite line of prayer in the Siddur is from *lecha dodi* [from the Friday night liturgy welcoming the Sabbath bride], where it reads, *Hitor'ri, hitor'ri, ki va oreich, kumi ori, uri uri shir dabeiri*.... [Awake, awake, your light has come! Arise, shine, awake and sing....] At night, with darkness descending, it is often hard to muster the energy it takes to hope, and yet it is precisely at this time when we sing out, "Arise and shine, your light has come!" To me, this is the light of hope and of God's love. When I sing this line of *lecha dodi*, I feel embraced and loved, even as the hour grows darker and darker.

RABBI ZOË KLEIN

A favorite prayer is from the weekday *Amidah*, may God "give us good counsel." Everything in life requires that, so I like to open myself up to the blessings of wisdom and ask assistance in making the right moves. It's not about bliss. To invite the *shefa* [divine flow] into those decisions is very beautiful.

RABBI NEHEMIA POLEN, PhD

Sometimes the best interpretation is no interpretation.

I don't think the tradition sees the words of the Siddur as metaphors. We say "metaphor" because that's a phrase that lets us feel more comfortable with language like this. How do we know that God doesn't somehow shape light as though it were clay? How is it to shape light? Well, this is a way of explaining to a limited human being that shaping light is like a potter shaping wet, fragrant clay that's black and that gets in your ears and coats your face! God did that with light. I don't know that God didn't. God has the power to do so. I think it's chutzpadic to say that these ideas are all metaphors and that the tactile world we know is foreign to God. I don't believe that.

RABBI RICHARD N. LEVY, DD

Skip the Offensive

These prayers weren't handed to us from God. It's one person's, or on occasion a small group of people's, experience of God. So if there's something that doesn't sit well, we can accept that this prayer is one person's take on it and we can appreciate it as that. And then we can interpret, but we don't have to accept it as fact. Let's say you're in a play and you're handed a script; that's what prayer is. We're supposed to play the role of "Jew praying." But in prayer we're not supposed to be playing a role; we're supposed to be experiencing the experience of Jew praying and have a real Method acting moment where we lose ourselves in it. I'm saying these words as if they're my words. But you have those moments where you say, "No, it's not my story, not my words." Some prayers work for me and not for you. And some work for you and not for me. It's an imperfect human endeavor. And it's a literature. You read a book and chapter 12 didn't work for you. The rest of the book was good, but not chapter 12. We can accept that much easier if we don't assign ourselves the role of believing every word as some kind of ultimate truth.

RABBI NAOMI LEVY

One of the great debates among contemporary liberal liturgists is the treatment of Jewish "chosenness." The founder of Reconstructionist Judaism, Mordecai Kaplan, famously banished all passages from the liturgy that portrayed the Jews as God's exclusive favorites. He sought full integration into modern, democratic society. Though quite close in worldview, many other liberal Siddurs kept the original Hebrew but softened the sting by playing loose with the English translation.

Liberal Jews in Israel do not have that choice, as Hebrew is the vernacular. So the authors of the Reform Movement's Siddur, *ha-Avodah she-be-Lev*, made a substitution. Instead of the traditional, "Who did not make us like other nations ... nor give us a portion like theirs," it reads, "Who separated us from those who go astray and gave us the Torah of truth … 'though all the peoples walk each in the names of its gods' (Micah 4:5)."[2] I like it because the uniqueness of Israel and the moral imperative for tolerance are both affirmed.

But leading services back in America, where liberal Jews struggle to learn the traditional prayers, I did not want to break the communal norm. And I often daven in more traditional settings. My solution: While the rest of the congregation is (presumably) praying the original, I am davenning, quietly and unobtrusively, the Israeli Reform alternative.

My former congregants in Wyoming are likely surprised to read these words, and traditionalists are no doubt cringing. There is much to be said for grappling and struggling with the traditional liturgy rather than giving up on it. That is what I usually do. Many people I respect disagree with my position, and I advise you to listen to their arguments. But after years of living in Israel, where messianic fundamentalists take such passages to justify antidemocratic politics, I simply cannot say them. In this case, other traditional Jewish teachings about justice and tolerance trump my love of, and responsibility for, the traditional liturgy. As long as it is out of conviction rather than convenience, I believe it is better to make (minor) changes in the liturgy rather than to stop praying.

Involve Your Body and Mind

Body Awareness

When I come to the Standing Prayer, the *Amidah,* I am quite conscious that my stance, my posture, is very intimately a part of the prayer I offer to God, and of the prayerful state that I seek to dwell in for a time. I take care to bring my feet together with great intention as I softly chant *Adonai sefatai tiftach* [O God, open my lips]. This gesture of opening my mind, my lips, and my heart to stand in the presence of God is completed when I bring my feet to a conscious stance, grounding my sometimes fidgety body. I stand with my two legs as one. From this silent and still place, the words of the *Amidah* arise from somewhere very deep inside of me. Many times, at some point during this prayer, I stop. The words drop away, and I am still, breathing, being with my God. Anchored in a body that is "gaiting" my awareness, I truly do find greater intimacy with my soul, with God.

RABBI MYRIAM KLOTZ

As described in the Preface and chapter 6, body awareness is an excellent way of bringing depth to prayer. See practices 4–6 and 20.

Visualization

Bowing all the way to the ground on Rosh HaShanah, I imagine myself in various places, in the First and Second Temples, in shul with Maimonides, in Brooklyn with my grandparents, in a shul in 2050, in front of God's throne of glory. These kinds of mental flights, I love; some of my favorite travel. You can't pray without imagination.

RABBI BRADLEY SHAVIT ARTSON

Adding visualization to your praying is like switching to high-definition TV. It requires more electricity (more effort up front), but the picture is brighter and clearer than you imagined possible. Everything is more alive, and there's no going back.

Giving the mind a second focus of attention on the prayer prevents distraction and keeps you connected to the liturgy. In other words, visualization yields instant *kavvanah*. It helps you put your intentions out into the world in a direct and effective way. And it's a lot of fun. There are no limits to where the imagination can take you.

One of my favorite times to employ this method is while praying the *Shema*. To embody the idea of unity, I close my eyes and call to consciousness the famous picture of the earth as seen from the moon, or imagine myself in the center of the Milky Way, looking out into the stars. Praying for peace, I visualize white light filling the hearts of everyone in the Middle East with love and respect for each other.

The most powerful visualization I know, however, accompanies the prayer for healing. I visualize the ill person for whom I am praying. I put awareness on my heart and then send *chiut,* divine energy, their way. As I pray, I imagine (that is, I image) a stream of light traveling from our minyan to the person in need of healing. This is a variation of practice 8, Jewish Blessings.

If you are inclined to dismiss this as nonsense, as I once did, may I respectively suggest that you suspend judgment and give it a try before coming to a final conclusion.

Here is another example of how visualization complements prayer.

> Before saying the *Shema,* I pause and hold the parts of me that are broken close to my heart. In order to be able to connect to *Hashem Echad* [the Name is One], I need to be able to feel a place of *echad* (oneness) within myself. I close my eyes and see two of the darkest moments in my life. I embrace myself as I was in those stages. I see myself holding them, kissing them, hugging them. Then I see my father, who left the world over twenty years ago, embracing all three faces of myself. The last stage of this image is feeling God hold all four of us—my two dark moments, myself as I am today, and my father. It is in this experience of the totality of who I am being embraced in God's face that I can then turn to say, *"Shema Yisrael Hashem Elokeinu, Hashem Echad."*
>
> REB MIMI FEIGELSON

Concentration

Do *everything* in the synagogue service without exception; and do everything with *kavvanah.* To keep the continuity, fill in any "gaps" in the service, when nothing is happening, with some kind of meditation: repeat a mantra of God's name or a use a verse from the Torah or Siddur, look around at people with love, study the Siddur or Torah portion; always do something to make the davenning continuous. The image I use is filling a jar with water. If you interrupt, it's like punching holes in the bottom. You're trying to accumulate spiritual power.

As you keep a continual focus, your mood deepens. That's a spiritual law, the spiritual principle behind any meditation, Jewish, Buddhist, Hindu; it's all the same. *Continuity produces depth.* As you maintain continuity, your focus increases and your mood deepens, until *you have an experience.* People go to synagogue and say it's boring. It's boring because they're not doing it! If you *meditate* by praying, which is the way the rabbis and rebbes say it's to be done, *something happens.* I guarantee it!

MAGGID YITZHAK BUXBAUM

19

Between Traditional and Personal Prayer

Traditional communal prayer is the structure. It's the house, with a foundation and a roof and walls. That's what keeps you safe. That's what keeps you solid. And God willing, it will be there a long time, long after we're gone. But if you never paint it, never hang a picture, or you never put in furniture and a rug, it's not a home. It's a house; it's not a home. Personal prayer makes it a home.

RABBI NAOMI LEVY

We have sung the praises of both personal and communal prayer. With Judaism's strong emphasis on communal prayer, how spontaneous prayer relates to Jewish services is not a small question.

To begin, we turn to scholar of Jewish liturgy Rabbi Lawrence Hoffman for some much-needed perspective.

We make the mistake of thinking the world always was the way it is today. We live in a heightened period of personalism, of individualism, to such an extent that people from one hundred years ago, even fifty years ago, would be shocked to see where we are today. Throughout the Middle Ages, the communal aspect was so paramount that individualism was hardly recognized. So the traditional Siddur as we have inherited it has little room for personal prayer. That wasn't always the case. The Bible is all personal prayer; no one repeats someone else's prayer. Hannah prays. David prays. Moses prays. Solomon prays for wisdom. Other kings don't say, let's pray Solomon's prayer, let's say a communal prayer for wisdom. That never happens. You have personal prayer for the individual and communal sacrifice for the group. The Siddur emerged in the Middle Ages, by which time sacrifice had long disappeared and the individual voice was lost. So coming into the modern period we didn't have much private prayer left in the service. Liberals in the nineteenth century did their best to restore private prayer into synagogues, and we have that now, but it's still not enough for our period, when we are so anxious to express our individuality. So, indeed, there is a great sense of needing to accent the individual. There are lots of places for it in the liturgy if you know it.

RABBI LAWRENCE A. HOFFMAN, PHD

Between biblical times, when prayers were not fixed at all, and the late Middle Ages, when so much of our liturgy was canonized as a result of general cultural conservatism and the invention of the printing press, we see that both personal and liturgical prayer have deep Jewish roots. The question is, how do the two interrelate?

We get tripped up when we expect communal prayer with the liturgy and individual, private prayer outside of synagogue to be the same. We suffer, then, from inappropriate expectations. The liturgy is meant to remind us of our history, our language, our sacred narrative, our Peoplehood and God's relationship to Israel. There are surely prayers said in the singular, but even then we pray primarily as individuals within the People Israel and in the context of a communal gathering. When we are alone we are free to follow the promptings of our own hearts. We can pray in any modality that suits us. Praying in community can save us from egotism, narcissism, and solipsism, but it can also be an obstacle to the very prayer we most need as individuals. We must remember when we join the community in prayer that *we are joining the community,* which doesn't exist to satisfy our individual sense of self. If we rely solely on our communal experience of prayer to satisfy our prayer needs, we will most likely be disappointed. To allow communal prayer to take its own authentic shape and nourish and surprise us with its particular beauty and blessing, we must develop a robust, regular personal prayer life outside the communal arena.

RABBI NANCY FLAM

As Rabbi Flam indicates, the tensions between personal and communal prayer can be used productively. The differences can be brought to serve the larger whole of a varied and whole spiritual practice.

The Siddur invites me to stand with a millennium of Jews who have been praying these words as I utter them today. I aspire when opening a Siddur to be able to hear these generations of davenners davenning with me. My personal prayer carries my voice; the Siddur carries my voice as it stands in the midst of my ancestors' voice.

REB MIMI FEIGELSON

Personal prayer without communal prayer has nothing to anchor it. The anchor is centuries of yearning and hoping. Being able to see that the human striving toward God and toward one another is as old as our people. Those ancient words. Our communal prayers, they're alive. They continue to resonate. And yet if all we have are the communal prayers, and we never put ourselves into the story, I think we're missing a rich part of what prayer can be.

RABBI NAOMI LEVY

In the end, a fruitful prayer life partakes fully of both.

There is a need to improvise in a personal way, to experience God and faith from your own perspective and to express that in some way, and there's a strong need to connect on a communal level. That moment of connection when the individual story and the communal story fit together is such a blessing. When the individual instrument connects up with the orchestra. Prayer is a living experience.

RABBI NAOMI LEVY

In practice, this plays out whenever we skillfully integrate communal and personal prayer. When we cultivate our personal prayer voice, we extend liturgical prayer into every facet of our lives by giving voice to our heart's yearnings directly. And when we compose our own prayers, when we confront the great challenge of putting heart into words, we can better appreciate the spiritual accomplishments of the liturgical composers.

As we have seen, many of our teachers pray spontaneously in synagogue services. Sometimes, it is the traditional prayers that catalyze personal prayer.

I can only do spontaneous prayer because traditional prayer has opened me up. On Shabbat, when I'm in the community where I can really pray and my heart is soaring and the traditional liturgy has opened me up, then my spontaneous prayer pours out. But I can't just start with personal prayer. I have trouble with that.

RABBI SHARON BROUS

For me, there's no difference between my words and the Siddur's words. Both are incredibly valuable. I think it's genius that the rabbis have us say the *Amidah* individually and then communally, where I'm not alone, drawing support from others, just as silent meditation with others is valuable. I make no distinction.

RABBI LAVEY YITZCHAK DERBY

Sometimes the best personal prayer is found in the traditional liturgy.

In my private prayer, I find it powerful to use the inherited words of communal prayer in a way that makes them my own. An example would be the last two lines of *adon olam,* a phenomenal prayer. In the first stanzas, God is the universal creator, distant. Then in fourth stanza, this is my God, *my* God, and then in the last two lines, "In God's hands I put my soul.... God is with me; I will not fear." A very personal statement. I trust my body and my soul to God. I say that every night. When my daughter was having brain surgery, she wanted a prayer. I taught her that and we said it as she went into surgery. I consider these grand compositions of our people to be a library of two thousand years of our greatest writers and thinkers. Knowing they've lasted all this time and they are part of my tradition, and thousands of people have said them, I make them my words, too; that gives me a great deal of comfort and hope.

RABBI LAWRENCE A. HOFFMAN, PHD

20

Advice for Beginners Redux

A s in chapter 9, our teachers offer counsel to those beginning to pray, only now, with regard to traditional Jewish prayer.

Looking for a Community

Find the Right Place

The most important thing is to find yourself in the right place. But many places are just bad places, that's all. It's like going to a great theater, but the director and the actors are terrible. I can say all I want about *Hamlet,* but if Hamlet misses the lines and mumbles, it's not going to be much of a play, and much of our worship is like that, unfortunately. You need to find a place with the right choreography, a sacred drama. You need a performance. That doesn't mean that it's a performance that's phony. I don't mean it in that way. Nor do I mean a performance where the cantor or rabbi says the prayers to a passive audience. I think of it as a performance that invites each one of the worshipers in to be part of the performance. We are all sacred actors in our inherited sacred drama of the centuries. The lines eventually become your lines. Once you find yourself into the experience of prayer and you say, "Oh this is good," then you're more likely to want to learn about it. I think it's a mistake to tell people, "Oh, it's your problem. Go learn it, then you'll get it." It's actually our problem, the Jewish People's problem, because the liturgy is supposed to carry us through the centuries. And if the people charged with the liturgy don't do their share, then it's all too easy to scapegoat the worshipers who don't know anything. Yeah, in theory, they should know, sure, but that's the ideal. In any event, the leaders of prayer have the responsibility to help other people care about prayer, by providing them with the opportunity to have a prayer experience that moves them.

RABBI LAWRENCE A. HOFFMAN, PHD

Ask for Help

Let someone know, "I'm new here. Can someone help me?" If you have the courage to do that, you're in good shape.

RABBI NAOMI LEVY

Look Around

If one stream doesn't work, try another, because there are many voices in Judaism, and you will find people like you somewhere. Don't judge everything by what you see at one place or your childhood experience.

RABBI SHAWN ZEVIT

It's a Process

All or Nothing

Jews suffer in this area as in other areas from an all or nothing mentality. When you owe money for taxes, if you write them a check for 50 percent, they'll throw you in jail. But I don't think God is like that, and I don't think mitzvah obligation is like that. I think we need to make people proud of taking baby steps.

RABBI BRADLEY SHAVIT ARTSON

Prepare for the Trip

If you were going to go to Italy, you would read a guide book before you went. You'd check out the highlights and check out a couple of phrases, like "Where's the bathroom?" because you would need some basic knowledge to get around. The same is true with a service at a synagogue. We need to come without the expectation, "This is mine; it should automatically make sense to me." Rather, we should say, "I'm coming to something that's new for me." Because really it is new, and it's helpful to read a guidebook in advance. The better you prepare, the better your trip will be.

RABBI NAOMI LEVY

A Three-Step Program

The first step is to raise awareness by naming the problem. If I don't know how to pray, or I know prayer but can't bring my heart to it, just own this. Name it as your prayer. Awareness is a beginning point. Then comes awkwardness. I have to practice. I can't hit a home run the first day. I need to have a realistic expectation. Find some place to connect and practice the behaviors and that leads to integration. It takes some time, but a year or two later, you're at home. Then you can start riffing.

RABBI SHAWN ZEVIT

Synagogues not only offer classes, many also offer a learner's minyan, where basic skills are demonstrated and the prayers are said at a slower pace. It takes time to master a skill.

It is no more difficult than the *Wall Street Journal.* Most Americans find that opaque as well. Business people learn how to navigate the *Journal*. Prayer-people learn how to navigate the Siddur.

RABBI LAWRENCE A. HOFFMAN, PHD

The Prayers Are a Means

Understand the Goal of Prayer

Our current prayer language, for most Jews, does the opposite of what it's meant to do. It's meant to be an invitation, to draw you into yearning, but instead, for many Jews, it places a barrier. Most non-Orthodox Jews don't believe in a God who fights for the good guys—that is, the Jews—and against everybody else. They don't believe in a God who magically heals the sick and who is going to rebuild the Temple in Jerusalem. So all of these ideas that were meant to be the entryway to the real juice, the emotional and the devotional, actually push us away.

What you see in a lot of progressive synagogues that take prayer seriously is an end run around that entry room, using drums or instruments, getting people dancing, getting them singing, the use of one-line chants to get around a lot of the Hebrew words and the old concepts that don't work for people. If we thought that the text of the prayer was the point, then these end runs would be pretty illegitimate, skipping the most important part. But I really do believe, and I have sources to back me up, that these words and concepts are just meant to help. They're a little bit like Hallmark greeting cards. If you can't think of something on your own, they get you started. They express the thought you're trying to express. And just as we could do without greeting cards if everyone could write their own poetry, so too, theoretically, we could do without liturgical prayer. But at the very least, if the language of the prayer isn't working, well, that's just the means, not the end. It shouldn't stand as an obstacle. For me, the language still usually works. But if it doesn't work, try different language. If language doesn't work, go to the end point, with silence or music. That's central. The way you get there is secondary.

JAY MICHAELSON

Find One Moment

I'm not going to connect every moment but I'm going to find one moment of light, of deep connection. So I don't treat myself like a failure if I'm not connecting, but I know that there will always be one moment where my heart is truly open.

RABBI SHARON BROUS

Walking through the Synagogue Door

In any human endeavor, what we expect colors what we experience. So it is appropriate to ask, which attitudes and expectations help people to pray well in synagogue?

It's unwise to come to a prayer service to be entertained. You come to a prayer service to have something asked of you, not something given to you.

RABBI DAVID J. WOLPE

Leave the Baggage at Home

Many people have no problem trying other people's stuff, even if they don't know the meanings of the words they're saying. But we have so much baggage. We need to explore Judaism like we would another culture—without judgment, for fun, with a good attitude.

RABBI SHAWN ZEVIT

Empty Out

I love the idea that the Siddur is a script, and that I am taking on the role of Jew. As a good actor, my job is to feel what the script would bid me feel. So there's a kind of emptiness that is required for Jewish prayer, but it's a productive emptiness. And I don't think we teach people that. I think we mislead them into "make your life meaningful by praying." There's so much ego in it, there's no room to become the character who uses that book. I like to encourage people to empty themselves so that they can be filled by the book.

RABBI BRADLEY SHAVIT ARTSON

Look for God Elsewhere

A lot of Jews go to synagogue to find God, and I'm really sad for them because I don't think they're going to find God in a synagogue. I think you go to synagogue after you find God. Find God in nature, in your family, in the Buberian I-Thou, in love, in powerful emotions. And then bring that to synagogue.

I go to reconnect, to say hello. And I go to be with other people who are also saying hello. It's kind of a powerful game of telephone. I bring my spirituality in. I give it as a gift and take a little from everybody else.

But that doesn't mean that I won't find God there. That's the message. I have found God many times in synagogue. It's the same as dating. If you date a person because you feel that you're half a person and they're going to complete you, that kind of relationship never works. That's a relationship based on need. So if you go into synagogue feeling that you don't have anything to offer, and you need to take take take, then you will be depressed, you will be upset. I think if you go in saying, "I'm going to offer my voice, my spirit, my passion, my commitment, and I'm going to take a little from everybody else's, too," then it's a much more satisfying experience. You have to walk in empty of preconceptions, empty of expectations of what you will receive. Because you don't know what will happen to you, or with you, or from you, before you walk in and actually experience it.

I'm never disappointed because I never have expectations other than, "Gee, what surprise is God going to have for me today?" That's why I can go to Orthodox services, Reconstructionist services, Jewish Renewal services. I just go to see, what does God have in store for me today?

And sometimes it's horrible. Sometimes I walk out of a synagogue and I say, "Oh, God, this should be illegal. How do they let people get away with this and get paid for it?" But, sometimes, it's just one thing, one word, one experience, one kid, one thing that happens.

RABBI ELYSE GOLDSTEIN

Big Wow, Little Wow
Prayer is a way of working for transformation in quiet ways. You can't expect fireworks every day. It's like any relationship. You know, when you're living with a partner, you're not going to have a candlelight dinner every night. But what those moments do is sustain you in the rush of everyday living. I think it's much like that in terms of prayer life. You really should go to a retreat, you should go to nature, where you'll experience prayer best, but you have to be patient and non-judgmental when you come back. It's not like that every day.

RABBI NEHEMIA POLEN, PhD

Be Hungry, Be Sincere
The ideal davenner comes in hungry. They're ready to go inside. This isn't just another Friday night but an opportunity to connect to our Jewish tradition, to explore passion and yearning. We're here to soften our hearts and leave here in a different state of consciousness. There's an old joke about Mrs. Goldstein: She's upset and complains to the rabbi, "My son learns Talmud and prays all day." "But that's what I do," responds the rabbi. "Yes, but he means it!" That's what I want, a congregation of people who mean it.

RABBI DAVID INGBER

Getting Started

Slow down

If people want to start praying, I believe that the only chance they have is not to be on the highway of prayer, but to be on the slow road.

RABBI ETHAN FRANZEL

Nature

Praying in wilderness has really helped my prayer life. Once those prayers became infused with meaning, I could carry that into a synagogue.

RABBI JAIME KORNGOLD

Befriend a Small Siddur

Zalman [Schachter-Shalomi] once said, get yourself a small prayer book, preferably the smallest one you can find, physically. Block out ten minutes a day to spend with it. That's how you start davenning. You can chew on the prayer book for ten minutes, you can lick the prayer book, you can tear out the pages, whatever you do with the prayer book counts. Classical Jewish prayer is you and the Siddur.

RABBI LAWRENCE KUSHNER

I can testify to the usefulness of this advice. In my years at yeshiva and rabbinical school, I carried my Siddur everywhere in my pocket. A pocket Siddur becomes a best friend, inseparable from you. Each day you hold it in your hand, and continue a dialogue that marks all the significant occasions of your life. It might travel with you to Asia, keep you company while you wait out a storm in your tent, or remind you of what's important when something goes wrong at work. Every dirt smudge and food stain and tattered page carries the record of your life, framing it in the history of our People, and the values we hold dear. Few things are as precious as a well-used Siddur.

Make It Real

I offer the *yotzer or* [creator of light] prayer when I open the shades for the first time in the morning. I just stand there, receive the light, and offer the entire blessing. There are places where our liturgy is connected to embodied experience, and we would do well to reclaim them. This is an important aspect of "making prayer real".

RABBI NANCY FLAM

Beginning to Pray

If you can't say words of the prayer book, say words of the heart. If you're saying words of the prayer book, go really slow. Don't try to stay with the congregation. Take your time with each word or phrase and rest with it, resonate with it. Let it call up images for you. Really pour your heart into the words. If you're saying "Please God," mean "Please God"; if you're grateful, pour gratitude into the words. Let each word percolate up and take you with it. If you come to a phrase that is challenging or pushes your buttons or seems intellectually untrue, just skip it. Don't say it.

RABBI LAVEY YITZCHAK DERBY

PART V

Building a Prayer Practice

Prayer has the power to lift us up, and it also has the power to settle us down when we're feeling lost, untethered, panicked, as so many of us do. Life goes faster and faster. Prayer on a daily basis offers us an opportunity to reconnect with God, our people, our souls, in a way that anchors us. And when you feel anchored, it's something that frees you up. The more rattled a person is, the more rigid he or she might become, or shut down. The more sensitive a person is, the more open and creative. Even a short period of prayer in the morning can change the way you experience the day. And a short period of prayer at night can change the way you face the darkness.

RABBI NAOMI LEVY

21

Starting a Daily Practice

As Rabbi Shefa Gold likes to say, there is no greater gift than giving oneself the gift of a morning practice. Indeed, prayer can work its wonders when it is regular.

> I urge people to start a morning practice with *modeh ani,* "I am thankful." I try to say *modeh ani* in the first moment of consciousness, perhaps before my eyes have opened. Sometimes something specific that I'm grateful for arises in my awareness. Sometimes it's just gratitude, a surprising, nonspecific gratitude. Sometimes there are questions about who or what I should be grateful for. Sometimes, if I'm in a grumpy mood, I don't feel very grateful, and I have to ask myself, "What do I do about that?" Any of those spiritual recognitions are valid ways of saying *modeh ani.* If I'm not feeling grateful, I need to acknowledge that that is my spiritual state and ask myself, "What do I have to do to move into a more grateful place? Or, what is it in my life or behavior that is keeping me from being grateful?" If a person is uncomfortable with Hebrew, they can say, "I'm grateful," and know that

that's connected to the traditional prayer. Another morning practice is to look at the list of traditional morning blessings and find the one that speaks to you that particular day and to contemplate that. What does it mean to open the eyes of the blind? What am I missing? What do I need to see more of? What am I grateful for that I'm able to see? What does it mean to really see?

DR. LINDA THAL

Some people prefer the evening as their time for daily prayer.

The prayers around the bedtime ritual are wonderful. I learned the practice of praying backwards through the day. I review the day backwards and notice those moments when I experienced blessing or the opposite, and just notice it. I keep a gratitude journal. I mentally note or write down the things I feel grateful for in this moment. And I have a tradition of saying out loud with my husband the angel blessing. It's just a really nice way of ending the day. Saying the bedtime *Shema* with children is something I urge my congregants to do, and then they can get the beauty of doing it themselves.

RABBI LAURA GELLER

There is great wisdom in the traditional practice of davenning three times a day. We break from routine and the mundane to make time for the sacred and the holy. Here is how Rabbi Nadya Gross lives the tradition.

What's important for me is to be in touch three times a day. The morning is about embodiment, remembering that I'm in conscious relationship with God, that the breath that breathes me is the gift of life that comes from a divine source. I have this body that works, my heart opens in praise, with gratitude for another day of life, and then I reaffirm my relationship with God, which is in the *Shema* and all the blessings that surround it. It's a way to access what I understand God to be.

Then I want to touch in later in the day. I align myself in the morning with all the best intentions, but life gets in the way. Anxiety and business and all the rest. So Minchah is a time to reconnect, to look at the day I've lived so far and be grateful for living in God's house, which is what I see as the central theme of the *ashrei* prayer, [said at the beginning of the afternoon service, from Psalm 84:5]. Realigning and noticing again.

Evening time is most important. I pray at the end of the day, with the bedtime *Shema,* as I surrender and entrust my soul to God. I try to live my day between those bookends. Every night I give it back, and every morning it's returned to me. This defines *this* day as a gift.

RABBI NADYA GROSS

Starting a practice is easy. Keeping a practice going is one of the most difficult challenges I have faced. Especially for those of us who are not "morning people," it can be exasperating. A morning practice is definitely preferable, as it is less likely to be threatened by contingencies at work or running out of energy at the end of the day. But even those who naturally rise early may have trouble finding time in the morning because of work and child-raising duties.

One key to building a successful practice is to start small and build from there. Doing a little regularly is likely to work better than doing a lot infrequently. Second, it's important to plan. In particular, it's wise to set a minimum daily practice and know what you add on when you have more time.

Personally, I try to devote at least an hour each morning to spiritual practice. I begin with the sun salutations from yoga and then practice qigong for up to a half hour. I put on my *tallit,* lay *tefillin,* say the morning blessings, and settle onto my meditation bench. I usually chant and sometimes meditate for another half-hour and then conclude with the *Shema,* the *Amidah,* and the *Aleynu.*

But, of course, I often don't have an hour. Sometimes I have ten minutes. Then I have to choose my priorities. For me, it's qigong, the *Shema,* personal prayer between the opening and closing blessings of the *Amidah,* and a closing chant.

Another key is to dedicate a particular place in the home for spiritual practice. Many adorn their practice space with photos, significant spiritual momentos, and sense-pleasing items such as embroidered cloth and flowers. Entering a space dedicated to prayer is an immediate *kavvanah* builder.

Frequent travel presents its own challenges to spiritual practice. I carry an embroidered cloth bag that holds my *kipa* (head covering; *yarmulke* in Yiddush), *tallit, tefillin,* a pocket-size prayer book, a small printed copy of the Torah, and whatever spiritual book I'm reading at the time. I can conveniently leave with it for synagogue, or the Tetons. Another important travel tool for me is memorization. I can say the *Shema* and her blessings, as well as the opening and closing blessings of the *Amidah,* by heart. Whether on a train or a plane, in a hotel room, or between meetings at a conference, I can put on my baseball hat and daven silently without drawing attention to myself.

Rabbis Debra Orenstein and Bradley Shavit Artson offer their advice on starting a daily practice.

> Many of our prayers started out as a *chatimah* (the final, brief blessings at the conclusion of a paragraph). The words that precede the final blessing were meant as a "way in," not as the final say. I recommend using the *baruch ata Adonai* formulations as an invitation to pray your own prayer about themes like ancestors (the *avot* prayer), peace (the *hashkiveynu*), and wisdom (the *chonen ha-da'at* blessing). Wherever you are in your knowledge and experience of prayer, you have something to add about these and other

themes that the *chatimah* addresses. Praying a fresh prayer each day based on the themes of the Siddur is traditional, creative—and potentially transformative. [See practice 21.]

RABBI DEBRA ORENSTEIN

Start with the *Shema* every night before you go to bed. In the morning, take one minute to stand in front of an open window and reflect on something loveable about yourself and say thank you to God for it by opening up the Siddur, saying the *Shema* and maybe one line from the *Amidah*. Then build on that. It's about linking the right emotional orientation with the doing of praying. To tell people to take an adult education class and memorize these prayers already defeats any possibility of praying. Start the day by asking, what do I want to say thank you for? And before you just roll over and say, "Good night, honey" and start to snore, think about the day. What was an unexpected gift that you received today? What was a moment where you exceeded your own expectation? Or where your worst fears didn't materialize? I think that training Jews to gratitude and to joy and to love is some of the most important work that we can be doing to help people learn to pray again. And then to tie it back to the prayer book.

RABBI BRADLEY SHAVIT ARTSON

Learning to pray as a Jew appears to be an overwhelming task. Just ask a Jew By Choice. But it doesn't need to happen in a day or a week or by the end of this month. As Rabbi Artson teaches, baby steps are just fine. When it comes to prayer, less is indeed more, if it is consistent.

Beginning to Pray

There are literally hundreds of prayer practices that you might employ to cultivate your prayer life. We have chosen just a few, and explained them in detail. They are purposely basic and simple. Most important, they are tried, tested, and effective.

As much as books like this one are important, spiritual practice is experiential. It is less like learning math or history and more like learning a skill, whether carpentry or a musical instrument. It is less book learning, and more apprenticeship training. Here are three pieces of advice to make the most out of the following practices.

> **Give it some time.** It's called "practice" because that is, indeed, what you need to do. Many teachers counsel that the effect of a practice cannot be gauged until it has been rehearsed for three months.

> **Don't be afraid to tweak a practice, but be cautious.** Different things work for different people. Having said that, if you find yourself constantly experimenting, you will never gain the effect of continued practice. Jumping around is often the result of impatience or neurosis. Especially at the beginning, it is wise to stick with a practice before tweaking it. Like so much else in spiritual practice, this is a judgment call.

> **Find a teacher.** Finding a role model with whom you can apprentice is ideal. Beginners in spiritual practice often become frustrated simply because they think they are doing something wrong, when in fact (as a teacher will point out) they are doing just fine. And when spiritual and emotional blocks arise, an experienced teacher can provide insight and suggest alternative practices based on their own experience.

Finding a teacher is not always easy, but most every city has teachers of prayer, chant, meditation, and other subjects. Look for them in the adult education programs at synagogues, Jewish community centers, and Jewish institutions of higher learning. See the Resources section for an array of helpful books, websites, and organizations offering classes and spiritual retreats.

Practices

Yearning

How do we cultivate yearning and longing? Reading the great poets (see the Resources section) or other inspirational literature is very fruitful. Almost any artistic endeavor helps us to stay in touch with that inner desire to connect with transcendence. We might give some thought to whether our art, whatever it is, points us toward holiness and God. Practice 1 articulates yearning through creative writing.

PRACTICE 1
Write a Psalm

For those who like creative writing, here is a practice to dialogue your longing. Poetry is a proven method to express yearning. The difference between a poem and a psalm is that the latter is directed in some way toward God. We move from desire to holy desire.

1. Write a poem that expresses your holy desire, your yearning and longing. It can be about anything.
2. In the language you find appropriate, bring your connection to transcendence and divinity into the writing.
3. Many people find it useful to employ second person, "You" language to address God in at least some of their poem.
4. Many find this exercise easier in the natural world.
5. Read your poem out loud in the place that inspired your writing.
6. For striking examples of contemporary psalms, see Rainer Maria Rilke's *Book of Hours* and David Whyte's *Fire in the Earth* (see the Resources section for full information about these books).

Gratitude

If you are like me, you wake up thinking about what needs to be done today. As a freelance teacher, I do not enjoy the security of knowing where my workday begins and ends. The constant question, "Can I get enough done today?" underlies my anxious thoughts. For many of us, starting the day with gratitude does not come naturally; it takes persistence. Fortunately, it is not an endeavor where satisfaction is delayed. You can tell the difference a gratitude practice makes from the very first day.

The basic principle is twofold: say thanks every day as part of your routine; do it in whatever way works for you. In addition to practices 2 and 3, you might try the following from Rabbi Karen Fox.

> When I end my morning meditation, I repeat a phrase from the liturgy, one that speaks of gratitude, and then I say five things I'm grateful for. Then I conclude with a prayer for God's compassion for me and for others, and ask, "How can I be compassionate today?"
>
> RABBI KAREN FOX, DD

PRACTICE 2
Gratitude List

1. Every day, think, speak, or write a number of things for which you are grateful.
2. To make this into a prayer, address your thanks to God. If you are not comfortable with God language, try thanking the universe.
3. Do this spontaneously, changing your list daily with whatever comes up.
4. Just after waking up in the morning and just before going to sleep are easy times to undertake this practice. At night, you can review the day and list the things for which you are thankful.

5. Choose a minimum number for your daily list. To start, try five.

6. You might start a gratitude journal to list them, and keep it at your bedside. This allows you to look back over time. If saying thanks spurs other thoughts, write on!

PRACTICE 3
Thank-You Walk

1. Take a walk around the neighborhood, your garden, or the house.

2. Approach a stone or plant or creature and direct your full attention toward it. You might take a moment to appreciate its beauty before speaking.

3. Say thanks, using your own words. "Thank you, flower, for the joy you bring me." To an old tree, you might say, "Thank you, grandmother, for your shade and shelter." Just saying "thanks" with sincerity is enough.

4. You might touch the pet or plant or stone while speaking.

On the virtues of using "you" language in addressing trees and mountains, see my *A Wild Faith: Jewish Ways into Wilderness, Wilderness Ways into Judaism* (Jewish Lights), chapter 4 and appendix 2.

Body Awareness

An experience of God, like any experience, can only be in the present. Mindfulness, concentrating on the here and now, is critical to prayer. But much of prayer is a mental process, an exercise in verbal and conceptual thinking, the very place we might drift into random thoughts of past and future. The antidote to mental boredom and distraction is to connect to our senses, placing at least part of our attention on what we hear, see, and feel on our skin. When we find a way to keep some of our attention on the body while praying, we can daven with greater focus and intensity.

If you practice yoga, tai chi, or other body awareness practices, I would not see them as competition to a Jewish spiritual practice. On the contrary, the more we are aware of the ways of the body, and the more skilled we are at focusing meditative attention on our senses, the better our prayer.

The following exercises cultivate body awareness specifically for prayer. Chant (see practice 20) is effective as well. For advice on working with the divine flow, with *chiut,* in prayer as I described in my essay in chapter 1, see my *A Wild Faith: Jewish Ways into Wilderness, Wilderness Ways into Judaism* (Jewish Lights), chapter 11.

PRACTICE 4
Soul Breathing

The simplest form of meditation is to follow the breath. Here we add the Hebrew words for breath and soul, *neshima* and *neshama.* They are almost identical, which adds a theological dimension as well as a rhyme, both parts of a useful mantra. I use this practice to quickly relax and drop into my body when davenning, both before and during the service.

1. Close your eyes and focus on your breath. You might listen for the subtle sound of breathing, or notice the rising and falling of the belly and chest, or focus on the sensation of air passing through the nostrils. When thoughts arise, gently let them go and return to the breath.

2. On the in-breath, say, "*Neshima,*" in your mind's voice. On the out-breath, say, "*Neshama.*"

3. Alternatively, integrate one or more of the names of God into your meditation. I often say *Yah*—the gender-neutral, abbreviated form of the four-letter name of God—on the in-breath, as it works nicely with *neshama.* You might try the divine name given at the Burning Bush, *Ehiyeh* (in-breath) *asher* (pause) *Ehiyeh* (out-breath), which means "I am that I am," or "I will be what I will be."

PRACTICE 5
25-25-50 Body Awareness

Originally, I developed this method of body awareness for mindful hiking in nature, where it is particularly effective. But it can be used anywhere. The meditative principle is simple. By giving our mind three different areas of focus in the present, it becomes too busy to entertain thoughts of past or future. We can better keep concentration on the object of our attention, and we bring our bodies into the process. Therapists and counselors often practice some version of this exercise to stay grounded and focus on their clients. You can use it to increase your concentration and awareness while doing anything from watching a play to cooking a meal to speaking with a friend. As described in the Preface, this is the practice I use to bring my body into prayer.

1. Close your eyes and focus on your breath, as in the previous practice.
2. After a minute, leave half your attention on your breath and place the other half on the bottoms of your feet or the feel of your backside on the chair. Feel the pressure of your body against the earth; notice the constant adjustments your muscles make to maintain balance.
3. After another minute, open your eyes while shifting your focus once again. Place 25 percent of your awareness on your breath, 25 percent on your feet or backside, and 50 percent on the world around you. If you are in nature, begin to walk, taking in all the sounds and sights of the land you are traversing. If you are in conversation, place your attention on the other person and the conversation. If you are praying, stay focused on the act of praying—a combination of awareness of the heart, the prayer, and beyond.
4. When your mind wanders and focus fades, try not to get angry at yourself. This happens to everyone, no matter how

experienced. Gently return your attention to the breath and to your body, and continue on.

5. The numbers 25-25-50 are to give you a general idea of where your attention should be focused. They are not meant to be followed literally. Another way to frame this practice is: place part of your attention on your breath, part of your attention on the feel of the earth against you, and most of your attention on the object(s) of your main focus. One woman mentioned that it was helpful to think of this as heart-earth meditation.

6. It might be too much to keep awareness on three loci. For some, it is better to simply keep some awareness on the bottoms of the feet, and not bother with breath. Some people prefer to keep awareness on the heart rather than the breath. The rule is, experiment and do what works for you. I find that when walking in nature, it helps to keep awareness on feet and heart. When praying, I keep some awareness on one or the other.

I often run into past participants from hikes with my organization, TorahTrek. Many volunteer that the 25-25-50 practice has affected them the most. Take it seriously, and you will notice a change in any activity to which you apply it.

PRACTICE 6

Heart Awareness

This practice is as powerful as it is simple. It is particularly effective while praying, as focus on the heart area not only keeps you aware of the body but also invites your emotional participation in the praying.

1. Whatever else you are doing, *keep part of your awareness on your heart*. Because of its simplicity, this is a good practice for staying grounded throughout the day, whatever the activity.

2. Before praying, place full awareness on your heart and listen in silence.

3. While praying, keep part of your awareness focused on the heart. Notice any sensations in the chest area. If you are davenning from the Siddur, feel your heart open up to the words of the prayer book. If you are praying your own prayer, feel your words coming from the heart and extending into the world.

4. Place your hand over your heart, as if you were saying the American pledge of allegiance. This helps maintain focus and facilitates the flow of *chiut,* divine energy, through the body. I especially love to do this during the Amidah and personal prayer.

Blessings

As discussed in chapter 11, blessings are a fruitful way to begin praying, as blessings always include awareness and gratitude. To begin a blessings practice, you might turn the Thank-You Walk (practice 3) into a Blessings Walk (practice 10). Simply add some variation of the *baruch ata* formula (see practice 8) into your thank-you prayer. I try to avoid generalities and get specific, as awareness of detail creates a stronger connection to what I am blessing and a stronger movement in my heart. So instead of thanking God for the blue sky, I might bless God, "who brings us fog in the morning and thunderclouds in the afternoon."

Second, you can learn the traditional blessings and use them (practice 9). I would begin with just a few. The blessings around food are a good place to start, as they are simple but varied, and we eat often. It is quite easy for blessings over food to become rote, the dark side of memorizing and habituating prayer. So blessings over food can be a testing ground and a knife-sharpener for honing your *kavvanah.* To combine traditional and personal blessings, try practice 10.

Whether spontaneous or traditional, blessings require our focus and concentration. A final reason for starting Jewish prayer with a blessings practice is that the techniques in the following exercise are the quickest, surest way I (and many others) know of learning how to connect heart to words. If you have time to try but one practice in *Making Prayer Real,* try practice 7.

PRACTICE 7
Blessings Practice

This practice is modeled on the Buddhist Metta, or blessing prayers, of vipassana or insight meditation, retreats. Prayer is a universal spiritual practice that arises in almost every culture, so blessings are hardly unique to Buddhism. But as is the Buddhist way in so many things, Buddhist blessings practice cuts to the core in its simplicity, and since the mind/body division is not part of Eastern culture, it does not ignore the physicality of good prayer. It begins by focusing on ourselves. The words are tweaked and adjusted to fit what is going on in your heart, as in spontaneous prayer, rather than the other way around.

1. Sit comfortably, close your eyes, and breathe deeply to become calm and still. If you know a meditation technique, you might want to use it for a few moments before you begin.
2. Relax your body and place awareness on your heart region. As you pay attention to the movement of your chest, notice your emotional state.
3. Visualize the person you would like to bless. Buddhists typically start with themselves and then move to family, friends, or a neutral person. The more challenging task is to bless a difficult or hostile person.
4. Bless the person you are holding by using the following formula:
   a. On the in-breath, say, "Please, God," or "Please, *Adonai,*" or "Please, *Yah,*" or "Please, *Shechinah.*"
   b. On the outbreath, say, "May you be ... " and fill in the sentence with your prayer for the one you are blessing. If you are praying for yourself, "May I be ... "

c. Start with four sentences and repeat them a minimum of five times, or set a timer for at least five minutes per person prayed for. You can add more sentences, but remember, the strength of this practice lies in its simplicity.

d. For example, you might pray, coordinated with your breath, "Please, God, may you be healthy. Please, God, may you be protected from inner and outer harm. Please, God, may you be at peace. Please, God, may you know love."

5. Choose the words that feel best, that your heart truly wishes, given what you know about the person. You might immediately see that a particular quality should be replaced by another. But once you get going, stick with the same words. Your thinking mind will intrude and break your *kavvanah* if you let it.

6. In the Torah, blessings are not only wishes for another; they are gifts. Typically, a father blesses his son with progeny, crops, leadership abilities, and more. Think of the wishes in your blessings as gifts, freely given, to become self-sustaining in the one you are blessing, expecting nothing in return.

7. Throughout, but especially when you are finished, notice your emotional state and the feeling in your heart region. Has anything changed?

8. Closure is good. Instead of just getting up and leaving, end with a chant, a song, or the prayer *Baruch ata ... shomea tefillah* (Blessed be You God, who hears prayer; see practice 11 for more on this).

9. There are many variations to this basic practice. An important one for me is to adapt the form to one of the morning prayers from the Siddur, *v'arastich li,* and give my blessings in Hebrew. Normally, the prayer is said when laying *tefillin.* From a passage in Hosea (2:19), it means, "I will betroth you to me forever; I will betroth you in righteousness and justice, in love and compassion." So, instead of, "Please, God, may you know peace," I will say, *"V'arasteecha"* on the inbreath, and *"B'shalom"* (May you be betrothed with

peace) on the outbreath. But even for me, fluent in Hebrew, it takes time to establish the connection between my heart and the words. It is much easier in your native language, so proceed to Hebrew only after you have gained some experience in your first language (unless, of course, you grew up speaking Hebrew!).

A more complete description of this practice can be found in Rabbi Jeff Roth's *Jewish Meditation Practices for Everyday Life: Awakening Your Heart, Connecting with God* (Jewish Lights), chapter 7.

PRACTICE 8
Jewish Blessings

This exercise is a direct continuation of practices 2 and 3. Here we put our gratitude practice into Hebrew language and Jewish form. Blessings practice is wonderful in nature, where you can hardly take a step without seeing a part of creation for which you might be grateful. But it is an even more powerful practice in places where gratitude may not arise naturally. Can you say blessings while contending with traffic, in the kitchen, or at the workplace?

1. Identify an activity or an entity or a living being you would like to bless.

2. You might start with the traditional blessing formula:

$$\text{בָּרוּךְ אַתָּה יְיָ ,אֱלֹהֵינוּ מֶלֶךְ הָעוֹלָם ...}$$

Baruch ata Adonai, Eloheinu melech ha-olam ...

Blessed be You Adonai, Sovereign of the world ...

Others are more comfortable with an alternative formula that includes feminine language and different images for God, such as:

$$\text{בְּרוּכָה אַתְּ יָהּ ,רוּחַ הָעוֹלָם ...}$$

B'ruchah at Yah, ruach ha-olam ...

Blessed be You Yah, spirit of the world ...

or

בְּרוּכָה אַתְּ יָהּ ,הַשְּׁכִינָה ...

B'ruchah at Yah, ha-Shechinah ...

Blessed be You, Yah, *Shechinah* (God's immanent presence) ...

3. Continue in English or, if you can, in Hebrew, and compose your blessing. Typical blessings might be as follows:

Baruch ata Adonai, Eloheinu melech ha-olam, ... for the feel of my cat's fur when she snuggles with me in the morning.

B'ruchah at Yah, ruach ha-olam, ... for the robins who join me in the backyard and the gift of sight to see them.

4. The more detail you include, the better. You are seeking to connect what is happening in your life to the presence of God. For most people, it is much harder to do so with formulas or generic statements.
5. Blessings should be said out loud, but a whisper will do.

PRACTICE 9
Learn the Traditional Blessings

While connecting to a liturgical formula is hard for most people (but not all) and you must also contend with the Hebrew, there are plenty of reasons to learn the traditional blessings and use them in your spiritual practice. When a tradition works, it opens us to an experience that we likely would not have reached on our own, and it give us the language and the ideas to appreciate it. Who would have thought to bless a trip to the restroom? But as we all learn at one point or another, the daily functioning of our complicated, intricate bodies is nothing short of a miracle and shouldn't be taken for granted. The traditional blessings are often beautiful and, as in the case of *baruch dayan emet* (said upon hearing of a death), give us words to express the inexpressible. Finally, by adopting the traditional form, we join a community of blessers. Our words are strengthened by the fact that they have been said for so long in so many places.

1. Study the traditional blessings, memorize as many as possible, and carry them with you. (They can be found in any Siddur, and in the books in the "Blessings" section of the Resources list.)
2. Where appropriate, recite them with *kavvanah*.

PRACTICE 10
Blessings Walk

To get the best out of both worlds, I like to combine personal and traditional blessings to start the day in a Blessings Walk.

1. Alternate the traditional morning blessings, found at the beginning of the morning service, with spontaneous blessings over what you are seeing, touching, and hearing in the moment.
2. For example, after reciting the traditional Hebrew morning blessing "Praised be You, God, Sovereign of the universe, who enables the blind to see," you might follow with, "Blessed be You, the Source of blessing, who in her wisdom places droplets of dew on pink-petaled roses."
3. You might continue with the next traditional blessing, this time phrased in the feminine: "Blessed be You, the *Shechinah* filling the universe, who dresses the naked," followed by, "Blessed be You, the Spirit of the universe, for clean clothes and warm socks."

Cultivating a Personal Prayer Voice

Cultivating a personal prayer voice is critical to developing a prayer practice. It allows us to connect directly to our hearts, and we learn the skills that make prayer effective in communal settings, as well. For many, the practices in this section ask us to take a risk, to try something out of our comfort zone, to do things that might not conform to the way we are used to thinking about God and prayer. Perhaps we're not so sure if this is a good idea. But like any body of practical skills and knowledge, we cannot know the benefit without actually doing it. Since we are not causing harm to ourselves or others, there isn't much actual risk, other than some minor embarrassment or uncertainty.

PRACTICE 11
Personal Prayer

This is the "just do it" exercise for cultivating your personal prayer voice. It is the easiest of exercises but perhaps the practice for which the most internal resistance must be overcome. If you are not ready to try it now, it would be wise to return in the future.

1. Find a private place where no one will make you feel self-conscious. A place in nature works best for many. Others prefer a chapel, but any quiet place will do.
2. Use practices 4–6 above or any other meditative practice you know (such as yoga) to get grounded in your body. Quiet your mind and enter receptive mode. Spend a moment listening to your heart. (Sometimes, you know what you need without practicing a specific mindfulness exercise, but in general, it's helpful.)
3. Compose your own prayer to God. The simplest way is to begin a sentence with, "Please, God ... " or "May it be ... " or "May I receive your help/wisdom/care ... " and let the rest follow. In praying for others, you might begin, "Please, God, may you be ... "
4. Be as honest as possible. What do you really need? (It isn't a Jaguar.) What do others really need? What are your best hopes for the world, for yourself? In prayer, simplicity is a virtue. The idea is to say words that, as much as possible, come directly from your emotional center. When prayer is heartfelt, it carries an emotional charge.

5. You might end with a traditional blessing, such as this:

בָּרוּךְ אַתָּה יְיָ, שׁוֹמֵעַ תְּפִלָּה.

Baruch ata Adonai, shomea tefillah.

Blessed be You, Adonai, who hears prayer.

Just as spiritual practice benefits from the setting of intentions, it also benefits from the emotional discharge and formal letting go—the closure—a blessing can provide.

PRACTICE 12
Talking to God—Rabbi Nachman's *Hitbodedut*

With some latitude, I translate *hitbodedut* as "alone time for spiritual purpose." This is the version of the practice that Rabbi Nachman of Breslov made famous. While you can do *hitbodedut* anywhere, Rabbi Nachman, aware of the supportive flow of *chiut* in natural settings, preferred the natural world. For many people, this is not an easy place to start. Don't be put off if it is difficult the first time around. You can return to it later. It is a very deep practice for those who take to it.

This practice is particularly useful in the work of *teshuvah*.

1. Find a place of solitude.
2. Talk out loud to God for a set period of time, and don't stop. A stopwatch or alarm is helpful so that you won't think about the time. Try starting with twenty minutes. Rabbi Nachman is said to have devoted an hour.
3. Speak, ask, figure things out, pray for guidance—whatever comes up, share it with God. Don't stop to think; just speak and do not quit.
4. Alternatively, do this exercise by writing in a journal. I don't know if Julia Cameron heard of Rabbi Nachman when she made this a core exercise in her program *The Artist's Way*, but it is the same idea. Open your journal and begin to write. Before you begin, set the number of journal pages that you will fill. Cameron recommends three 8½-by-11 ruled pages.

This practice can be difficult at first, but getting over the inhibition of talking out loud to God is not particularly hard. Rather, the problem is that you will quickly run out of what to say. But you must keep speaking. (See Dr. Linda Thal's comment on p. 111.) This is where it gets interesting. You will find yourself saying things that you had no idea were in you. In psychological terms, you have cleared room for your subconscious to send whatever it needs you to know into the light of day.

PRACTICE 13
Write a Letter to God

In this journal practice popularized by Rabbi Elie Kaplan Spitz, we address God directly. And we give God a chance to respond. Like practice 12, this practice is particularly useful in the work of *teshuvah*.

1. Find a place of solitude and take a moment to quiet down.
2. When you are ready, open your journal. Write the most honest thing you can to God. You might describe your wishes for yourself, or for your family and friends. You might write about the things you need most. You might ask for guidance.
3. When you are finished, sit for a moment or two in silence, perhaps in meditation. Listen, in contemplative silence (see practice 15).
4. Using your imagination, write yourself a response from God's perspective. At the very least, you will access the God of your mind's eye. And if your theology allows for God to be found within, perhaps this is much more.
5. You might conclude with a prayer for what you need and gratitude for what you have.

PRACTICE 14
God Says

This practice, from Rabbi Nadya Gross, takes seriously the mystics' view that God can be found inside all of us, and when we still ourselves from mental clutter and our ego-driven desires, we can listen to what God might be telling us. This exercise in discernment (see chapter 8) is a variation of Rabbi Nachman's *hitbodedut* in journal form, only this time from the side of God. Here is Rabbi Gross's explanation in her own words.

> When I'm sleeping, my ego is asleep, so I feel I'm closest to getting clear discernment of God's guidance in those first moments of waking. I put on *tefillin,* since this is a way of connecting the physical and unphysical, of binding God to me, a kind of soul-unification process after the unconscious journeys of the night. With the prayer, of betrothing myself to the Creator, I go into a meditative state and express gratitude. Then I open my journal, write the date, and write, "God says," and then I just write. I try to make it not a thought process, but an open-hearted expression of whatever comes. Often, images from dreams will arise. Some message or awareness or understanding will come through. The more you journal, the more you distill things down to their essence. You find yourself writing things you didn't know you thought, or you knew, by just doing the practice. It shouldn't be such a difficult thing. It's not like I'm waiting for God to move my hand; it's just that in those moments before I've gotten entangled in the day and what I have to do, those thoughts are the closest I come to pure, unencumbered thought. That's how I get in touch with that guidance.
>
> RABBI NADYA GROSS

PRACTICE 15
Contemplation

As Dr. Linda Thal taught us in chapter 7, contemplation is the practice of listening directly for God. It is a good follow-up to many of the other practices, including personal prayer and chant. It is also a simple practice that people find difficult and frustrating if they approach it incorrectly.

1. Follow the 25-25-50 body awareness meditation instructions (practice 5).
2. While keeping some awareness on body and breath,
instead of focusing most of your awareness on the objects
around you, keep your eyes closed, your sensual awareness open-ended, and your attention loosely focused on
everything around you.
3. Many find it helpful to repeat a short mantra, such as "Only
You," to set the intention and keep the mind focused on
listening.
4. This form of awareness is subtle. The idea is to listen for what
may be coming to you from outside of yourself, even if it
comes through what you are feeling or thinking inside. So
unlike insight meditation, where we are inquiring into our
mental and emotional states by examining them closely and
learning how they manifest, here we might also observe our
thoughts and emotions, but we are attending to what is feed-
ing them or affecting them from beyond. We are listening
for what might be coming to the heart from outside, from
God. Our focus is more diffuse, and at times, may not center on the inner movements of mind and emotion at all. (If
this sounds confusing, you are not alone.)
5. Alas, people can also become frustrated by inappropriate
expectations of what they are listening for. As in many spiritual practices, we only get what we desire in contemplation
if we let go of expectations and results. We have no control
over what God may send our way. So expectations of getting
an insight or "message" on any given day are inappropriate.
What we can and should expect is that if we follow the technique properly, we can let go of small self and enter *mochin
d'gadlut,* expanded awareness. This is a great reward in itself,
and a prerequisite for receiving a profound, heartfelt insight.
6. For me, as usual, the state of the body is critical. Making
room for God is an exercise of "dropping into" your body
and allowing your mind to slow down. Nothing can happen

without relaxation. If you feel yourself getting tight and tense, or just plain feeling antsy, it's a clear sign that you need to relax and let go. You should aim for a calm alertness that enables your heart to reach out in relaxed awareness.

7. Reread number 5.

8. A response from God might come in the form of a thought, an image, a feeling, a body sensation, an emotion, an insight, or just the sweetness of sitting in undisturbed "I don't need anything to be different" silence. There is no better way to sabotage this practice than to wait with a preconceived notion of what should happen and give up in frustration after ninety seconds. It is enough to be in a state of mindfulness, of *mochin d'gadlut*. This should be your only expectation. Whatever else comes is frosting on the cake.

This is an advanced practice; it is helpful to learn with a teacher and other students. But it is not the equivalent of a black belt (more like orange or green). Anyone who practices consistently can learn the skills of spiritual discernment.

Coping with Loss

The following three exercises, Practices 16–18, from Rabbi Anne Brener follow up on her essay in chapter 14.

PRACTICE 16

Tears

Let us return to the ruins of the Temple, and imagine ourselves sitting in its ashes. On the ninth of Av, the day that commemorates the Temple's destruction, observant Jews traditionally sit on the ground after sunset, light a candle, and recite the book of Lamentations. When a loss has occurred, one of the things that we must do is come to terms with a difficult truth: some things can't be fixed. These losses call for presence and lamentation. Sit on the floor and light a candle. Hold an image of who or what is lost in your heart and let the tears come. This is the beginning of prayer.

PRACTICE 17
Words

> To further find your own voice of prayer, let's revisit Rabbi Johanan's list of synonyms for prayer: *cry, lament, groan, sing, encounter, trouble, call, fall, pray,* and *supplicate.* These words give us permission to express our deepest feelings, directing them to the deity or force that has brought such pain into our lives, or expressing our frustration with the current state of affairs. Without censoring yourself, imagine yourself confronting God (whether you understand God as the laws of the universe, the power that runs the universe, a force in the universe, or Being itself), and speak your truth, giving vent to the language of your soul.

PRACTICE 18
Meditation

> Sit comfortably, breathing out and breathing in. As you empty yourself with an out-breath, hear yourself say, "Please," as you ask for what it is you most desire. As you breathe in, filling yourself again with breath, hear yourself say, "Thank you." Despite the fact that you will not likely get what you pray for, over time this practice may facilitate a deeper movement toward gratitude. As your breath is restored to you, you might discover the blessings that still flow to you, despite the pain of loss.

PRACTICE 19
Give It to God

> Often there is no solution to the problems and dilemmas that we face in life. It is not in our power to cure a disease; we cannot change a difficult or troubled person; sometimes we have little or no ability to resolve a challenging situation. In these circumstances, when our hearts are heavy with grief or anger or frustration, it often feels as if we are holding up the world all by ourselves. But we need not carry our burdens alone. We can share our troubles with friends, and we can turn to God.

1. In a comfortable position, close your eyes. Sense in your body the pain of your situation. Be with it. No doubt, memories will come into your mind—of a past incident, a suffering friend, a difficult situation. Instead of letting them go as in other meditations, sit with the image and feel it resonate in the body. Watch it with compassion for yourself and others.

2. Try to visualize the feeling. You might see a color, or perhaps an image that symbolizes your pain or grief. Sit with this to make sure it feels right. Your initial image might give way to a more appropriate one.

3. When you are ready, ask God to share this with you. (If you feel tightness or constriction, consider doing this exercise at a later time.) Much as our ancestors raised their sacrifices at the Temple in Jerusalem, take your situation or the image symbolizing it, and with words of prayer, offer it to God. For example, "Please, God, take this struggle and share with me the anguish it causes."

4. In your mind's eye, you might visualize two hands holding the idea or image and raising it upward.

5. Express your feelings to God.

6. You might conclude with a song, such as *oseh shalom,* or a blessing, such as *shomea tefillah* (see practice 11).

Teshuvah

As discussed in chapter 13, *teshuvah* is the art of self-analysis and self-change, usually associated with the High Holidays, especially Yom Kippur. It is easy to describe, and very difficult to do. Prayer aids when it helps us to get honest with ourselves, discover and reveal our deepest motivations, and guide us to a different perspective on our actions. The traditional liturgy and practices 11–14 are useful in the analytical work of *teshuvah,* of understanding our stories and setting the intention to change. Jewish chant (practice 20), meditation and the other mindfulness practices (4–6, 15) support *teshuvah* by helping us to gain a wider perspective on our lives, move beyond our stories, and attune ourselves to the ways of holiness. For a full treatment of the process of *teshuvah* and additional practices, see my *A Wild Faith: Jewish Ways into Wilderness, Wilderness Ways into Judaism* (Jewish Lights), chapter 13.

Engaging the Body in Traditional Prayer

Yoga, tai chi, meditation, or any other practice that heightens awareness, particularly of the body, helps you to prepare for prayer. During prayer, you can use the body awareness techniques discussed above (practices 4 and 5). Placing awareness on the heart area (see practice 6) is simple and often very helpful.

In addition, the traditional liturgy engages the body in several ways. We start with the breath. The *elohai neshama* prayer at the beginning of the morning service has several words in a row that end with a hard "hah" sound. Clearly, each word was meant to be said with the end of a breath in rhythmic cadence (*Ata v'raTAH, ata y'tzarTAH, ata n'fachTAH* ...). A common meditation practice is to say the six words of the *Shema* slowly, one word per breath. Practice 4, "Soul Breathing," is an excellent way to concentrate and focus your awareness on the body before and during services.

Many of the prayers are accompanied by movements— bowing for the *Barchu* and the first and last two blessings of the *Amidah,* stepping forward three steps before saying the *Amidah* and stepping back three steps upon completion, rising off the heels and onto the toes during the *Kedushah.* Shuckling, swaying back and forth during prayer, is quite common. Another physical part of Jewish prayer is covering the head and wearing *tallit* and *tefillin.* They effectively draw body awareness into all aspects of a service.

I was resistant to wearing a *tallit* because it felt so male to me. There was also something that was drawing me toward it. I heard it described as wrapping yourself in God's light; I knew I wanted that. What pushed me over the edge of hesitation was a teacher who asked, "How are you going to prepare for High Holiday services? How, in the midst of everyone greeting each other and speaking about their summer vacations, are you going to get into the frame of mind for prayer?" All of the sudden, I knew that I needed a *tallit*. It became a way of creating a private space for personal recentering and for conversation with God. Now, morning prayers without a *tallit* seem very strange to me. It was awkward at first, but now it's very comforting; there's a sense of embrace and the creation of a sanctified space.

Dr. Linda Thal

For a video demonstration of the choreography of the traditional Jewish prayer service, go to www.MakingPrayerReal.com. Consult the Resources section for additional books and websites.

PRACTICE 20
Jewish Chant

As discussed in chapter 6, chant is a an effective way to join heart and body to the traditional liturgy. While we cannot teach chant from a book, we can mention some of the principles that transform an entertaining song into a chant. Here are a few simple techniques from Rabbi Shefa Gold that can help us to get the most out of chanting.

1. Choose an appropriate chant. A good chant melody is simple enough to sing easily (which varies from person to person). When you sing it for the first time, it's as if you already knew the melody.
2. Be clear on your intention for singing a particular chant. Different words and different melodies are appropriate for different moments in our lives. It can be useful to bring to

the chant a question that you are hoping to resolve, or to ask for guidance. Perhaps you are in need of a quality mentioned in the words, such as love, awe, peace, or patience. More on this below from Rabbi Gold.

3. Listen well to the music and words as you chant. We are not trying to gain an intellectual understanding of the words, but to embody them.

4. Chant the chant too many times. The aim is to bore the thinking mind, so that the intuitive, creative, artistic part of the mind comes to the fore. Repeat it over and over, at least ten to fifteen times to get the full effect. To prevent yourself from having to think about it, set a timer.

5. Keep part of your awareness on your body to stay grounded and to stay focused on the chant. I place part of my attention on the feel of the bottoms of my feet against the ground, or my backside on the chair. Sometimes chants come with hand or other body motions, or you can make them up. Again, this helps the chant to pulse through the body, and sometimes, it's part of the message (such as raising your hands to the sky when singing a chant about transcendence).

6. The most important moment of a chant is not when you're chanting. It's the moment when you stop and go into silence. The silence after a chant is just as much a part of the chant as when you are singing. This is where you listen for a response. This is where you can place your awareness on yourself and notice what has changed. This is the opportunity to harvest the fruits of your chanting. Since the thinking mind is ready to jump back in as soon as it can, it is especially important to maintain concentration as the chant ends. I do this by staying focused on my body using the 25-25-50 body awareness practice, and/or continuing to hear the chant in my mind's ear. You might repeat a short phrase in your mind, such as "Only You," to maintain a contemplative state of awareness (see practice 15).

Here is an example of how Rabbi Gold works with a phrase from the prayer book in her chanting practice.

As the *Shema* is central, I pay special attention to the phrases leading me into that prayer. One of them reads, *v'yached levaveynu, b'ahava u'veyirah, et shemecha,* (May our hearts, with love and with awe, unify Your name). It is meant to open me to unity during the *Shema.* So I look inside myself and know that my heart is often compartmentalized and divided, that one part of me has experiences that often contradict another part of me, and that I need to bring them together in my own heart so that I can experience God's unity during the *Shema.* And then I look at the history of the phrase and I learn that it's a revision of a psalm (Psalms 86:11). The liturgist added love. So he is saying you can't just unify your heart with the quality of awe or fear; you have to integrate that which you love. It points toward a certain work that I need to do inwardly, which is to identify the place of love in my heart and the place of awe in my heart, and to see if I can bring them together and feel them at once before this Mystery.

One of the rules of chant is that I am not talking about something when I chant; I'm embodying that. So if I say, *"v'yached levaveynu"* (May our hearts unify), I need to use those words to ride into the depths of the heart. When I say *"b'ahava"* (with love), I'm feeling in my body, my breath, that flowing love, that open, sweet, delicious heart quality, *ahaaavaah.* Then *yiraaah.* I switch. I'm not thinking about that awe, I'm recalling it inside me. The way my breath catches the word, feeling a slight tremble. I might even use a memory of a time when I experienced that. I call it up, so I embody the quality of awe, and when I say *"shemecha"* (Your name), I try to feel both at once—two experiences that might never have come together. I need to put in the work to explore and integrate the phrases of the liturgy.

So I practice with it until I have a moment of experiencing the unity of my own heart despite all its contradictions. That's what I have to do to bring that phrase alive. And then when I come across it in a prayer service, it will light up the memory in my body of that state. I need that in order to come to the *Shema* in my wholeness. It's an exercise, working with the inner muscles of my spiritual life.

For a chant lesson with Rabbi Shefa Gold and me, see www.MakingPrayerReal.com.

Befriending the Traditional Prayers

As you know, I believe it is better to understand the spiritual dynamics of prayer in general and engage personal prayer before learning the history and theology of the Siddur, as this may hinder rather than help a person beginning to pray. But once we understand the power of prayer, and the more we wish to claim Jewish forms of prayer for ourselves, then the more we want to know about Jewish liturgy and the more joy we receive when we study the Siddur. To that purpose, a variety of study aids are listed in the Resources section.

In part IV we discussed many attitudes and techniques to get the most out of traditional Jewish prayer. Here we offer a few additional practices to bring the Siddur to life. In each, our goal is not only to learn the informational content of the prayer, but also how to engage it in spiritual dialogue. First, we want to understand why it may have been written the way it was. Can we place ourselves into the shoes of the author? Then we seek to bridge the distance between the author's perspective and our own. Often, as in the case of nature prayers, it doesn't take much. We can appreciate a sunset in much the same way as biblical or medieval Jewish writers. Other times we need to play with the words and find our own interpretations. It helps to meet a prayer outside of a synagogue service, when we can take the time to appreciate its poetic beauty and resonate with its sounds, allusions, and ideas.

Previous practices—chant (practice 20) and Jewish blessings (practices 8–10)—have addressed the challenge of praying the traditional prayers with *kavvanah* and integrity. In addition, we offer the following practices.

PRACTICE 21

Improvise with the *Chatimah*

We know that parts of the Jewish liturgical tradition are ancient. The *Shema*, for instance, was said as part of the Temple service, minimally two thousand years ago, probably centuries earlier. So when was the first Jewish prayer book compiled? Twenty-five hundred years ago? Surprisingly, the first prayer book–like documents go back to eighth-century Babylonia, not much more than a thousand years ago. And prayer from books didn't really take off until the invention of the printing press, only five hundred years ago. So how did Jews pray for most of Jewish history? For one thing, with a lot more spontaneity than we do today.

In Talmudic times, the *chatimah*, (the "seal," the ending blessing of many Rabbinic prayers) was standardized, but each prayer leader, and sometimes each praying Jew, was expected to fill in the content of the prayer themselves. So the *chatimah* might read, "Blessed are You God, who heals the sick." This functioned like a headline, or a statement of the theme of the prayer. But it was up to the individual to put the request for the healing of loved ones or themselves into their own words. We can adopt that practice ourselves.

1. Find the weekday *Amidah* in the Siddur of your choice.
2. If you have little knowledge of these prayers, take some time to familiarize yourself with them.

3. Pray the *Amidah* as they did in Talmudic times. Identify the theme of the blessing. Pray your own words on the theme and conclude with the *chatimah,* the traditional blessing that seals the prayer.

PRACTICE 22

Ask the Siddur a Question

1. Is something on your mind as you begin to pray, such as a difficult relationship, a challenge at work, or a troubling pattern in your life?
2. Rest with this a bit, allow the thought to germinate if it needs to, and then phrase a question. I might ask, "What can I do to get on better with X?" or "Why am I struggling with Y?"
3. See if a particular phrase from the liturgy evokes an insight during the service. Perhaps a relevant thought will arise while davenning the prayers.

PRACTICE 23

Visualization

Visualization is an excellent way to infuse prayer with a sense of play and adventure. Using your imagination in prayer is also an instant *kavvanah* creator. As you focus both on the prayer and on the images you draw up from memory, your mind is too occupied to wander far.

1. Before praying, think of the images that best express your intention when saying a particular prayer.
2. As you pray the prayer, bring those images to mind.
3. If new images appear uninvited, or if you feel the need to search for another while praying, feel free to do so.

This exercise is light and playful. If you find yourself tensing up over getting the "right" image, it is getting in the way rather than helping your prayer. See chapter 18 for more on visualization and prayer.

PRACTICE 24
Dialogue a Prayer

Here are several ways to enter into a conversation with a traditional prayer.

Resonate with the Power *Pesuk* (Verse)

1. Pray through the prayer in a light, listening, receptive state of mind.
2. When a verse or a phrase resonates with you, stick with it. Roll it around your mouth and your mind. See what associations come to the fore.
3. You might specifically search for the verse that best sums up the theme of the prayer or strikes you as the most meaningful.
4. You might keep the power *pesuk* with you like a necklace for the rest of the day and see if more images or meanings come up. If you keep a journal, you might want to write about your verse.
5. Before sleep, revisit the verse and see if it has said anything further to you.
6. You might notice that on a different day, a different verse will capture your attention.

Find the Key Hebrew Roots

1. As explained by Linda Motzkin in chapter 17, it is possible to learn the basic meanings of words without understanding their specific grammatical function. You can tell, for instance, that words with the letters *shin-mem-ayin* relate to hearing and listening, even if you don't know whether a specific word is a verb or a noun.
2. Many prayers are extended wordplays on just two or three roots. Identifying them can give you deeper insight into the poetry and the message of the prayer.

3. An interlinear Siddur, where specific Hebrew words are next to their English translation, can help.

Dialogue the Verses

1. Write out the verses of a prayer, in English, on a sheet of paper, leaving a few inches of blank space after each.
2. Read the first verse and, without thinking, write a response. It might include your thoughts on the subject matter, a contemporary way of stating the same idea, a new idea that the verse provokes, a desire or vow to do something differently in your life, whatever your spirit sends forward.
3. Continue with the rest of the verses.

Learn the Story of the Prayer

Every prayer is a literary work; it has a beginning, a middle, and an end. And each verse was carefully selected. It could have been different.

See if you can enter the author's mind, as it were, by tracing the story of the prayer, verse by verse. What are the main points that the author makes with regard to the overall theme? How does the idea of a given verse in the prayer relate to the verse before and the verse after? Does the author build any dramatic or literary tension into the prayer? How might you have done it differently?

In my experience, each of these exercises is best done in the classical method of Jewish study called *chevruta*. You might notice that this Aramaic term has the same root as the Hebrew *chaver* (friend, companion). Try undertaking the above practices with a partner.

For a detailed exposition and downloadable worksheets on how to undertake the above practices with the *yotzer or* prayer (immediately after the *Barchu* in the morning liturgy), go to www.MakingPrayerReal.com.

Letting God In

A few months after I became a rabbi, a terrible tragedy occurred in my congregation in New York. An active member of the synagogue, a junior in college, was crossing the street in her university after finishing a final exam when she was struck by a car and left in critical condition for a week, with little chance of survival. The whole community was paralyzed and devastated. "What can we do?" I asked my rabbi. "Pray," he said. "Pray with all your heart. Pray as if there is no such thing as a medical certainty. Pray as if anything is possible. Pray without ambivalence. Pray without doubt in God's capacity to heal. Pray as if the whole world depends on your prayers." That Shabbat, I closed my eyes and sang out with all of my heart. Halfway through *Kabbalat Shabbat* [Friday evening service], I realized that I was no longer singing—I was praying. I was soaring. That experience changed my life. It is when I realized that prayer can be a moment in which we suspend doubt and disbelief, in which we allow ourselves to hope and to believe that anything is possible. Since then, I don't sing; I pray.

RABBI SHARON BROUS

Would an active prayer life really improve your overall life? Could it really change you for the better? I am certain that the answer is yes. This sounds arrogant but I think it's important to say.

I am certain that if an inactive person begins daily exercise, and does so with proper guidance and wisdom—if such a person turned up enough resistance on the exercise bike and did intervals rather than just move their legs while reading a magazine, if such a person worked up a sweat every day for three months—the exercise would have a profound effect.

In the same sense, I am certain that if a person does the Jewish Blessings practice as instructed for fifteen minutes every day for three months, the effect will be profound. I say this from personal experience and from the testimony of others. The method is tried and tested. There is no magic here, no risk, and no need for doubt. All that is needed is a commitment of time and effort. All that is needed is a willing heart.

We Jews, it seems, can make prayer into something complicated and difficult. But it can also be so very, very simple. I suggest and hope that you find an uncomplicated place to start, and go from there.

Becoming a prayer-person, in the end, is not about making life more complex and convoluted. It's about slowing down. It's about the (difficult but simple) decision to let God's presence become a force in our lives. It's about letting the demands of transcendence and the reality of God's love find a home in our hearts. It's about becoming the kind of person who makes godly priorities into human priorities.

Perhaps like Rabbi Sharon Brous, we will learn liturgy and discover the emotional keys that allow it to unlock our hearts. My prayer is that this book might help us to do so without a traumatic event to tear down the walls, whatever they may be, that surround our hearts.

Prayer and the Jewish People

Some Jewish leaders claim that from the viewpoint of Jewish "continuity," there is no purpose in writing a book like *Making Prayer Real*. Championing personal religiosity plays to the idea that

Judaism is private and optional rather than a matter of public duty. Besides, it is not spirituality or theology that determine whether people come to synagogue services; it is sociology. For reasons having to do with the general culture, providing bar mitzvahs for children is mandatory and Shabbat services are optional. Another book on spirituality won't change that.

There is truth to these claims, but I disagree with the conclusion.

The Jewish People, along with the Chinese, are the only first-world cultures with a continuous history over three millennia old. Back then, there was no separation between a nation's political identity and religious identity. If your country was defeated, so were its gods, and you adopted the religion of the conqueror. Unique in the West today, we Jews are a "people," a combination of national and religious elements. That's why Israel is the only country where conversion to a religion entitles you to citizenship.

The upshot is that, for better and for worse, even though Jewish identity is largely ethnic for many Jews, Jewish life in the diaspora will always center around Judaism as a religion. The main Jewish activity in the home is the Pesach Seder, and the main institution of diaspora Jewry is the synagogue. The local Jewish community center has not displaced the local temple, and no amount of bagels or Jewish comedians will displace Yom Kippur as the locus of diaspora Jewish activity.

The core activity at synagogues will always be, can only be, prayer services. The irony is that even if very few people show up, we'll never stop doing them.

It is often the case, and it can always become the case, that the social fabric of the synagogue and the development of its leadership are linked to the services. This is where the community within the larger community often gravitates, where people can express their Jewish identity best, where people find the most benefits from synagogue membership, where a real social community exists.

My point is this: if the number of people who pray regularly in synagogue were to double, the positive effect on synagogue leadership and increased activity would not be twofold, it would be five- or tenfold. If the number of people who sincerely pray were to double, with all the effects that genuine prayer would have on them, the number of volunteer leaders and the quality of their commitment would transform diaspora Jewish life. For the Jewish People, what happens in the individual hearts of Jews is much more than a matter of personal piety.

Making Prayer Real

As I wrote in the Preface, leading High Holiday services in Jackson Hole was a difficult experience for me. After five years, I came to the synagogue board with a confession. In my love and zeal for the traditional liturgy, I had imposed a far too traditional service on a community that wasn't ready for it. I was ready to change. Who, I asked, would serve on a committee with me to rethink High Holiday services? I expected a wave of excitement to sweep the people around the table. Instead, I was met with nothing. I couldn't get anyone to serve on the committee and eventually gave up. Finally, the lay cantor explained it to me.

Everyone knows what it's like to have a rabbi who's just going through the motions. They're reminded every time you lead a responsive reading in English. People aren't as concerned with the effect on them of changing this or that prayer as much as they're afraid of what will happen to you. You love the prayers and they love the fact that when you lead services, you really pray. That's what inspires others to pray.

Of course. The liturgy, the sermon, the music, the potluck lunch—it all matters. But as a prayer leader, the most important thing that I could do for my congregation was to pretend no one else was there, and really pray.

Notes

PREFACE

1. I daven at the Shtibl Minyan in Los Angeles.
2. *JPS Hebrew-English Tanakh: The Traditional Hebrew Text and the New JPS Translation* (Philadelphia: Jewish Publication Society, 1999), 1552.
3. *The Holy Scriptures* (Jerusalem: Koren Publishers, 1983), 782.

INTRODUCTION

1. For an excellent summary of the relevant science, see Jill Bolte Taylor, *My Stroke of Insight: A Brain Scientist's Personal Journey* (New York: Viking Penguin, 2008).

CHAPTER 1

1. Leon D. Stitskin, ed., *Studies in Torah Judaism* (New York: Yeshiva University, 1962), 26, 28–29.
2. Ibid., 31.
3. Midrash Rabbah, Parshat Vaetchanan 20.
4. *Caring: A Feminine Approach to Ethics and Moral Education*, 2nd ed. (Berkeley: University of California Press, 2003), chapter 2.

CHAPTER 2

1. Michael Strassfeld, "Reconstructing Prayer," *The Reconstructionist* 71, no. 1 (Fall 2006), 36.

CHAPTER 6

1. Abraham Joshua Heschel, *God in Search of Man* (New York: Farrar, Straus and Giroux, 1955), 75.

CHAPTER 11

1. Marcia Prager. *The Path of Blessing: Experiencing the Energy and Abundance of the Divine* (Woodstock, Vt.: Jewish Lights Publishing, 2000), 172.
2. Shulchan Aruch, Orach Chayyim 46:3.
3. Babylonian Talmud, Menachot 43b.

CHAPTER 15

1. Michael Strassfeld, *A Book of Life: Embracing Judaism as a Spiritual Practice* (New York: Schocken, 2002), 183.
2. Heschel, *God in Search of Man,* 46.
3. Ibid., 77
4. Ibid., 48.

CHAPTER 16

1. Jacob's second name, given to him by the mysterious man who wrestled with him on the banks of the Jabbok river (Genesis 32).

CHAPTER 18

1. Strassfeld, "Reconstructing Prayer," 36.
2. Translation from *The Prophets: A New Translation of the Holy Scriptures According to the Masoritic Text* (Philadelphia: Jewish Publication Society, 1978), 835.

Waiting for You at
www.MakingPrayerReal.com

- Video demonstrations on chant (with Rabbi Shefa Gold) and other practices, the choreography of Jewish prayer, wearing *tefillin,* and more;
- Study guides and suggestions for using *Making Prayer Real* in the classroom;
- Information on bringing Rabbi Mike Comins and *Making Prayer Real* contributors to teach the theory and practice of Jewish prayer in your community;
- Continually updated Resources list;
- New essays and additional quotes from contributors and the author;
- Additional prayer practices from contributors, the author, and readers;
- Reviews;
- Rabbi Mike Comins's teaching schedule.

To Join the Discussion

Share your ideas, questions, reflections, and inspiration on the practice of Jewish prayer at the *Making Prayer Real* page on Facebook.

Glossary

This glossary has been adapted from the *My People's Prayer Book: Traditional Prayers, Modern Commentaries* series (Jewish Lights), edited by Rabbi Lawrence A. Hoffman, PhD. For a concise explanation of the major prayers and parts of the traditional Jewish prayer service, see Chapter 16.

Aleynu (pronounced ah-LAY-noo): The first word and, therefore, the title of a major prayer compiled in the second or third century as part of the New Year (Rosh HaShanah) service, but from about the fourteenth century on, used also as part of the concluding section of every daily service. *Aleynu* means "it is incumbent upon us" and introduces the prayer's theme: our duty to praise God.

Amidah (pronounced either ah-mee-DAH or, commonly, ah-MEE-dah): One of three commonly used titles for the second of two central units in the worship service, the first being The *Shema* and Her Blessings. It is composed of a series of blessings, many of which are petitionary, except on Sabbaths and holidays, when the petitions are removed out of deference to the holiness of the day. Also called *haTefillah* (The Prayer) (Eighteen) and *Sh'moneh Esreh*. *Amidah* means "standing" and refers to the fact that the prayer is said standing up.

Baal Shem Tov (1698–1760): Rabbi Israel ben Eliezer, the founder of Hasidism, often called the Baal Shem Tov (Master of the Good Name). He led a popular revolution in Eastern European Jewish communities that emphasized personal piety and joyful Jewish practice.

Birchot ha-Shachar (pronounced beer-KHOT hah-SHAH-khar): Literally, "Morning Blessings," the title of the first large section in the morning prayer regimen of Judaism; originally said privately upon arising in the morning, but now customarily recited immediately upon arriving at the synagogue. It is composed primarily of benedictions thanking God for the everyday gifts of health and wholeness, as well as study sections taken from the Bible and Rabbinic literature.

Barchu (pronounced bah-r'-KHOO or, commonly, BOH-r'khoo): The first word and, therefore, the title of the formal call to prayer with which the section called The *Shema* and Her Blessings begins. *Barchu* means "praise," and it introduces the invitation to the assembled congregation to praise God.

Buber, Martin (1878–1965): An Austrian-born Jewish thinker best known for his philosophy of dialogue, based on the distinction between I-Thou and I-It relationships. His wide range of work influenced German letters, philosophy, psychology, and Jewish studies.

Chiut (pronounced khee-OOT): The Hasidic name for the flow of divine energy, the emanation of God into the world, popularized by earlier Jewish mystics (Kabbalah).

Davennen (pronounced DAH-vehn-ehn): This Yiddush term for prayer has been Yinglishized into "daven," "davenners," "davenned," "davenning," and more.

Devekut (pronounced DEH-veh-koot): A Hebrew word for "bonding" or "cleaving;" it became the Hasidic term for keeping the awareness of God constant in all activities.

Hasidism (Hasidic [adj.]): The Hasidic movement, started by Rabbi Israel ben Eliezer, (also known as the Baal Shem Tov), was a response to persecution and the scholastic Jewish culture in eighteenth-century Eastern Europe. Hasidism reinterpreted and revitalized Jewish mystical belief and emphasized the role of "rebbes," rabbinical leaders. Hasidism promoted spiritual awareness and joy in Jewish practice.

Heschel, Abraham Joshua (1907–1972): One of the leading Jewish theologians and Jewish philosophers of the twentieth century. The heir of two rabbinical families, he was raised in Poland and studied at the University of Berlin. Hebrew Union College rescued him from the Nazis in 1939, and after five years in Cincinnati, he moved to New York and taught at the Jewish Theological Seminary until his death. Known for his poetic writing style, he became a spiritual leader of American Jewry with books on Jewish theology and prayer, and his beloved short classic, *The Sabbath*. An early opponent of the Vietnam War, he marched into Selma at the shoulder of Dr. Martin Luther King Jr. in 1965.

Hitbodedut (pronounced HEET-boh-d'DOOT): Literally "to be alone"; the name of the practice popularized by Rabbi Nachman of Breslov, where a person finds a place of solitude, particularly in nature, and speaks directly to God. Other solitary spiritual practices, such as meditation and personal prayer, can also fall under the rubric of *hitbodedut*.

Kabbalah (pronounced kah-bah-LAH, or, commonly, kah-BAH-lah): A general term for Jewish mysticism, but used properly for a specific mystical doctrine that began in western Europe in the eleventh or twelfth century; was recorded in the Zohar in the thirteenth century; and then was further elaborated, especially in the Land of Israel (in Safed), in the sixteenth century. From a Hebrew word meaning "to receive" or "to welcome" and, secondarily, "tradition," implying the receiving of tradition from one's past.

Kaddish (pronounced kah-DEESH, or, more commonly, KAH-dish): One of several prayers from a Hebrew word meaning "holy," and therefore the name given to a prayer affirming God's holiness. This prayer was composed in the first century but later found its way into the service in several forms, including one known as the Mourners' Kaddish and used as a mourning prayer.

Kavvanah (pronounced kah-vah-NAH): From a word meaning "to direct," used to denote the state of directing one's words and thoughts sincerely to God, as opposed to the rote recitation of prayer.

Kedushah (pronounced k'-doo-SHAH, or, commonly, k'-DOO-shah): From the Hebrew word meaning "holy," and one of several prayers from the first or second century occurring in several places and versions, all of which have in common the citing of Isaiah 6:3: *kadosh, kadosh, kadosh* ... (Holy, holy, holy is the Lord of hosts. The whole earth is full of His glory).

Ma'ariv (pronounced mah-ah-REEV, or, commonly, MAH-ah-reev): From the Hebrew word *erev* (pronounced EH-rev), meaning "evening"; one of two titles used for the evening worship service (also called *Arevit*).

Mi Chamocha (pronounced MEE Khah-MOH-khah): A verse from the Song of the Sea (Exodus 15:11) celebrating the crossing of the Red Sea, this prayer celebrates God's redemptive powers. It is the signature line of the prayers connecting the two major units of Jewish liturgy, the *Shema* and the *Amidah*.

Mi Sheberach (pronounced, commonly, MEE sheh-BAY-rakh): Prayer for healing. A standard blessing beginning, "May the One who blessed [our ancestors] ... ," which could be adapted for any number of instances. This set of prayers requesting God's blessing on those who receive an *aliyah* to the Torah or on their family members is perhaps the best-known addition to the service. When mentioned on its own, the reference is usually to the blessing for healing.

Midrash (pronounced meed-RAHSH, or, commonly, MID-rahsh): From a Hebrew word meaning "to ferret out the meaning of a text," and therefore a Rabbinic interpretation of a biblical word or verse. By extension, a body of Rabbinic literature that offers classical interpretations of the Bible.

Minchah (pronounced meen-CHAH, or, more commonly, MIN-chah): Originally the name of a type of sacrifice, then the word for a sacrifice offered during the afternoon, and now the name for the afternoon synagogue service usually scheduled just before nightfall. *Minchah* means "afternoon."

Minyan (pronounced meen-YAHN, or, commonly, MIN-y'n): A quorum of ten, the minimum number of people required for certain prayers. Minyan comes from the word meaning "to count."

Mitzvah (pronounced meetz-VAH, or, commonly, MITZ-vah; plural, *mitzvot*, pronounced meetz-VOTE): A Hebrew word used commonly to mean "good deed" but in the more technical sense denoting any commandment from God, and therefore, by extension, what God wants us to do. Reciting the *Shema* morning and evening, for instance, is a mitzvah.

Mochin d'gadlut (pronounced moh-KHEEN d'gahd-LOOT): An Aramaic, Hasidic term for "expanded consciousness." It refers to the open, mature, listening, caring state of awareness that is considered in itself an experience of divine presence. Contrasted to *mochin d'katnut* (small consciousness), when one is self-occupied and looking out for oneself, the term is connected to *devekut* (see above).

Musaf (pronounced moo-SAHF, or, commonly, MOO-sahf): The Hebrew word meaning "extra" or "added," and therefore the title of the additional sacrifice that was offered in the Temple on Shabbat and holy days. It is now the name given to an added service of worship appended to the morning service on those days.

Nachman of Breslov, Rabbi (1772–1810): A grandson of the Baal Shem Tov and the founder of the Breslov Hasidic dynasty. So beloved, his followers refused to appoint another rabbi in his stead when he died without an heir. He is famous for popularizing *hitbodedut* as the practice of speaking directly to God.

Pesukei d'Zimra (pronounced p'-soo-KAY d'-zeem-RAH, or, commonly, p'-SOO-kay d'-ZIM-rah): Literally, "verses of song," and therefore the title of a lengthy set of opening morning prayers that contain psalms and songs, and serve as spiritual preparation prior to the official call to prayer.

Refuah shleimah (pronounced r'-foo-AH sh'lay-MAH, or, commonly, r'-FOO-ah sh'LAY-mah): Literally, "a complete healing," and the title of the eighth blessing of the daily *Amidah*, a petition for healing.

Shacharit (pronounced shah-khah-REET, or, commonly, SHAH-khah-reet): The name given to the morning worship service; from the Hebrew word *shachar* (SHAH-khar), meaning "morning."

Schachter-Shalomi, Rabbi Zalman (b. 1924): Commonly known as Reb Zalman. One of the major founders of the Jewish Renewal movement. Raised in Vienna, he fled to the U.S. in 1941. Ordained a Chabad rabbi, he left Orthodoxy in the late 1960s to lead prayer groups and teach the path that became the Jewish Renewal movement. His innovative teachings helped to popularize Jewish mysticism in North America. He is the spiritual mentor of many of the contributors to this book.

Shechinah (pronounced sh'-khee-NAH or, popularly, sh-KHEE-nah): Both a Talmudic and (later) mystical term for the immanent, feminine aspect of God that is experienced by human beings in this world. From the same root as *mishkan* (the Tabernacle), meaning to "inhabit" or "dwell."

Shema (pronounced sh'-MAH): The central prayer in the first of the two main units in the worship service, the second being the *Amidah* (see *Amidah*). The *Shema* comprises three citations from the Bible, and the larger unit in which it is embedded (called The *Shema* and Her Blessings) is composed of a formal call to prayer (see *Barchu*) and a series of blessings on the theological themes that, together with the *Shema*, constitute a liturgical creed of faith. *Shema*, meaning "hear," is the first word of the first line of the first biblical citation, "Hear O Israel, Adonai is our God; Adonai is One," which is the paradigmatic statement of Jewish faith, the Jews' absolute commitment to the presence of a single and unique God in time and space.

Siddur (pronounced see-DURE, or, commonly, SIH-d'r): From the Hebrew word *seder,* meaning "order," and by extension, the name given to the "order of prayers," or prayer book.

Tachanun (pronounced TAH-khah-noon): A Hebrew word meaning "supplications," and by extension, the title of the large unit of prayer that follows the *Amidah* and that is largely supplicatory in character.

Tallit (pronounced tah-LEET; plural: *tallitot,* pronounced tah-lee-TOTE): The prayer shawl equipped with tassels on each corner, and generally worn during the morning (*Shacharit*) and additional (*Musaf*) synagogue services.

Talmud (pronounced tahl-MOOD, or, more commonly, TAHL-m'd): The name given to each of two great compendia of Jewish law and lore compiled over several centuries, and ever since, the literary core of the rabbinic heritage. The *Talmud Yerushalmi* (pronounced y'-roo-SHAHL-mee), the "Jerusalem Talmud," is earlier, a product of the Land of Israel generally dated about 400 CE. The better-known *Talmud Bavli* (pronounced BAHV-lee), or "Babylonian Talmud," took shape in Babylonia (present-day Iraq) and is traditionally dated about 550 CE. When people say "the"

Talmud without specifying which one they mean, they are referring to the Babylonian version. Talmud means "teaching."

Tetragrammaton: The technical term for the four-letter name of God that appears in the Bible. Treating it as sacred, Jews stopped pronouncing it centuries ago, so that the actual pronunciation has been lost. Instead of reading it according to its letters, it is replaced in speech by the alternative name of God, Adonai.

Tefillah (pronounced t'-fee-LAH, or, commonly, t'-FEE-lah): A Hebrew word meaning "prayer" but used technically to mean a specific prayer, namely, the second of the two main units in the worship service. It is known also as the *Amidah* or the *Sh'moneh Esreh* (see *Amidah*). Also the title of the sixteenth blessing of the *Amidah*, a petition for God to accept our prayer.

Tefillin (pronounced t'-FIH-lin, or, sometimes, t'-fee-LEEN): Two cube-shaped black boxes containing biblical quotations (Exodus 13:1–10; 13:11–16; Deuteronomy 6:4–9 and 11:13–21) and affixed by means of attached leather straps to the forehead and left arm (right arm for left-handed people) during morning prayer.

Teshuvah (pronounced t'shoo-VAH, or, commonly t'SHOO-vah): Literally, "repentance," and the title of the fifth blessing in the daily *Amidah*, a petition by worshipers that they successfully turn to God in heartfelt repentance.

Resources

This eclectic list of resources reflects my particular knowledge and experience. It is by no means exhaustive. Further resources, including your suggestions, are listed at www.MakingPrayerReal.com. Website addresses of organizations are not listed, as they often change and they are easily attained with any Internet search engine.

LEARNING TO PRAY

Where can you learn to pray in Jewish context? In North America, the following national programs specialize in teaching the art of personal and communal prayer. If you are looking for a place to begin or to revitalize your prayer life, try one of these excellent programs.

Awakened Heart Project
See below under "Silence and Meditation."

C-Deep
The Center for Devotional, Energy & Ecstatic Practice sponsors Rabbi Shefa Gold's retreats and chant workshops around the country (a schedule can be found on their website), including the Kol Zimra Chant Leadership Training Program. In addition to her numerous CDs, you will find recordings of Rabbi Gold's latest chants and chanting practices (including lyrics and practice instructions) on her website.

Davennen' Leadership Training Institute
Rabbis Marcia Prager and Shawn Zevit teach participants the fine art of davenning, and leading davenning, in this cutting-edge program.

Elat Chayyim, The Jewish Spiritual Retreat Center
The groundbreaking retreat center provides a home for innovative, in-depth spiritual learning in all areas of Jewish practice.

The Institute for Jewish Spirituality
The IJS offers programs to deepen Jewish practice through contemplative prayer, meditation, yoga, chant, and more. In addition to annual retreats for laypeople, their Vetaher Libeynu: Curriculum for Adult Jewish Spiritual Growth is available for use in synagogues. Ask your clergy to teach it in your community. Their web site also features instruction for practice in

podcasts and other resources. One of their latest initiatives is "The Prayer Project" (www.ijs-online.org/prayer.php).

Rabbinical Assembly of Canada (Conservative) Institute for Jewish Liturgy and School for Shamashim

This two-month program (one-month sessions over consecutive summers) focuses on learning the skills to lead traditional davenning, so it is not for beginners. But it is one of the few opportunities for laypeople to immerse themselves in the study and practice of daily prayer over a significant period of time.

Much of the action in Jewish spiritual circles is regional and local. In any large city, and in plenty of not-so-large communities, you are likely to find synagogues, prayer groups, and retreat centers offering prayer services, retreats, classes, and beginner's prayer groups. Check your local Jewish community websites and newspapers. For a continually updated list of regional programs, go to www.MakingPrayerReal.com.

PLACES TO PRAY

The following conferences serve as hothouses for inspiring prayer. Often, courses in various facets of Jewish prayer are offered as well.

Aleph Kallah

The biennial conference of the Jewish Renewal movement, offering week-long classes and workshops in Jewish spirituality, features many of the contributors to this book.

Limmud

Spreading out from England, where two thousand people gather together each year to study, pray, and celebrate over winter break, Limmud offers trans-denominational conferences around the world.

National Havurah Committee Summer Institute

Daily prayer in the context of weeklong classes and workshops on a variety of Jewish subjects.

Ruach Ha'aretz

Jewish spirituality retreats in the style of Jewish Renewal across North America, under the direction of Rabbis Nadya and Victor Gross.

URJ Kallah

This annual Union of Reform Judaism conference features daily davenning around in-depth classes from top scholars.

There are many books, websites, and CDs, as well as additional programs and conferences, that can support our prayer lives. My favorites are organized below according to the topics in *Making Prayer Real.*

YEARNING
Books

Not surprisingly, yearning is the realm of poets. The ability of Jehuda Halevi, Rainer Maria Rilke, and Rumi (one Jew, one Christian, one Muslim) to articulate their passion for God is unsurpassed. I've also included the works of two contemporary poets who write what I think of as contemporary psalms.

Barks, Coleman. *The Essential Rumi.* New York: HarperCollins, 1995.

Brody, Heinrich. *Selected Poems of Jehudah Halevi.* Philadelphia: Jewish Publication Society, 1974.

Oliver, Mary. *House of Light.* Boston: Beacon Press, 1990.

Rilke, Rainer Maria. *Rilke's Book of Hours: Love Poems to God.* Trans. Anita Barrows and Joanna Macy. New York: Riverhead Books, 1996.

Whyte, David. *Fire in the Earth.* Langley, Wash.: Many Rivers Press, 2002.

GRATITUDE
Books

The title of Ryan's little gem of a book has become cliché. The message is not.

Ryan, M. J. *Attitudes of Gratitude.* New York: MJF Books, 1999.

Steindl-Rast, David. *Gratefulness: The Heart of Prayer.* Mahwah, N.J.: Paulist Press, 1984.

BLESSINGS
Books

In addition to Marcia Prager's contemporary classic on the spiritual wisdom encoded in Jewish blessings, you will find a comprehensive treatment on the how and why of blessings in my *A Wild Faith: Jewish Ways into Wilderness, Wilderness Ways into Judaism* (Jewish Lights), chapters 8 and 9.

Prager, Marcia. *The Path of Blessing: Experiencing the Energy and Abundance of the Divine.* Woodstock, Vt.: Jewish Lights Publishing, 2003.

ENGAGING THE BODY
Books

Jay Michaelson offers a comprehensive treatment of Jewish spiritual practice that emphasizes the physical dimensions of the commandments. Tamar Frankiel and Judy Greenfeld's contributions bring spirit, mind, and body together in prayer.

Frankiel, Tamar, and Judy Greenfeld. *Entering the Temple of Dreams: Jewish Prayers, Movements and Meditations for the End of the Day.* Woodstock, Vt.: Jewish Lights Publishing, 2000.
———. *Minding the Temple of the Soul: Balancing Body, Mind, and Spirit through Traditional Jewish Prayer, Movement, and Meditation.* Woodstock, Vt.: Jewish Lights Publishing, 1997.
Michaelson, Jay. *God in Your Body: Kabbalah, Mindfulness and Embodied Spiritual Practice.* Woodstock, Vt.: Jewish Lights Publishing, 2007.

Websites
www.otiyot.com

At Otiyot Hayyot, tai chi master Yehudit Goldfarb offers a series of gentle, flowing movements based on the shapes of the Hebrew letters.

NATURE
Books

As I hope you have found in reading *Making Prayer Real*, bringing wilderness into your spiritual practice is a highly effective way of enriching your prayer life. The insights gathered in the natural world are important everywhere. In my thoroughly biased opinion, the following two books have much to offer any spiritual seeker. (Hiking boots are not required to read them.)

Comins, Mike. *A Wild Faith: Jewish Ways into Wilderness, Wilderness Ways into Judaism.* Woodstock, Vt.: Jewish Lights Publishing, 2007.
Korngold, Jamie S. *God in the Wilderness.* New York: Doubleday Religion, 2007.

Programs
Adventure Rabbi, Rabbi Jamie Korngold

The Adventure Rabbi program's three rabbis offer the Adventure Bar and Bat Mitzvah class and holiday retreats (such as Passover in Moab, Utah), as well as Shabbat services on skis (in the winter) or on hiking trails (in the summer). Based in Boulder, Colorado, Adventure Rabbi attracts singles, couples, and families with children from around the country.

Hazon Food Conference, Nigel Savage
The annual festival of Jewish environmental learning and activism, including earth-centered ritual, prayer, and Shabbat observance.

Institute for Jewish Wilderness Spirituality, Rabbi Mike Comins
IJeWS offers leadership training programs for Jewish professionals and wilderness guides.

TorahTrek Spiritual Wilderness Adventures, Rabbi Mike Comins
TorahTrek pushes the envelope of Jewish spiritual practice in wilderness, mainly in North America.

Wilderness Torah, Zelig Golden
Holiday retreats, Jewish Vision Quest, and other programs in the natural world from the Bay Area of California.

CHANT
Along with the following resources, a video lesson in chant with Rabbis Shefa Gold and Mike Comins is available at www.MakingPrayerReal.com.

Books
Gold, Shefa. "That This Song May Be a Witness: The Power of Chant." In *Meditation from the Heart of Judaism: Today's Teachers Share Their Practices, Techniques, and Faith*, ed. Avram Davis. Woodstock, Vt.: Jewish Lights Publishing, 1999.
Hernandez, Ana. *The Sacred Art of Chant: Preparing to Practice.* Woodstock, Vt.: SkyLight Paths Publishing, 2005.

Programs
See Rabbi Shefa Gold's *C-Deep* above in "Learning to Pray."

YOGA
While Yoga, like chant, is best learned with a qualified teacher, the following resources support a lively, Jewish prayer practice.

Books
Bloomfield, Diane. *Torah Yoga: Experiencing Jewish Wisdom through Classic Postures.* San Francisco: Jossey-Bass, 2004.
Rapp, Steven A. *Aleph-Bet Yoga: Embodying the Hebrew Letters for Physical and Spiritual Well-Being.* Woodstock, Vt.: Jewish Lights Publishing, 2002.

Websites

www.TorahYoga.com
Meet Diane Bloomfield, the first woman to take the intersection of Torah and yoga public. The site includes a directory of teachers and free video lessons.

www.YogaMosaic.org
An international directory of Jewish yoga teachers and events.

CDs

Klotz, Myriam. *Preparing the Heart: Yoga for Jewish Spiritual Practice.* Institute for Jewish Spirituality.
————. *In All Your Ways Know God: Beginning Yoga On and Off the Mat.* Institute for Jewish Spirituality.

SILENCE AND MEDITATION
Books

This list includes a collection of essays from leading practitioners in the field (Davis), the most complete collection of Jewish meditation practices from a particularly insightful spiritual teacher and skilled writer (Cooper), and a beloved classic (Kaplan). It also includes an excellent introduction for beginners (Fink) and a comprehensive approach to the theology and practice of Jewish blessings and meditation (Roth). Something for everyone.

Cooper, David A. *The Handbook of Jewish Meditation Practices: A Guide for Enriching the Sabbath and Other Days of Your Life.* Woodstock, Vt.: Jewish Lights Publishing, 2000.
Davis, Avram, ed. *Meditation from the Heart of Judaism: Today's Teachers Share Their Practices, Techniques, and Faith.* Woodstock, Vt.: Jewish Lights Publishing, 1999.
Fink, Nan. *Discovering Jewish Meditation: Instruction and Guidance for Learning an Ancient Spiritual Practice.* Woodstock, Vt.: Jewish Lights Publishing, 1999.
Kaplan, Aryeh. *Jewish Meditation: A Practical Guide.* New York: Schocken, 1995.
Roth, Jeff. *Jewish Meditation Practices for Everyday Life: Awakening Your Heart, Connecting with God.* Woodstock, Vt.: Jewish Lights Publishing, 2009.

Program and Website

The Awakened Heart Project for Contemplative Judaism, Rabbi Jeff Roth
In addition to articles, podcasts, and practice instructions from Rabbi Jeff Roth and friends on the website, Awakened Heart offers one-day to multi-week meditation and prayer retreats.

CDs

Peltz Weinberg, Sheila. *Preparing the Heart: Meditation for Jewish Spiritual Practice.* Institute for Jewish Spirituality.

Firestone, Tirzah. *The Women's Kabbalah: Ecstatic Meditation CD Program.* Sounds True Tapes.

CULTIVATING YOUR PERSONAL PRAYER VOICE
Books

Precious little has been written in the contemporary Jewish world on spontaneous, personal prayer, but the books we have are superb. Aryeh Ben David's (unfortunately) little-known book provided inspiration for this one. He takes your hand and walks with you down the path of deep introspection before God through prayer. For inspiration, I turn to two artists of personal prayer. Marcia Falk's book is a groundbreaking collection of innovative blessings and poetic, new translations of traditional blessings. After a wonderful introduction on the art of personal prayer, Naomi Levy demonstrates her artistry with prayers on all facets of life. The bookshelf of useful volumes from the non-Jewish world is long and deep. You will find my favorites listed on the *Making Prayer Real* website.

Ben David, Aryeh. *The Godfile: 10 Approaches to Personalizing Prayer.* Jerusalem: Devora Publishing, 2007.

Falk, Marcia. *The Book of Blessings.* Boston: Beacon Press, 1999.

Levy, Naomi. *Talking to God: Personal Prayers for Times of Joy, Sadness, Struggle, and Celebration.* New York: Doubleday, 2002.

THE POWER OF YOU
Books

Start with Buber's classic, *I and Thou,* and proceed from there. The volumes of commentary on Buber's book could fill many a bookshelf. My favorites are listed on the *Making Prayer Real* website. Rabbi Lawrence Kushner not only convinced me that my mind could let my heart experience God, he also helped me to realize that I had been feeling God in my life all along. Here are three of his many books; I suggest reading them in the order they appear.

Buber, Martin. *I and Thou.* London: Hesperides Press, 2008.

Kushner, Lawrence. *God Was in This Place & I, i Did Not Know: Finding Self, Spirituality and Ultimate Meaning.* Woodstock, Vt.: Jewish Lights Publishing, 1993.

————. *The River of Light: Jewish Mystical Awareness*. Woodstock, Vt.: Jewish Lights Publishing, 1981, 1990.

————. *The Way Into Jewish Mystical Tradition*. Woodstock, Vt.: Jewish Lights Publishing, 2001.

TESHUVAH (REPENTANCE)

Books

From the revered, late leader of Modern Orthodox Judaism in North America, Rabbi Joseph Dov Soloveitchik's treatise on *teshuvah* stands alone. Solomon Schimmel presents a scholarly and moving account of the intricacies of *teshuvah* in Judaism, Christianity, and Islam. Both are sometimes difficult but worthwhile reads. Ira Stone and Alan Morinis describe the nitty-gritty of inculcating the moral virtues through Mussar practice.

Morinis, Alan. *Everyday Holiness: The Jewish Spiritual Path of Mussar*. Boston: Trumpeter, 2007.

Newman, Louis E. *Repentance: The Meaning and Practice of Teshuvah*. Woodstock, Vt.: Jewish Lights Publishing, 2010.

Peli, Pinchas H. *On Repentance: The Thought and Oral Discourses of Rabbi Joseph Dov Soloveitchik*. Northvale, N.J.: Jason Aronson, 1996.

Schimmel, Solomon. *Wounds Not Healed By Time: The Power of Repentance and Forgiveness*. Oxford: Oxford University Press, 2002.

Stone, Ira. *A Responsible Life: The Spiritual Path of Mussar*. New York: Aviv Press, 2006.

RECOVERY

Books

The following books bring Judaism to bear on Twelve-Step recovery programs and the psychological roots of addiction.

Olitzky, Kerry M., and Stuart Copans. *Twelve Jewish Steps to Recovery*, 2nd ed.: *A Personal Guide to Turning from Alcoholism and Other Addictions*. Woodstock, Vt.: Jewish Lights Publishing, 2009.

Shapiro, Rami. *Recovery—the Sacred Art: The Twelve Steps as Spiritual Practice*. Woodstock, Vt.: SkyLight Paths, 2009.

Twerski, Abraham J. *Addictive Thinking: Understanding Self-Deception*, 2nd ed. Center City, Minn.: Hazelden, 1997.

————. *The Spiritual Self: Reflections on Recovery and God*. Center City, Minn.: Hazelden, 2000.

Programs

JACS: Jewish Alcoholics, Chemically Dependent Persons and Significant Others
Since 1978 JACS has driven a new self help/mutual support movement of
recovering Jewish people empowering themselves, talking to their communities and advocating for services on behalf of addicted Jews and families.

COPING WITH LOSS: HEALING
Books

These volumes explore the Jewish and psychological dimensions of dealing with illness and healing from loss with great empathy and skill. Naomi
Levy's moving memoir recounts the senseless murder of her father, and her
spiritual path since.

Frankel, Estelle. *Sacred Therapy: Jewish Spiritual Teachings on Emotional
   Healing and Inner Wholeness.* Boston: Shambhala, 2003.
Levy, Naomi. *To Begin Again: The Journey Toward Comfort, Strength, and
   Faith in Difficult Times.* New York: Alfred A. Knopf, 1998.
Spitz, Elie Kaplan. *Healing from Despair: Choosing Wholeness in a Broken
   World.* Woodstock, Vt.: Jewish Lights Publishing, 2008.
Wolpe, David J. *Making Loss Matter: Creating Meaning in Difficult Times.*
   New York: Riverhead Trade, 2000

Programs

National Center for Jewish Healing
The National Center for Jewish Healing helps communities better meet the
spiritual needs of Jews living with illness, loss, and other significant life
challenges. They offer consultation, resource material, publications, training, and referrals to community resources. Most important, you will find
links to the many **regional Jewish healing centers** and programs
throughout North America.

COPING WITH LOSS: MOURNING
Books

The following three books walk the mourner through the grieving process.
Anne Brener's best-selling volume offers numerous spiritual practices to
cope with the loss of a loved one.

Brener, Anne. *Mourning and Mitzvah: A Guided Journal for Walking the
   Mourner's Path through Grief to Healing*, 2nd ed. Woodstock, Vt.: Jewish
   Lights Publishing, 2001.

Olitzky, Kerry M. *Jewish Paths toward Healing and Wholeness: A Personal Guide to Dealing with Suffering.* Woodstock, Vt.: Jewish Lights Publishing, 2001.

Wolfson, Ron. *A Time To Mourn, a Time to Comfort: A Guide to Jewish Bereavement,* 2nd ed. Woodstock, Vt.: Jewish Lights Publishing, 2005.

THE SPIRITUAL DYNAMICS OF THE SIDDUR
Books

The resources here include Abraham Joshua Heschel's not-to-be-missed classic text on Jewish prayer, Lawrence Hoffman's relevant and readable general introduction to Jewish prayer, and Yitzhak Buxbaum's practical advice on praying with passion and *kavvanah*. If you can find it in your local Jewish library, Jakob Petuchowski's book is an excellent introduction to the issues of traditional Jewish prayer, followed by a collection of essays from the leading spiritual thinkers of the previous generation. The books by Barry Holtz, Jonathan Slater, and Michael Strassfeld have very useful chapters on prayer. The best single essay on Jewish prayer I've ever read, Heschel's "On Prayer," is included in Petuchowski and Susannah Heschel's anthology.

Buxbaum, Yitzhak. *Real Davvening: Jewish Prayer as a Spiritual Practice and a Form of Meditation for Beginning and Experienced Davveners.* The Jewish Spirit Booklet Series, 1996.

Heschel, Abraham Joshua. *Man's Quest For God.* Santa Fe, N.M.: Aurora Press, 1998.

———. "On Prayer." In *Moral Grandeur and Spiritual Audacity: Essays, Abraham Joshua Heschel.* Susannah Heschel, ed. (New York: Noonday Press, 1996).

Hoffman, Lawrence A. *The Way Into Jewish Prayer.* Woodstock, Vt.: Jewish Lights Publishing, 2000.

Holtz, Barry W. *Finding Our Way: Jewish Texts and the Lives We Live Today.* New York: Schocken, 1990.

Petuchowski, Jakob J. *Understanding Jewish Prayer.* New York: Ktav, 1976.

Slater, Jonathan. *Mindful Jewish Living: Compassionate Practice.* New York: Aviv Press, 2004.

Strassfeld, Michael. *A Book of Life: Embracing Judaism as a Spiritual Practice.* Woodstock, Vt.: Jewish Lights Publishing, 2006.

Hasidic Wisdom
Books
The Hasidic movement's revitalization of Jewish prayer continues to this day. Yitzhak Buxbaum has written the definitive collection of the practical techniques created and used by Hasidic rabbis. Two anthologies—one by Barry Holtz and Art Green, the other by Lawrence Kushner and Nehemia Polen—distill the wisdom of Hasidism on prayer for the contemporary reader. Finally, a resource to learn directly from the contemporary neo-Hasidic master, Rabbi Zalman Schachter-Shalomi, who has profoundly influenced the current generation of Jewish spiritual teachers.

Buxbaum, Yitzhak. *Jewish Spiritual Practices.* Lanham, Md.: Rowman and Littlefield, 1999.

Green, Arthur, and Barry W. Holtz. *Your Word Is Fire: The Hasidic Masters on Contemplative Prayer.* Woodstock, Vt.: Jewish Lights, 1993.

Kushner, Lawrence, and Nehemia Polen. *Filling Words with Light: Hasidic and Mystical Reflections on Jewish Prayer.* Woodstock, Vt.: Jewish Lights, 2004.

Schachter-Shalomi, Zalman. *Jewish with Feeling: A Guide to Meaningful Jewish Practice.* New York: Riverhead Books, 2005.

Websites
www.NeoHasid.org
Rabbi David Seidenberg's earth-based neo-Hasidic teachings, prayers, and songs.

Learning the Siddur
Check your local synagogue or Jewish community center for classes. Many large cities host a Jewish college or seminary. Usually you will find classes to learn Hebrew and liturgy. Hebrew College (Boston) and Siegal College of Judaic Studies (Cleveland) have distance learning programs. Many Jewish learning institutions publish podcasts on Jewish subjects, including prayer and liturgy. In particular, look for American Jewish University, The Jewish Theological Seminary of America, The Skirball Center for Adult Jewish Learning at Temple Emanu-El, and the Pardes Institute in Jerusalem.

Books
Evelyn Garfiel, Rueven Hammer, and Adin Steinsaltz offer one-volume introductions to the history and theology of Jewish liturgy. Joel Lurie Grishaver's book is the best source for learning the narrative context of the traditional Jewish prayers. Jewish Lights Publishing's *My People's Prayer Book: Traditional Prayers, Modern Commentaries*, in ten volumes, edited

by Rabbi Lawrence A. Hoffman, PhD, is the gold standard for Siddur study in our generation. While Hoffman provides the macro of Siddur history, structure, and development, commentaries on each prayer from multiple contributors give us the micro, including Hebrew usage, traditional Jewish law and practice, Hasidic interpretations, liberal practice, feminist understanding, and more. This National Jewish Book Award winner looks intimidating if you place all the volumes together, but the series is, in fact, readable and informative for layperson and rabbi alike. The more serious you are about Jewish prayer, the more volumes will appear on your bookshelf.

In keeping with Rabbi Zalman M. Schachter-Shalomi's advice in chapter 20, acquiring and befriending a pocket-size Siddur is highly recommended. This is easier with an all-Hebrew Siddur, as English translation adds bulk. Various Israeli editions are available from across the ideological spectrum. As for English/Hebrew pocket prayer books, many are available (American ultra-Orthodox *Artscroll*, British Orthodox *Koren Sacks*, American Conservative *Sim Shalom*, British Reform *Forms of Prayer*, and American Reform *Mishkan T'filah*).

Garfiel, Evelyn. *Service of the Heart: A Guide to the Jewish Prayer Book.* Northvale, N.J.: Jason Aronson, 1994, 1989.

Grishaver, Joel Lurie. *Stories We Pray: Windows into the Inner-Workings of Jewish Prayer.* Los Angeles: Torah Aura Productions, 2010.

Hammer, Rueven. *Entering Jewish Prayer.* New York: Schocken Books, 1994.

Hoffman, Lawrence A. *My People's Prayer Book: Traditional Prayers, Modern Commentaries*, Vols. 1–10. Woodstock, Vt.: Jewish Lights Publishing, 1997–2007.

> Vol. 1—*The Sh'ma and Its Blessings.* Woodstock, Vt.: Jewish Lights Publishing, 1997.
>
> Vol. 2—*The Amidah.* Woodstock, Vt.: Jewish Lights Publishing, 1998.
>
> Vol. 3—*P'sukei D'zimrah (Morning Psalms).* Woodstock, Vt.: Jewish Lights Publishing, 1999.
>
> Vol. 4—*Seder K'riat Hatorah (The Torah Service).* Woodstock, Vt.: Jewish Lights Publishing, 2000.
>
> Vol. 5—*Birkhot Hashachar (Morning Blessings).* Woodstock, Vt.: Jewish Lights Publishing, 2001.
>
> Vol. 6—*Tachanun and Concluding Prayers.* Woodstock, Vt.: Jewish Lights Publishing, 2002.
>
> Vol. 7—*Shabbat at Home.* Woodstock, Vt.: Jewish Lights Publishing, 2004.
>
> Vol. 8—*Kabbalat Shabbat (Welcoming Shabbat in the Synagogue).* Woodstock, Vt.: Jewish Lights Publishing, 2005.

Vol. 9—*Welcoming the Night: Minchah and Ma'ariv (Afternoon and Evening Prayer)*. Woodstock, Vt.: Jewish Lights Publishing, 2005.

Vol. 10—*Shabbat Morning: Shacharit and Musaf (Morning and Additional Services)*. Woodstock, Vt.: Jewish Lights Publishing, 2007.

Steinsaltz, Adin. *A Guide to Jewish Prayer*. New York: Schocken Books, 2000.

Programs

Several week-long programs teach the skills involved in leading services and give participants a chance to pray daily in a spirited, devotional atmosphere. The Union of Reform Judaism (American) offers the *Had'rachah Seminar* for aspiring prayer service leaders and *Hava Nashira* for songleaders. United Synagogue (American Conservative) offers *Imun* for future davenning leaders.

Websites

www.myjewishlearning.com

Basic explanations and numerous essays on all facets of Jewish liturgy.

www.urj.org/learning/torah/ten

The Union for Reform Judaism offers a daily e-mail learning program on various facets of Jewish life, including, "Delving into Liturgy."

CDs

Kimelman, Reuven, and Sergiu S. Simmel. *The Hidden Poetry of the Jewish Prayerbook: The What, How and Why of Jewish Liturgy*. Our Learning Company, 2005.

OVERCOMING THE HEBREW BARRIER

Books

Linda Motzkin has participated in the writing of prayerbook Hebrew primers three times in the last two decades. While all are good, she considers her latest effort from the URJ Press the most effective for busy adults. It puts into practice the principles she outlined in chapter 17. Her project with Simon Resnikoff is a comprehensive biblical Hebrew grammar, used in some colleges and seminaries as a year-long introduction to classical Hebrew. While it requires time and dedication, it is a good resource for those who want to learn more than select pieces of Hebrew grammar; it contains full paradigms and conjugations, written in nontechnical language. Edith Samuel's book, an excellent companion to the work of Linda Motzkin, brings together on one page the many words derived from the same Hebrew root that you will encounter in Torah and the Siddur. Finally, some advice from my wife, Jody. She finds the *Artscroll Siddur* with inter-linear translation an invaluable resource. The Hebrew words and the English translation appear directly side-by-side throughout.

Motzkin, Linda. *Aleph Isn't Tough: An Introduction to Hebrew for Adults, Book 1*. New York: URJ Press, 2000.

————. *Aleph Isn't Enough: Hebrew for Adults, Book 2*. New York: URJ Press, 2002.

————. *Bet Is for B'reishit: Hebrew for Adults, Book 3*. New York: URJ Press, 2003.

————. *Tav Is for Torah: Hebrew for Adults, Book 4*. New York: URJ Press, 2003.

Resnikoff, Simon, and Linda Motzkin. *The First Hebrew Primer: The Adult Beginner's Path to Biblical Hebrew*. Oakland, Calif.: EKS Publishing Co., 1992.

Samuel, Edith. *Your Jewish Lexicon: Some Words and Phrases in Jewish Life and Thought in Hebrew and in English*. New York: URJ Press, 2006.

Programs

National Jewish Outreach Program

An independent, non-profit organization dedicated to "providing, through educational courses and experiential programs, a basic Jewish education for every Jew in America." It offers free classes in learning to read Hebrew letters ("Read Hebrew America" and "Hebrew Crash Courses").

One final comment. In future editions of this book and on the *Making Prayer Real* website, I will gladly include the name of any relevant Orthodox organization that references relevant liberal resources.

About the Contributors

Rabbi Bradley Shavit Artson (www.bradartson.com) holds the Abner and Roslyn Goldstine Dean's Chair of the Ziegler School of Rabbinic Studies at American Jewish University, Los Angeles, where he is vice president. He is the author of more than two hundred articles and nine books, most recently *The Everyday Torah: Weekly Reflections and Inspirations* (McGraw Hill).

Rabbi Aryeh Ben David is the founder and director of *Ayeka:* Bringing God Back to the Conversation (www.ayeka.org.il). He taught at the Pardes Institute for twenty years and was the educational director of Livnot U'Lehibanot in Jerusalem. He is the author of *Around the Shabbat Table* (Jason Aronson) and *The Godfile: 10 Approaches to Personalizing Prayer* (Devora).

Rabbi Anne Brener, LCSW, is a Los Angeles-based psychotherapist, a spiritual director, and a frequent scholar-in-residence who assists institutions in creating caring communities. A prolific writer, she is the author of the acclaimed *Mourning & Mitzvah: A Guided Journal for Walking the Mourner's Path through Grief to Healing* (Jewish Lights) and has contributed chapters to *LifeCycles: Jewish Women on Personal Milestones and Life Passages*; *Jewish Pastoral Care: A Practical Handbook from Traditional and Contemporary Sources*; *Jewish Spiritual Direction: An Innovative Guide from Traditional and Contemporary Sources* (all Jewish Lights); and many other publications. A frequent columnist for the *Los Angles Jewish Journal,* she teaches at the Academy for Jewish Religion, Los Angeles, and is on the faculty of Yedidya's Morei Derekh—Jewish Spiritual Direction Program.

Rabbi Sharon Brous is the founder of IKAR, a Jewish spiritual community in Los Angeles that integrates spiritual and religious practice and the pursuit of social justice. She serves on the faculty of REBOOT, teaches at Hebrew Union College–Jewish Institute of Religion, and sits on the rabbinic advisory board of American Jewish World Service and the regional council of Progressive Jewish Alliance. Sharon has been a guest on NPR's *Speaking of Faith* and is a panelist on *Newsweek* and the *Washington Post*'s "On Faith."

Maggid Yitzhak Buxbaum—the word "maggid" refers to an inspirational speaker and storyteller—specializes in Jewish mysticism and Hasidic tales. He directs the Jewish Spirit Maggid Training Program, which operates by conference calls and occasional live gatherings. He is the author of ten books, including *Jewish Spiritual Practices*; *Real Davvening: Jewish Prayer as a Form of Meditation*; and *The Light and Fire of the Baal Shem Tov*. His website, the Jewish Spirit Online, is at www.jewishspirit.com.

Rabbi Mike Comins, the founder of *TorahTrek* Spiritual Wilderness Adventures (www.Torahtrek.com) and the Institute for Jewish Wilderness Spirituality (www.ijws-online.org), is author of *A Wild Faith: Jewish Ways into Wilderness, Wilderness Ways into Judaism* (Jewish Lights; www.awildfaith.com). A native of Los Angeles and a graduate of UCLA, Rabbi Comins made *aliyah* and lived in Israel for fifteen years. He studied classical Jewish texts at the Pardes Institute, earned his MA in Jewish education from Hebrew University, and was ordained in the Israeli rabbinical program of Hebrew Union College. He was a founding member and the first director of education at Kehilat Kol Haneshama in Jerusalem. Finding his calling in life, Rabbi Comins became a licensed Israeli desert guide and led *Ruach HaMidbar* desert trips in Israel and the Sinai. He participated in the Mindfulness Leadership Training program at Elat Chayyim, the Jewish Spiritual Retreat Center, the first rabbinical cohort of the Institute for Jewish Spirituality, and the Kol Zimra: Chant Leader's Professional Development program. He founded *TorahTrek* while serving the Jewish Community of Jackson Hole, Wyoming. Currently, Rabbi Comins lives, teaches, and writes in Los Angeles; he leads *TorahTrek* programs and serves as a scholar-in-residence around the country.

Rabbi Elliot J. Cosgrove, PhD, is the senior rabbi at Park Avenue Synagogue. In 2008, Rabbi Cosgrove earned his doctorate in the history of Judaism from the University of Chicago. He is the editor of *Jewish Theology in Our Time: A New Generation Explores the Foundations and Future of Jewish Belief* (Jewish Lights).

Rabbi Lavey Yitzchak Derby is the eighth-generation direct descendent of Reb Levi Yitzchak of Berditchev, for whom he is named. Currently the senior rabbi of Congregation Kol Shofar in Tiburon, California, he has also served as director of the Council on Jewish life, the premiere think tank and outreach department of the Jewish Community Federation of Greater Los Angeles, and as director of Jewish education at the 92nd Street Y in New York. He is on the faculty of the Wexner Heritage Foundation, an adjunct faculty member at the Institute for Jewish Spirituality, and the founder of the IDRA: A Center for Jewish Spiritual Growth and Practice.

Cantor Ellen Dreskin (www.dreskin.us) has served as the program director of Synagogue 2000 and the associate dean of Hebrew Union College–Jewish Institute of Religion and is currently the assistant cantor of Temple Beth El of Northern Westchester, New York. She teaches courses in liturgy, mysticism, and synagogue transformation and travels to various synagogues as a scholar-in-residence.

Rabbi Diane Elliot is the spiritual leader of the Aquarian Minyan in Berkeley, California. Previously she performed internationally as a modern dancer, taught dance and improvisational movement, and choreographed more than thirty original works. A certified practitioner and teacher of Body-Mind Centering®, Rabbi Elliot has been in private practice as a somatic (body-based) therapist since 1986 and is the author of numerous essays, articles, and poems, among them "Hannah's Tears" in *Rosh Hashanah Readings: Inspiration, Information, Contemplation,* edited by Dov Peretz Elkins (Jewish Lights); "Two Great Lights, The Spiritual Potency of the Teacher-Student Relationship" (*Currents,* Winter 2006); and "The Torah of the Body" (*New Menorah,* Spring 2001).

Reb Mimi Feigelson (www.zieglerpodcasts.com) is the *Mashpi'ah Ruchanit* (spiritual mentor) and lecturer in rabbinic literature and Chassidic thought at the Ziegler School of Rabbinic Studies at American Jewish University, Los Angeles. She was previously the associate director of Yakar, Jerusalem, and director of its women's Beit Ha'midrash. She is an international teacher and storyteller.

Rabbi Tirzah Firestone is the spiritual leader of Congregation Nevei Kodesh in Boulder, Colorado, as well as a Jungian therapist and the cochair of Rabbis for Human Rights, North America. She has authored *With Roots in Heaven: One Woman's Passionate Journey into the Heart of Her Faith* (Plume); *The Receiving: Reclaiming Jewish Women's Wisdom* (HarperOne); and *The Women's Kabbalah: Ecstatic Meditation CD Program* (Sounds True Tapes).

Rabbi Nancy Flam served for five years as the founding director of the Institute for Jewish Spirituality, where she is currently codirector of programs. The cofounder of the Jewish Healing Center in San Francisco, she lectures widely on the topics of Judaism, healing, and spirituality, and has written on these issues for *Reform Judaism* magazine, *CCAR Journal,* and *Sh'ma: A Journal of Jewish Responsibility.* She has also contributed to *Wrestling with the Angel: Jewish Insights on Death and Mourning,* edited by Jack Riemer; *Jewish Pastoral Care: A Practical Handbook from Traditional and Contemporary Sources;* edited by Dayle Friedman (Jewish Lights), and *Best Contemporary American Jewish Writing,* edited by Michael Lerner. She was the founding series editor for *LifeLights,* a series of informational, inspirational pamphlets on challenges in emotional and spiritual life published by Jewish Lights.

Rabbi Karen Fox, DD, serves Wilshire Boulevard Temple in Los Angeles. She holds a doctor of divinity and is a licensed marriage and family psychotherapist. She coauthored *Seasons for Celebration* (Putnam), a user-friendly guide to Jewish holidays, and has published articles on women's issues, health, and healing and Jewish spirituality.

Dr. Tamar Frankiel, dean of academic affairs and professor of comparative religion at the Academy for Jewish Religion, California (www.ajrca.org), received her PhD from the University of Chicago Divinity School. She is the author of *The Gift of Kabbalah: Discovering the Secrets of Heaven, Renewing Your Life on Earth* (Jewish Lights) and *She Rises While It Is Still Night: Exploring the World of Dreams* (e-book, Generosity Incorporated), and coauthor of *Minding the Temple of the Soul: Balancing Body, Mind and Spirit through Traditional Jewish Prayer, Movement and Meditation* and *Entering the Temple of Dreams: Jewish Prayers, Movements, and Meditations for the End of the Day* (both with Judy Greenfeld, Jewish Lights).

Rabbi Ethan Franzel serves Main Line Reform Temple Beth Elohim in Wynnewood, Pennsylvania. A long-time practitioner of meditation and chant, he teaches courses around the country on Kabbalah, Hasidism, Jewish spirituality, and meditation.

Rabbi Elyse Frishman serves the Barnert Temple in Franklin Lakes, New Jersey. She is the editor of *Mishkan T'filah,* the new Siddur for the American Reform movement. Other publications include *Haneirot Halalu, These Lights Are Holy, A Chanukah Home Prayerbook,* (CCAR); online Torah commentary on the book of Numbers for *Ten Minutes of Torah,* (URJ website); and articles in several publications including *The Women's Torah Commentary: New Insights from Women Rabbis on the 54 Weekly Torah Portions* (Jewish Lights), *Duties of the Soul* (URJ Press), and *The Tot Shabbat Handbook* (URJ Press); and she has done editorial work on *A Children's Haggadah* (CCAR) and *The Five Megillot* (CCAR).

Rabbi Laura Geller, senior rabbi of Temple Emanuel in Beverly Hills, is the third woman to be ordained in the Reform Movement and the first woman to be selected to lead a major metropolitan synagogue. She served as executive director of the American Jewish Congress, Pacific Southwest Region, where she created the Jewish Feminist Center, and as director of Hillel at the University of Southern California, where she co-organized the award-winning national conference "Illuminating the Unwritten Scroll: Women's Spirituality and Jewish Tradition." She has contributed to many books and was on the editorial board of the groundbreaking *The Torah: A Woman's Commentary* (URJ Press), in which she has two essays. She was also featured on the PBS documentary *The Jewish Americans*.

Rabbi Neil Gillman, PhD, is the Aaron Rabinowitz and Simon H. Rifkind Emeritus Professor of Jewish Thought at the Jewish Theological Seminary. He is the author of many books, including *Sacred Fragments: Recovering Theology for the Modern Jew* (Jewish Publication Society); *The Death of Death: Resurrection and Immortality in Jewish Thought* (Jewish Lights); and *Doing Jewish Theology: God, Torah, and Israel in Modern Judaism* (Jewish Lights).

Rabbi Shefa Gold (www.rabbishefagold.com) is the director of CDEEP: Center for Devotional, Energy and Ecstatic Practice and of the *Kol Zimra* Chant Leaders Professional Development Program, and she serves on the faculty of the Institute for Jewish Spirituality. A prolific composer, she has written chants that are sung in synagogues around the world. She travels widely, leading retreats and teaching the art she has pioneered: the practice of Jewish chant. In addition to her many CDs (available on her website), she is the author of *Torah Journeys: The Inner Path to the Promised Land* and *In the Fever of Love: An Illumination of the Song of Songs* (both from Ben Yehuda Press).

Rabbi Elyse Goldstein is the director of Kolel: The Adult Centre for Liberal Jewish Learning, an adult education institute she founded in Toronto in 1991. She is one of seven women featured in the Canadian National Film Board documentary *Half the Kingdom*. Her first book, *ReVisions: Seeing Torah through a Feminist Lens* (Jewish Lights), received the Canadian National Jewish Book Award. She is also the editor of *The Women's Torah Commentary: New Insights from Women Rabbis on the 54 Weekly Torah Portions* and *The Women's Haftarah*

Commentary: New Insights from Women Rabbis on the 54 Weekly Haftarah Portions, the Five Megillot and Special Shabbatot (both Jewish Lights). Her new book, *New Jewish Feminism: Probing the Past, Forging the Future*, was a finalist for the National Jewish Book Award. She received the Covenant Award for Exceptional Jewish Educators.

Joel Lurie Grishaver, a recipient of the Covenant Award, is the cofounder and the creative chairperson of Torah Aura Productions. He is the author of numerous books, including *Shema Is For Real* and *40 Things You Can Do to Save the Jewish People* (Alef Design Group), and the forthcoming *Stories We Pray: Windows into the Inner-Workings of Jewish Prayer* (Torah Aura Productions).

Rabbi Nadya Gross serves Pardes Levavot: A Jewish Renewal Congregation in Boulder, Colorado. She is *Yoetzet* and associate director of HASHPA'AH (www.aleph.org/hashpaah.htm), the ALEPH Ordination program in spiritual direction/guidance, and co–project director of Ruach Ha'Aretz, a project of ALEPH (www.ruachhaaretz.com).

Rabbi Jill Hammer, PhD, is the director of spiritual education at the Academy for Jewish Religion. She is also the director of Tel Shemesh (www.telshemesh.org), a community celebrating earth-based Jewish traditions, and the cofounder of Kohenet Hebrew Priestess Institute (www.kohenet.com), a training program in women's spiritual leadership. She is the author of *The Jewish Book of Days: A Companion for All Seasons* and *Sisters at Sinai: New Tales of Biblical Women* (both from the Jewish Publication Society).

Melila Hellner-Eshed, PhD, teaches Jewish mysticism at the Hebrew University in Jerusalem. She is a senior fellow at the Shalom Hartman Institute, a faculty member of the Institute for Jewish Spirituality, and author of *A River Flows From Eden: The Language of Mystical Experience in the Zohar* (Stanford University Press).

Rabbi Lawrence A. Hoffman, PhD, is the Barbara and Stephen Friedman Professor of Liturgy, Worship, and Ritual at the Hebrew Union College–Jewish Institute of Religion in New York. In 1994 he cofounded Synagogue 2000 (now Synagogue 3000), a transdenominational project to transform synagogues into moral and spiritual centers for the twenty-first century. He is a past president of the North American Academy of Liturgy, the professional and academic organization for Christian and Jewish liturgists in the United States and Canada, and a recipient of that organization's annual *Berakhah* Award, for outstanding lifetime contributions to his field. He is the author and editor of more than thirty books, including the *My People's Prayer Book: Traditional Prayers, Modern Commentaries* series (Jewish Lights), a ten-volume edition of the Siddur with modern commentaries and a winner of the National Jewish Book Award; *Rethinking Synagogues: A New Vocabulary for Congregational Life* (Jewish Lights), a finalist for the National Jewish Book Award; *The Way into Jewish Prayer* (Jewish Lights); and *The Art of Public Prayer* (SkyLight Paths).

Rabbi David Ingber founded and serves Romemu, a community dedicated to Judaism for body, mind, and spirit in New York City. After yeshiva studies, his personal search led him to study Buddhism and Hinduism; immerse himself in the works of integral philosopher Ken Wilber and psychologist Carl Jung; and engage deeply in tai chi, Pilates, gyrotonic, and yoga. Rabbi Ingber was moved to re-engage with Jewish life when he found his teacher, Rabbi Zalman M. Schachter-Shalomi.

Rabbi Zoë Klein (www.zoeklein.com) is the senior rabbi of Temple Isaiah in Los Angeles. She is the author of two fictional works, *Drawing in the Dust* (Simon and Schuster), a novel about the discovery of the remains of the prophet Jeremiah, and *The Scroll of Anatiya* (Resource Publishing), the poetic teachings of a prophetess.

Rabbi Myriam Klotz is the director of yoga and embodied practices for the Institute for Jewish Spirituality and codirector of the yoga and Jewish spirituality teacher training program at the Elat Chayyim Center for Jewish Spirituality. She serves as a spiritual director for the Reconstructionist Rabbinical College. Her CDs include *Preparing the Heart: Yoga for Jewish Spiritual Practice* and *In All Your Ways Know God: Beginning Yoga On and Off the Mat* (both from the Institute for Jewish Spirituality).

Rabbi Jamie Korngold is the founder of Adventure Rabbi (www.adventurerabbi.org), based in Boulder, Colorado. She is the author of *God in the Wilderness: Rediscovering the Spirituality of the Great Outdoors with the Adventure Rabbi* (Doubleday) and the forthcoming children's books *Breakfast in the Sukkah, Sadie and the Big Mountain,* and *Ori and the Super Shames* (all from Kar-Ben).

Rabbi Lawrence Kushner (www.rabbikushner.org) is the Emanu-El Scholar at Congregation Emanu-El of San Francisco. Previously, he served as rabbi-in-residence at Hebrew Union College–Jewish Institute of Religion in New York City, where he taught spirituality and mysticism and mentored rabbinical students, and as the rabbi of Congregation Beth El in Sudbury, Massachusetts. He is the author of *Kabbalah: A Love*

Story (Doubleday/Morgan Road), *Filling Words with Light: Hasidic and Spiritual Reflections on Jewish Prayer* (with Nehemiah Polen; Jewish Lights), and *God Was in This Place and I, i Did Not Know* (Jewish Lights), among many others. He is also a contributor to the *My People's Prayer Book: Traditional Prayers, Modern Commentaries* series (Jewish Lights).

Rabbi Naomi Levy is the spiritual leader of Nashuva, a groundbreaking outreach organization in Los Angeles (www.nashuva.com). She is the author of *To Begin Again: The Journey Toward Comfort, Strength, and Faith in Difficult Times* and *Talking to God: Personal Prayers for Times of Joy, Sadness, Struggle, and Celebration* (both from Knopf).

Rabbi Richard N. Levy, DD, is rabbi of the synagogue and director of spiritual growth as well as director of the Rabbinic School at the Los Angeles Campus of the Hebrew Union College–Jewish Institute of Religion. He was president of the Central Conference of American Rabbis from 1997–99, when he shepherded passage of the Statement of Principles for Reform Judaism, the "Pittsburgh Principles." He is the author of *A Vision of Holiness: The Future of Reform Judaism* (URJ Press), and he is editor and primary contributor to *On Wings of Awe: A High Holyday Machzor* (KTAV).

Rabbi Sheryl Lewart serves Kehillat Israel Reconstructionist Congregation, Los Angeles. She is a spiritual teacher who lectures and leads workshops and seminars in mystical Judaism (Kabbalah, Hasidism, and Mussar) and values-based decision making. She is the author of *Change Happens: Owning the Jewish Holidays in a Reconstructionist Tradition* (Cherbo Publishing).

Jay Michaelson is the author of *Everything Is God: The Radical Path of Nondual Judaism* (Shambhala) and *God in Your Body: Kabbalah, Mindfulness, and Embodied Spiritual Practice* (Jewish Lights) and other books. He is a columnist for the *Forward*, the *Huffington Post, Zeek, Hadassah*, and *Reality Sandwich* magazines and the executive director of Nehirim: GLBT Jewish Culture and Spirituality. He is completing his PhD in Jewish thought at the Hebrew University of Jerusalem and was a recent visiting professor at Boston University Law School.

Rabbi Linda Motzkin is corabbi, together with her husband, Rabbi Jonathan Rubenstein, at Temple Sinai in Saratoga Springs, New York, and Jewish chaplain at Skidmore College. She is the author of the four-volume adult Hebrew curriculum published by the Union for Reform Judaism Press (*Aleph Isn't Tough, Aleph Isn't Enough, Bet Is for B'reishit,* and *Tav Is for Torah*), as well as coauthor of *The First Hebrew Primer: The Adult Beginner's Path to Biblical Hebrew* and *Prayerbook Hebrew: The Easy Way* (both from EKS). She is also a scribe, currently in the process of writing a Torah scroll (www.templesinai-saratogasprings.org/Bread_and_Torah/Soferetx.pdf).

Rabbi Debra Orenstein, an award-winning teacher and writer, is the editor of *Lifecycles 1: Jewish Women On Life Passages and Personal Milestones* and *Lifecycles 2: Jewish Women on Biblical Themes in Contemporary Life* (both Jewish Lights). A frequent scholar-in-residence across North America, she serves as spiritual leader of Makom Ohr Shalom in Tarzana, California. The website www.rabbidebra.com features her audio teaching CDs, along with other spiritual resources.

Rabbi Nehemia Polen, PhD, is professor of Jewish thought and director of the Hasidic Text Institute at Hebrew College, Boston. He is the author of *The Rebbe's Daughter* (Jewish Publication Society), winner of the National Jewish Book Award; *Filling Words with Light: Hasidic and Mystical Reflections on Jewish Prayer* (with Lawrence Kushner; Jewish Lights); and *The Holy Fire: The Teachings of Rabbi Kalonymus Shapira, the Rebbe of the Warsaw Ghetto* (Jason Aronson) and is a contributor to *My People's Prayer Book: Traditional Prayers, Modern Commentaries* series (Jewish Lights). He received his PhD from Boston University, where he studied with and served as teaching fellow for Nobel laureate Elie Wiesel.

Rabbi Marcia Prager is director and dean of ordination programs for ALEPH: Alliance for Jewish Renewal, and rabbi for the P'nai Or Jewish Renewal communities of Philadelphia, Pennsylvania, and Princeton, New Jersey. A creator of innovative approaches to prayer and liturgy, she is the author of *The Path of Blessing: Experiencing the Energy and Abundance of the Divine* (Jewish Lights) and the unique *P'nai Or Siddurim* for Shabbat. She developed and codirects the Davvenen' Leadership Training Institute at Isabella Freedman/Elat Chayyim, the Jewish Spiritual Retreat Center.

Rabbi Jeff Roth is the founder and director of the Awakened Heart Project for Contemplative Judaism (www.awakenedheartproject.org). He is the cofounder of Elat Chayyim, the Jewish Spiritual Retreat Center, where he served as executive director and spiritual director for thirteen years. He is the author of *Jewish Meditation Practices for Everyday Life: Awakening Your Heart, Connecting with God* (Jewish Lights).

Rabbi Zalman M. Schachter-Shalomi, the founder of Jewish Renewal and the spiritual guide of many of the contributors in this book, is the author of numerous books and articles, including *A Heart Afire: Stories and Teachings of the Early Hasidic Masters* (with Netanel Miles-Yepez; Jewish Publication Society) and *First Steps to a New Jewish Spirit: Reb Zalman's Guide to Recapturing the Intimacy and Ecstacy in Your Relationship with God* (Jewish Lights).

Rabbi Rami Shapiro (www.rabbirami.com) is an award-winning author, poet, essayist, and educator whose poems have been anthologized in more than a dozen volumes, and whose prayers are used in prayer books around the world. A congregational rabbi for twenty years, he is currently adjunct professor of religious studies at Middle Tennessee State University. He writes a regular column for *Spirituality and Health* magazine called "Roadside Assistance for the Spiritual Traveler" and blogs at http://rabbirami.blogspot.com. The author of many books, including *Tanya, the Masterpiece of Hasidic Wisdom: Selections Annotated and Explained; Hasidic Tales: Annotated and Explained; The Hebrew Prophets: Annotated and Explained; Ethics of the Sages: Pirkei Avot—Annotated and Explained; The Sacred Art of Lovingkindness: Preparing to Practice*; and *Recovery—The Sacred Art: The Twelve Steps As Spiritual Practice* (all SkyLight Paths).

Rabbi Jonathan P. Slater is codirector of programs of the Institute for Jewish Spirituality and teaches meditation at the JCC in Manhattan and elsewhere. He is the author of *Mindful Jewish Living: Compassionate Practice* (Aviv Press). He also offers web-based Hasidic text study programs (www.ijs-online.org/resources_cdstudy.php).

Rabbi Elie Kaplan Spitz is the spiritual leader of Congregation Bnai Israel in Tustin, California, and a member of the Rabbinical Assembly's Committee of Jewish Law and Standards. He is the author of *Does the Soul Survive? A Jewish Journey to Belief in Afterlife, Past Lives, and Living with Purpose* and *Healing from Despair: Choosing Wholeness in a Broken World* (both Jewish Lights).

Rabbi Ira Stone has been the spiritual leader of Temple Beth Zion-Beth Israel in Philadelphia since 1988. He is also adjunct instructor in Jewish thought at the Reconstructionist Rabbinical College, and he established the Mussar Leadership Programs at BZBI (www.mussarleadership.org). He is the author of *Seeking the Path to Life: Theological Meditations on God, and the Nature of People, Love, Life and Death* (Jewish Lights),

Reading Levinas/Reading Talmud (Jewish Publication Society), and *Living a Responsible Life* (Aviv Press).

Rabbi Michael Strassfeld serves the Society for the Advancement of Judaism, a synagogue in Manhattan. He is the author of *A Book of Life: Embracing Judaism as a Spiritual Practice* (Jewish Lights), and coauthor of *A Night of Questions: A Passover Haggadah* (Reconstructionist Press), and *The Jewish Catalog* (Jewish Publication Society).

Dr. Linda Thal is codirector of the Yedidya Center for Jewish Spiritual Direction and its Morei Derekh training program. She offers spiritual direction both privately and to rabbinic students at Hebrew Union College, New York; serves on the faculty of Makom, the Center for Mindfulness at the JCC in Manhattan; and conducts a program on Jewish spirituality for psychotherapists. She is the primary author of *Vetaher Libeynu: The Institute for Jewish Spirituality's Curriculum for Adult Spiritual Development* (IRJ) and has recently contributed chapters to *Jewish Spiritual Direction: An Innovative Guide from Traditional and Contemporary Resources* (Jewish Lights) and *What We Know about Jewish Education* (Torah A'ura). She earned her doctorate in religion and education in a joint program at Union Theological Seminary and Columbia Teachers College.

Rabbi Abraham Twerski, MD, is a psychiatrist who lectures frequently on a broad range of topics, including spirituality and self-esteem. He is the author of more than fifty books, including *Happiness and the Human Spirit: The Spirituality of Becoming the Best You Can Be*, *A Formula for Proper Living: Practical Lessons from Life and Torah* (both Jewish Lights), *Twerski on Prayer* (Shaar Press), and *The Spiritual Self: Reflections on Recovery and God* (Hazelden). He is the founder and medical director emeritus of Gateway Rehabilitation Center in Pittsburgh.

Rabbi Sheila Peltz Weinberg is a founder and outreach director of the Institute for Jewish Spirituality. Over the last nineteen years, Rabbi Weinberg has studied mindfulness and introduced meditation into the Jewish world as a form that can enliven and illuminate Jewish practice, ideas, and community.

Rabbi Zari M. Weiss (www.rabbizariweiss.com) works one-on-one with individuals as a spiritual director and has been at the forefront of bringing spiritual direction to the Jewish community. She has published several articles and chapters on this topic, including "Spiritual Direction as a Contemplative Practice," in *Jewish Spiritual Direction: An Innovative*

Guide from Traditional and Contemporary Resources (Jewish Lights), as well as "The Place on Which You Stand Is Holy Ground" in *Tending the Holy* (Morehouse Publishing). She is the chair on the committee of rabbinic spirituality of the Central Conference of American Rabbis.

Rabbi David J. Wolpe serves Sinai Temple in Los Angeles, California. He previously taught at the Jewish Theological Seminary of America in New York, American Jewish University in Los Angeles, and Hunter College and currently teaches at UCLA. He regularly writes for many publications, including the *Los Angeles Times,* the *Washington Post's* "On Faith" website, the *Huffington Post, New York Jewish Week,* Beliefnet.com, the *Jerusalem Post,* the *L.A. Jewish Journal,* and others. He is the author of seven books, including the national bestseller *Making Loss Matter: Creating Meaning in Difficult Times* (Riverhead Trade). His new book is entitled *Why Faith Matters* (HarperOne).

Rabbi Shawn Israel Zevit is the director of outreach and *tikkun olam* for the Jewish Reconstructionist Federation. An educator and musician, he is a founding member of Shabbat Unplugged, codirector of the Davennen' Leader's Training Institute (www.dlit.homestead.com), and a spiritual director for the ALEPH HASHPA'AH program (www.aleph.org/hashpaah). He is the author of *Offerings of the Heart: Money and Values in Faith Communities* (Alban Institute). See www.rabbizevit.com for music links, articles, and more information.

Index of Contributors

Notes

Notes

Notes

Notes

About Jewish Lights

People of all faiths and backgrounds yearn for books that attract, engage, educate, and spiritually inspire.

Our principal goal is to stimulate thought and help all people learn about who the Jewish People are, where they come from, and what the future can be made to hold. While people of our diverse Jewish heritage are the primary audience, our books speak to people in the Christian world as well and will broaden their understanding of Judaism and the roots of their own faith.

We bring to you authors who are at the forefront of spiritual thought and experience. While each has something different to say, they all say it in a voice that you can hear.

Our books are designed to welcome you and then to engage, stimulate, and inspire. We judge our success not only by whether or not our books are beautiful and commercially successful, but by whether or not they make a difference in your life.

For your information and convenience, at the back of this book we have provided a list of other Jewish Lights books you might find interesting and useful. They cover all the categories of your life:

Bar/Bat Mitzvah	Life Cycle
Bible Study / Midrash	Meditation
Children's Books	Men's Interest
Congregation Resources	Parenting
Current Events / History	Prayer / Ritual / Sacred Practice
Ecology / Environment	Social Justice
Fiction: Mystery, Science Fiction	Spirituality
Grief / Healing	Theology / Philosophy
Holidays / Holy Days	Travel
Inspiration	12-Step
Kabbalah / Mysticism / Enneagram	Women's Interest

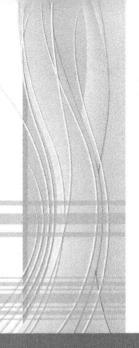

Rabbi Mike Comins, the founder of *TorahTrek* Spiritual Wilderness Adventures (www.TorahTrek.com) and the Institute for Jewish Wilderness Spirituality (www.ijws-online.org), is the author of *A Wild Faith: Jewish Ways into Wilderness, Wilderness Ways into Judaism* (Jewish Lights). He studied classical Jewish texts at the Pardes Institute, earned his MA in Jewish education from Hebrew University, and was ordained in the Israeli rabbinical program of Hebrew Union College. He was a founding member and the first director of education at Kehilat Kol Haneshama in Jerusalem. He lives, teaches, and writes in Los Angeles, and serves as a scholar-in-residence for schools and synagogues around the world.

Also Available

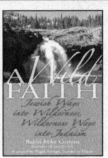

A Wild Faith
Jewish Ways into Wilderness, Wilderness Ways into Judaism
By Rabbi Mike Comins; Foreword by Nigel Savage
Comprehensive how-to guide to the theory and practice of Jewish wilderness spirituality unravels the mystery of Judaism's connection to the natural world and offers ways to enliven and deepen spirituality through nature.
6 x 9, 240 pp, Quality PB Original, 978-1-58023-316-3

The Way Into Jewish Prayer
By Rabbi Lawrence A. Hoffman, PhD
Opens the door to three thousand years of Jewish prayer, making available all you need to feel at home in the Jewish way of communicating with God.
6 x 9, 208 pp, Quality PB, 978-1-58023-201-2

Also Available: **Teacher's Guide**
By Rabbi Jennifer Ossakow Goldsmith
8½ x 11, 42 pp, PB, 978-1-58023-345-3
Download a free copy at www.jewishlights.com

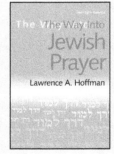

For People of All Faiths, All Backgrounds

JEWISH LIGHTS Publishing
www.jewishlights.com

Printed in the USA
CPSIA information can be obtained
at www.ICGtesting.com
LVHW021352261023
762111LV00005B/119